A–Z GUIDE TO
BRITISH
MOTORCYCLES
from the 1930s to the 1970s

A–Z GUIDE TO
BRITISH
MOTORCYCLES
from the 1930s to the 1970s

Cyril Ayton

BAY VIEW
BOOKS

Published 1991 by
Bay View Books Ltd
13a Bridgeland Street
Bideford, Devon EX39 2QE

Reprinted 1992

Jacket pictures by Andrew Morland
Designed by Gerrard Lindley
Typeset by Lens Typesetting, Bideford

ISBN 1 870979 19 2

Printed in Hong Kong

Foreword

The entries in the following pages deal with the majority of the manufacturers, and most of their models, in British motor cycling in the years from 1930 to the virtual extinction of the home industry in the 60s and 70s. It is a period that presently coincides, approximately, with the Vintage Motor Cycle Club's varying code of eligibility. Inevitably, it seems, vintage has a connotation of excellence. This can be misleading: never more so than in the case of some of the motor cycles reviewed here.

This book differs from Bay View Books' companion A-Z guides on cars. It is not a survey of *all* the machines that were available during 40 years. On the contrary. It is selective, and it is far from being impartial. One estimable model may be dealt with by a 10-line entry while another, objectively of no greater merit, receives extended treatment.

It is appropriate to record again my indebtedness to, above all, C.E. – Titch – Allen, who was generous with his knowledge and opinions, largely based on first-hand experience; to the authors, known but too numerous to list, of the host of published marque histories; and to those anonymous journalists who laboured mightily to fill so many column inches of the technical press with all the facts (and scarcely a criticism) pertaining to the hundreds of models which made up what was once the world's leading motorcycle industry.

Cyril Ayton
December 1990

ABJ

This one deserves little attention other than for its seating arrangement which in 1948, long after everybody else in the business was using soft, spring saddles, remained pure "pedal cycle", with a small Brooks atop a long, adjustable pillar. However, the engine was only 98cc; comfort was not a priority.

ABJ 98cc, 1950.

AMC: AJS

As far as the entries in this book are concerned, AJS was mainly Matchless. Or the other way round, depending on your sympathies. Rationally, Matchless should take precedence for this was the firm that saved the AJS name in 1931 and thereafter called the tune.

AJS began in Wolverhampton around the turn of the century, when the Stevens brothers were making ic engines for use in other people's motorcycles. The eldest brother was Albert John, and it was his initials that identified the firm of A.J. Stevens Ltd., formed in 1911, and appeared on the tank of the bike entered for the IoM Junior (up to 300cc) TT of that year. This AJS was 292cc, a side-valve, with two speeds and belt drive.

In the year the First World War began, AJS 350s – full size this time, to meet new TT limits, and equipped with two-speed primary drive, plus countershaft, to give four gears – swept the Junior Race, taking the first two places, third, fourth and sixth. As well as providing a great victory for the firm, these 70mph side-valve singles broke the stranglehold which twin-cylinder racers had appeared to establish in the TT and other speed events held during the Edwardian era.

Racing successes can breed sales. The 1914 TT effort brought an immediate increase in AJS orders and set the firm on the move, to bigger premises in Wolverhampton and, later, a multitude of new models, planned and developed while engaged in wartime work for the Government.

The 1920, '21 and '22 Junior TTs were AJS affairs, dominated by progressively improved 350s having overhead valves and the first hemispherical combustion chamber seen in British motorcycling. In addition, AJS took the Senior Race of 1921 with a

Junior-class bike giving away 150cc to assorted Indians. Sunbeams, Douglases and Nortons. The rider was Howard R. Davies, of later HRD fame. He beat Freddie Dixon on a mighty American Indian. It was not done by luck, or even by superior riding: the little AJS seemed actually to be faster than the 500s.

By 1922 the racing AJSs had acquired their name of "Big Port", describing a new aluminium-piston engine with 1⅝ inch diameter exhaust port and even larger exhaust pipe. Other developments over the years included a change to internal-expanding drum brakes, a three-speed gearbox and dry-sump lubrication.

AJS 349cc E6 "Big Port", circa 1925.

Production machines were selling well. There were 6hp (800cc) vee-twins and 350 and 500 singles, all side-valve. AJS was a leading manufacturer of "ordinary" motorcycles, always with a racing slant. In 1927 came the first ohc design, for a 350, with drive to the single camshaft by a Weller-tensioned chain carried in a closed casing on the right (offside) of the cylinder.

Neat, reliable and fast, the "cammy Ajay" was rather overshadowed by Norton's new ohc 500, and to an extent by another camshaft 350, from Veloce. It was 1930 before the AJS won a TT race, and then the bike was a specially built 250 and the race was the

Harry Collier, a founder of the Matchless concern, on a 1911 297cc JAP-engined Matchless.

Lightweight. By that time there was a 500cc version . . . and the firm was in financial trouble. It was a case of too many products – motorcycles, cars, commercial vehicles, radios – backed by too little money. Looking around for new money, or new owners, the Stevens brothers approached several firms in the industry – including BSA, who appeared to be interested. But nothing came of it. AJS seemed certain to go to the wall, like so many other medium-to-big Midlands firms. Then the Collier brothers, with their Matchless works in London, stepped in and dictated terms. Within weeks AJS were out of Wolverhampton and on their way, with what remained of their unsold stock, to the busy environs of the Arsenal at Woolwich, in south-east London. The Stevens brothers were not part of the deal. They stayed on at Wolverhampton, in smaller premises, and turned out engines for other bikes.

Through the 1930s AJS bikes became increasingly Matchless lookalikes, while continuing to bear the AJS name on the tank. What individuality remained was displayed almost exclusively in racing, which the Colliers agreed to support on a restricted budget as a probable aid to sales of the production bikes. Thus the 350 and 500cc overhead-camshaft singles were offered again. They became the brightest stars in a dim constellation that, year by year, took on more of a Matchless colouration – and not merely its colours: technically, too, there came to be virtually nothing between the two makes.

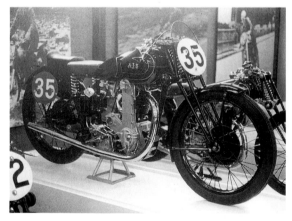

A 1936 Matchless-made 350 ohc AJS on display at the National Motorcycle Museum.

There were isolated exceptions, of course, as and when the Colliers believed there might be extra publicity, and sales, to be won by giving an AJS an exclusive identity. Soon after the takeover they brought out a 350, catalogued as the Big Port to stir memories of the AJS models that carried that name in the 20s . . . though in those days it had been more of a nickname than an official title; Wolverhampton never mentioned a "Big Port" in any brochure or advertising material. The "Matchless" AJS followed the example of the earlier machines in having an oversize exhaust port and pipe, but there was little of the "get-up-and-

go" quality of the original. It was a "tax-cheater", earning a £1 10s a year tax rating because of its low weight (under 224lb).

In 1936 the first version of a supercharged vee-four was produced, and tested, when it overheated, being subsequently converted to watercooling. In this form it continued to overheat, though not as badly as before, and carried its considerable bulk and weight – plus Jock West and on other occasions Walter Rusk – through several grands prix. Outclassed by Italian and German multis, it lacked not so much power as reasonable handling and reliability. However, it managed a well-publicized 100mph lap of the Ulster Grand Prix on the Clady circuit and served as a guinea pig of sorts for the 500 twin racer conceived during the war that was intended to flatten continental (and Norton) opposition when racing resumed.

AJS supercharged vee-four of 1939, with water cooling, now owned by Sammy Miller.

AJS "Porcupine" racer, 1949, Leslie Graham in the saddle. It was designed wih supercharging in mind.

The new racer was called "Porcupine" on account of its spiky engine finning. It was designed, as the four had been, for supercharging. When race supercharging was banned in 1945, the Porcupine was left high and dry. It was modified to run in normally aspirated form but never produced significantly more power than the outdated singles from Norton.

After the war, AJS and Matchless were virtually identical. To justify his choice between the two, the Ajay fan could say that he preferred having the magneto in front of the cylinder (on the singles) and that black-and-gold was more classy than having a chrome-plated "M" on the tank. Perhaps (if he was given to fantasizing, and did not appreciate the realities of modern industry) he would point to the 7R AJS, the 350ohc racer introduced in 1948, and by association try to make a case for AJS *road* bikes being, somehow, especially favoured. This line of reasoning was faulty, but the compiler recalls it being offered with every show of inside knowledge. It was finally scuppered when the management put "Matchless" on the tank of the 500 racers.

AMC (Associated Motor Cycles Ltd.) took over the Colliers' Matchless and AJS titles in 1938. The early postwar 350 and 500 singles had engines almost identical to the 1939 units. AMC relied on the "Teledraulic" front fork, developed for the wartime Matchless 350, to give a semblance of modernity. Not that anybody said the bikes were old-fashioned. They were; but there were waiting lists for AMC bikes, while a new design, the Sunbeam, remained unsold.

AJS 347cc single, 1946: finish was black, in place of wartime khaki.

Modernity arrived in 1948 with new 500cc twins in pivoted-fork frames, enlarged by the late 1950s to 592cc as the Model 30. From AMC's cramped, multi-storey factory in Plumstead came news each year of dozens of modifications to improve the line... dualseat in place of saddle, hairpin valve springs for the singles, light-alloy cylinder heads, alternators in place of dc generators, an AMC-made gearbox to replace the Burman. In 1958 a 250 was included in the programme and was the basis, a couple of years later, for a fresh 350 design, the Model 8, or Light 350. With a new line and a new name on the stocks, the existing models became known as the Heavyweights. Single-tube frames gave way to duplex, and brakes were shrouded in full-width hubs.

In 1962 the ohc 7R – the "Boy Racer" – was dropped. A general slackening of interest in sport was confirmed by a close-down at the competitions shop at Woolwich which had spawned the bikes used by so many of the stars in postwar trials and moto-cross – men such as Hugh Viney and Gordon Jackson, Bob Manns, Geoff Ward and Bill Nilsson.

In 1967, sales having fallen disastrously, AMC became part of newly formed Norton Villiers. Very soon the name "AJS" was only to be seen, and then but rarely, on a middling-successful two-stroke scrambler.

AJS S3 transverse vee-twin

In 1931 the Stevens brothers were forced to cast around for a buyer for their business, which had run perilously short of ready cash. In the same year they produced the S3 transverse vee-twin which, claimed the promotional literature, "struck a new note in motor cycle design." Clearly, the two events were related, probably as cause and effect. The question remains – which way round? Did AJS hope to fight its way out of financial trouble with a sales success for a model that was so different from anything previously turned out by this (in a motorcycle sense) conventionally minded firm? Or was the S3 the glittering straw that broke a back already weakened by

AJS S3 496cc transverse vee-twin, 1931. Note the uncluttered handlebar.

AJS S3 side-valve engine: cylinder heads are in light-alloy.

supporting a spread of enterprises – car and van and radio manufacture, among other things – that was unique in the industry? The truth (in the prosaic way of truth in most similar situations) probably was between the two. The S3 was a last fling that did not come off; and its expense, so ill affordable in the circumstances, hastened the end of A.J. Stevens and Co. (1914) Ltd.

The vee-twin, all relaxed, vibration-free power, is of course a rock in the edifice of motorcycle design; when arranged longitudinally in the frame, that is, where its narrow crankline and reasonable length conveniently tie in with a single track. AJS had manufactured some worthy examples in the 20s. But there have been – continue to be – few examples of the vee-twin set *across* the frame. For the Stevens brothers in 1931 there was only one major predecessor in the genre, and that was the P. and M. Panthette, which had turned out a pretty miserable failure. The attractions of the layout are few, though compelling: cooling cannot be easier, with cylinders poking out in the breeze, and the crankshaft, being in line with the wheelbase, is ideally angled for a shaft final transmission. AJS were won over by the idea of trouble-free cooling but hedged their bets, with an eye to the unadventurous public, by going to the trouble of right-angling the drive, with bevel wheel and pinion, to facilitate use of a chain to the rear wheel.

The side-valve engine had cylinders at 50° to each other, with alloy heads, and individual valve chests set in their outer faces. The camshafts, somewhat distant from the crankshaft, were driven by Weller-tensioned chains. The clutch was not on the end of the mainshaft, as might be expected, but to the rear, on the gearbox, where it established a reputation for ineradicable drag, no matter how skilled the double-declutcher in the saddle.

Set low in a specially produced frame with widely splayed front tubes, the vee-twin produced enough quiet power to take the 330lb tourer up to an easy lope in the 50s, when the twin fishtail silencers – like scaled-down versions of a Brooklands can – emitted a sonorous burble that was a mite out of keeping with the manufacturer's oft-repeated claims for an "unobtrusive passage".

The handlebars were clear of all impedimenta other than clutch and brake controls. It was a time when AJS, not alone among the motorcycle makers, were moved by a vision of a world in which the motorcycle, having outgrown its adolescent, tearaway years, might be endowed with respectability. Nothing, thankfully, came of this; but a token gesture by AJS had involved a cleaning-up operation in the environs of the handlebar. Everything best sited on or around the steering head was moved to a panel in the tank top. All minor controls formerly convenient to a thumb or finger on the handlebar were engineered out of sight, and easy reach, under the bar. Even the newly introduced throttle twistgrip, with blessedly simple direct action, was modified to a complex, worm-and-peg (and slow) rotation, in the interest of good looks.

The lubrication system of the S3 showed how familiar the Stevens brothers were with the prejudices of their customers, who in the early 30s were sold on the dry-sump system, popularized by its use in the most successful racers. AJS, however, were determined to carry on with the tried and proved "total-loss" system. A by-pass was arranged from the pump, to send back a dribble of oil to the under-saddle tank. This was enough to convince any enquiring owner that he was riding an up-to-the-minute dry-sump model, while AJS could look forward to a minimum of guarantee claims arising from oil-starved bearings.

It was a pity that the S3, introduced at a "loss-leader" price of £68, did not catch on. If it had been a success, when no doubt a tenner would quickly have been added to the price, perhaps the sell-out to Matchless, and the long trek south, would have been avoided. But perhaps not.

Specification, S3 (1931): Vee-twin transverse cylinder, sv, 496cc (65 × 75mm). Three-speed gearbox. 3g fuel. Tyres, 3.25 × 19in. 65mph.

AJS Trophy ohc

Cammy AJS models of the 30s owed their existence to trials and road-race rider George Rowley, who travelled down to Plumstead with plant and machinery when the old Wolverhampton concern was taken over by the Collier family's Matchless company.

AJS under the Stevens brothers had a sporting reputation, with a long history of TT entries. The Colliers, however, producing a determinedly bread-and-butter range of motorcycles, could see no reason to change their "no-racing" policy. It was decreed that the new "Plumstead" AJS models should fall into line. George Rowley was to receive no factory support in sport.

George Rowley on his ohc AJS at Brooklands in 1930. With him are Bert Denley (left) and entrant Nigel Spring.

It was all very frustrating for Rowley, a born competitor. Intensely loyal to AJS – in a long career he never rode another make – he remained at Plumstead and carried on an under-cover sporting life by riding his own AJS. He has explained how he nudged the Colliers into racing . . . "In '32 an old cammy racer was shipped into Dover. There was £10 to pay on it in freight charges. The office wouldn't come up with the cash so it looked as if the racer was going to moulder in a dock shed. I made up my mind, went to Dover and paid the fee. They handed the bike over and I took it to Plumstead where I kept it out of the Colliers' sight. A few things needed to be sorted out but it was basically all right. I entered it for the 100-mile grand prix at Brooklands . . ."

Frank Longman with his 349cc ohc AJS in the 1929 IoM Junior TT.

It was at this point that Harry Collier became acquainted with Rowley's plans, when write-ups on Brooklands practice appeared in the weekly press. Was this, the Green 'Un enquired, the beginning of a new race programme at Plumstead? Collier was not amused. Rowley feared for his job. But the row blew over and he was allowed to race, scoring fifth and seventh places. The unpredictable nature of the boss mentality then surfaced, with the Colliers declaring themselves delighted by Rowley's showing – and why wasn't the firm involved in the racing game?

Redesigning of the old cammy AJS was put in hand. The magneto was moved from in front of the engine (the traditional place for it on Ajays, and retained long afterwards on the overhead-valve models) to the rear, which was the "Matchless" position. For the rest, the engine remained much as before, with large light-alloy enclosure on the right side for the Weller-tensioned chain to the single overhead camshaft.

The frame was strengthened and the gearbox fitted with a positive-stop foot-change. In Trophy form – the

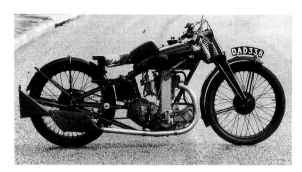

AJS 349cc overhead-camshaft R7, 1930.

description stemming from Rowley's inclusion in the British ISDT Trophy team – the ohc 350 was offered with a 7.5:1 cr piston and upswept exhaust pipe. As an out-and-out racer it ran on a higher compression ratio, with an open pipe. All these changes were masterminded by Phil Walker, who had designed the original ohc AJS in 1926-27 and was to be responsible for the postwar cammy 7R.

It was, in all its forms, a very satisfactory motorcycle deserving of parity, or something near, with Norton and Velocette.

Specification, 350 ohc (1931): Single-cylinder, ohc, 346cc (70 × 90mm). Three-speed gearbox. 3g fuel. Tyres, 3.00 × 19in. 81mph. £80.

AJS 500 V4

One of the most interesting motorcycles to appear at an Olympia show was the AJS vee-four which many have since categorized as a racer pure and simple. It was, however, a very impressive-looking *roadster* in the form in which it was first shown in London, in 1935. The intention was to produce it during the following year and sell it at 85 guineas. Nothing came of these plans. Perhaps the public had a lucky escape. The engine was complicated, highly tuned and able to give of its best only when expertly tended.

As *Motor Cycling* pointed out, when granted access to the machine at Plumstead, it appeared at first sight to be a vee-twin. The confusion arose because the four cylinders were arranged as a double vee, set at an included angle of 50 degrees. Only one camshaft drive – by chain, in customary AJS fashion – was employed although each cylinder had its own camshaft. All this, reported *Motor Cycling*, was ". . .most ingeniously arranged, the single chain, driven from a half-time pinion on the crankshaft, being carried between the front and rear banks of cylinders to the tops of the cylinder heads and then led down again to the centre of the crankcase, where it passes under a jockey sprocket and thence to the other cylinders. Only one sprocket is used for each pair of cylinder heads, two separate camshafts being connected by Oldham couplings".

The rocker gear was completely enclosed, while hairpin valve springs were exposed beneath the camboxes. The crankcase was remarkably compact despite having to support four separate cylinders. Generally there was rather less clutter by way of pipes and ancillaries (four short oil pipes, two magnetos) than was the case with the later Vincent/Irving Series A vee-twin.

Bearings for the big-ends were of roller type, the crankshaft, with two throws, being carried on five main bearings. One of the pair of connecting rods on each crank was forked. A dry-sump lubrication system was fed from a six-pint container, with extended filler neck, below the seat stays.

As to performance, AJS appeared anxious to steal some of the new Ariel 1000 Squariel's thunder. While Selly Oak were touting their bike's "10 to 100 on top", AJS publicists were making the same claim on behalf of the vee-four. Plumstead finally could go one better, however, for provision had been made for a supercharger to be fitted at a later date on the AJS, in the place initially occupied by the dynamo. Ariel had no answer to this one-upmanship.

Specification: V4 (1935): Four-cylinder, ohc, 495cc (50 × 63mm). Four-speed gearbox. 3½g fuel. Tyres, 3.00 × 19in(fr). 3.25 × 19in(r). 90mph. £89 5s.

AJS Model 16/Matchless G3L

The Model 16 and the G3L, the L denoting the telescopic front fork which was the main difference between 1939 and early postwar AMC singles, were available as new bikes in the late 1940s only to those who had joined waiting lists at their local getting-rich-quickly dealers. Not many manufacturers were in such a happy position. AMC enjoyed this good fortune for

several years after resuming civil production in 1945.

It was not clear why you could buy a B31 BSA pretty much as you pleased while having to wait months, perhaps a year, for an AJS/Matchless 350. Prices were close, and quality was on a par. But being hard to get is a certain way of building a reputation. Deservedly in this case, for the AMC singles were impeccably made even if, in 1945, they were still basically army motorcycles treated to a coat – several coats – of lustrous black in place of khaki.

By 1946/47 wheel rims were chrome-plated but the front brake, though effective, remained a puny-looking 6in in diameter. The headlamp was supported by pressed-steel strips, mudguards were of simple D form and the saddle was set at a fixed height.

Many changes were introduced for the 1948 season: an 8in diameter front brake, powerful enough to squeal the tyre on one-finger application, domed and ribbed mudguards, a wire-wound piston for smaller clearance, less running noise, improved handlebar fittings, saddle-height adjustment. The modifications, none particularly radical, must have numbered 50 or more.

AJS Model 16/Matchless G3L, 1962

More than a decade later, in the early 1960s, the "heavyweight" AMC singles had not changed appreciably. The frame had become a duplex (in

AJS Model 16 347cc, 1962: new frame, revised electrics.

Matchless 347cc G3L, 1947: almost a double, apart from magneto position, of the 350 AJS.

AJS Model 16C scrambler, 1964: potent but heavy.

1960), ignition was by coil (1958), the "tin-pressing" primary-chain case was a large cast-aluminium enclosure, the mudguards were gently valanced. Little else was different: and certainly not the power output, which had an additional 50lb to heave along, resulting in a drop in top speed to under 70mph.

The AMC frame, being common to both 500 and 350, was rather large for the smaller engine. In single-tube form, this was not so apparent as it became on the change to a duplex design, when the 347cc long-stroke unit appeared marooned in space.

Specification, Model 16/GL3: single-cylinder, ohv, 347cc (69 × 93mm). Four-speed gearbox. Coil ign/ alternator. 4g petrol, 4pt oil; dry sump. Telescopic/pf. Tyres, 3.25 × 19in. 400lb. 65mph.

AJS Model 20/Matchless G9

AMC's move into the vertical-twin arena occurred in 1948, in company with Royal Enfield and Norton. What chiefly distinguished their design was the use of an additional middle bearing to support the crankshaft. Of plain split type, it lay between twin flywheels and was intended to aid outer roller bearings in minimizing flexing of the one-piece alloy-iron crankshaft assembly. This it did perhaps too well for at high rpm thwarted out-of-centre movement of the crank was transmitted through the crankcase and frame as a deep-seated vibration.

At first available only for export, and finished in chrome and bright colours at a time when home-market singles were restricted to black, the 498cc twin had separate iron cylinders, a light-alloy head with cast-in valve seats, and light-alloy forged connecting rods with plain big ends and wire-wound pistons. Electrics comprised separate gear-driven auto-advance magneto and dynamo, respectively front and rear of the engine. The gearbox was separate, and the primary chain was enclosed in AMC's long-favoured "tin-pressing" which retained a half-pint of oil, essential to the smooth functioning of the engine-shaft shock absorber, for a period that depended on an owner's skill in dealing with the casing's friable sealing strip.

Though it had a true (mean) top speed of no more than 84mph, a late 1940s/early 1950s twin was a prodigious before-the-wind or downhill revver. In the "right" conditions – for example, during a long descent of a Highland pass – it would reach 100mph. The compiler writes here from personal experience but recalls also that following several highland flings at around 100mph his twin had the good sense to blow a gasket, when it was returned to London from Inverness by train.

Specification, Model 20/G9: Twin-cylinder, ohv, 498cc (66 × 72.8mm). 26bhp. Four-speed gearbox. Magneto/dynamo. 3½g petrol, 4pt oil; dry sump. Telescopic/pf. Tyres, 3.25 × 19in (fr), 3.50 × 19in (r). 380lb. 84mph.

AJS 30 CSR/Matchless G11CSR

The 30CSR Sports Twin was a tuned version of the 1956-introduced 592cc model, which was an enlargement of the original 1948 twin.

The tuning was the work of AMC development engineer Jack Williams, who increased the compression ratio of the standard 600 to 7.8:1, "rubbed the camshaft a little here and there", modified the inlet ports, and arranged the exhaust system in siamesed fashion, in place of the separate-pipes layout. All this helped to boost power from 34 to 39.5bhp at 6,000rpm, and enabled a production Matchless Sports Twin to cover over 100 miles in one hour during a celebrated outing on the industry's proving track at Nuneaton. This performance becomes even more creditable when it is realized that top speed of the Matchless varied only between 100mph and 109mph, according to wind direction, indicating that the twist-grip was held almost permanently against the stop during the 60 minutes.

The Sports Twin had a scrambler frame, variable (according to use) tyre equipment and quickly detachable lighting equipment.

AJS Model 20 500 twin: expensive, well-made, vibratory.

AJS Model 592cc 30, 1956: smooth, pleasant tourer.

AJS 31 CSR/Matchless G12CSR

Following good sales for the 600 from 1956 to 1958, with some slackening in the last few months, AJS/Matchless did what came naturally to the British motorcycle industry in those days, and enlarged the engine. Making the stroke 79.3mm in place of 72.8mm, and keeping the bore at 72mm, gave a swept volume of 646cc. The model number of the Matchless was G12CSR. Later, when sales of this one too were dropping, it was saddled with the name of Monarch, as well as the number; but nobody was ever heard to call a sports 650 anything other than a CSR. (In the USA owners of the few CSRs imported there called the machine an Apache.)

Matchless 646cc G12CSR, 1959: useful, long-distance racer.

Matchless G12CSR at speed on the MIRA track, 1962. Rider is journalist Vic Willoughby.

Externally there was little to distinguish a 1961 CSR from the 600 Sports Twin: a twin-downtube frame, a slightly altered angle for the leftside exhaust pipe as it bent to join the main exhaust on the offside, a bigger enclosure for the battery. . .

In spite of vibration, endemic in most AMC twins, the 650 gave a good account of itself in long-distance racing, winning the Thruxton 500-Miler in 1960 and, three years later, an important 1000km event at Brands Hatch.

Specification, 31 CSR/G12CSR: Twin-cylinder, ohv, 646cc (72 × 78.3mm). 46bhp/6,500rpm. Four-speed gearbox. Magneto/dynamo. 4g petrol, 4pt oil; dry sump. Telescopic/pf. Tyres, 3.25 × 19in (f), 3.50 × 19in (r). 430lb. 108mph.

AJS Model 14S/Matchless 250CSR

AMC's Phil Walker-designed lightweight singles were given the CSR treatment in May 1962. The improvements to 14S (AJS) and G2 (Matchless) were based on experience with the Woolwich scramblers and made impressive reading. The over-square engine was given a bigger inlet valve, bigger-choke carburettor (1¼in), higher (8:1) compression ratio, hairpin valve springs, steel flywheels and a larger crankpin. The crankcase and gearbox continued as separate items, though this was not obvious, for both were enveloped by large, polished cheeks, that on the right holding the 2½-pint oil tank and the other covering the primary chain.

The specification was distinctly "sporting", yet on the road the bike disappointed. A brave attempt to match the power if not the refinement of the Honda Dream recently released to the UK market, the 14S/CSR was hamstrung by a shortage of revs and therefore of speed. Perhaps the silencing was unduly restrictive, or the carburettor over-large, for stripped-out versions of the bike proved to be very fast.

Specification, Model 14S/250CSR: Single-cylinder, ohv, (70 × 65mm). 20bhp. Four-speed gearbox. Coil ign/alternator. 3¼g petrol, 2½pt oil. Telescopic/pf. Tyres, 3.25 × 17in. 320lb. 72mph.

AJS 250 Model 14S of 1964 was a disappointing performer.

AJW

Originated by Arthur John Wheaton, whose publishing family provided much of the founding money, the AJW concern created something of a sensation at the Olympia show of 1928 with a watercooled, side-valve four. The engine was a car-type Anzani in a massive chassis constructed mainly in steel channel and carrying a crude form of hub-centre steering. No orders were accepted, which was probably just as well. The Anzani-AJW – it was called the Super Four – never went into production though it reappeared, tantalizingly, at the 1929 show with various modifications to the exhaust system and gearbox, and with a supercharger tacked on, to underline the maker's claims of 100+mph. Sensibly, the big four was allowed to drop out of sight. In its place, in 1929-30, came 500, 680 and 980cc twins, their engines from Anzani and JAP. Later, four-valve Python engines were ordered from Rudge Whitworth.

Other AJW 500s, hardly slower than the Rudge-engined models, were powered by ohv singles from Stevens and JAP. Through the Depression years motorcycles sales slumped, but the Wheaton text books business remained buoyant, subsidizing the bikes. Towards the end of the decade Mr Wheaton, like so many proprietors at the poorer end of the industry, was happy to avail himself of the services, as selling agents, of Messrs Pride and Clarke, in London. By then, however, AJWs were rarely 500s. Instead, they were for the most part inexpensive 250s, their Villiers engines installed in rather unsightly frames made up of lengths of angle iron, tubing and plate. It has to be said, though, that these frames proved capable of coping with all the stresses imposed by 30bhp Ulster-tune Python engines, on the few occasions when customer demand dictated assembly of small batches of "hot-stuff" AJWs. The firm managed to survive until the war. In the 1940s it was sold to one Jack Ball of Bournemouth who opened after the war with publicity for a JAP vertical-twin side-valve, to be known as the Grey Fox.

Supplies of the engine were sporadic, and not many examples of the Grey Fox took to the road. In later years, up to the 1970s, what few AJWs were sold were powered by Italian-made two-stroke engines of 50, 80 and 125cc.

AJW Grey Fox

AJW began postwar production in 1949 with the Grey Fox, powered by a 500cc twin side-valve JAP engine. A telescopic front fork and plunger rear suspension contributed to the picture of an attractive motorcycle. "Picture" is significant here, for the compiler of these notes never saw a Grey Fox on the road.

AJW Grey Fox of 1949 had a JAP twin sv engine of 494cc.

AJW Lightweights

Always reliant on proprietory engines, AJW produced, around 1955, a 125 JAP two-stroke-powered lightweight. The engine was conventional but the frame was of unusual design, for a low-speed roadster, in having a large-diameter main tube carrying at one end the headstock for the front fork, with brackets midway along from which depended the engine.

Later AJWs, given the name of Fox Cub, were fitted with the Italian FBM 48cc engine but retained something of the spine-frame layout originated for the 125 – plus a telescopic front fork, pivot-fork rear suspension, full-width hubs and direct lighting.

In the 1970s the range was enlarged to include 80 and 125 variations, with engines from Minarelli of Italy. The importers came up with Wolfhound as the name

Pre-war AJW powered by a 500 ohv JAP.

AJW 50cc Fox Cub, 1960: as fast as a 98cc Villiers.

for the bigger bikes. Top speed for the 80 was 60mph – very creditable in view of the small capacity but hardly surprising when the engine's 9.5bhp/13,000rpm (DIN) output is considered in relation to the dry weight of 140lb.

AMBASSADOR

Managed by one-time racing driver Kaye Don, Ambassador was formed in early 1947 and existed throughout its 15-year life in premises not a minute's canter from Ascot race course, in Berkshire.

Kaye Don was a commanding, irascible personality who switched to motorcycles when his import business for American Pontiacs faltered in the bleak trading conditions of early postwar Britain. While motorcycles were selling well, in the 1950s, Mr Don was happy. He avoided costly innovation. Instead he produced well-finished lightweights of rigorously conventional design powered by whatever was available from Villiers.

When sales struck hard times he did not allow sentiment to slow his reaction, which was to sell off the motorcycle side of the business and turn to other, more profitable, pursuits.

Ambassador 197 for 1951, with simple rear springing.

Ambassador Supreme

Ambassador went up market in 1951 and introduced their simply named Supreme finished in grey and chromium. (The saddle was grey, and so were the control cables, the battery and the tyre pump.)

The Supreme was important for the makers in being the first Ambassador to be sold with rear springing. This was a plunger-type in steel forgings that permitted an undamped 1½in movement and contributed less to rider comfort than did the extra-large Lycett saddle with vynide top. Splashing out on this last item was a shrewd move by the management who reasoned that the average owner would attribute any ride improvement, more properly due to the saddle, to the new frame and thus be reassured that extra

expenditure (around £10) for the "springer" had been worthwhile.

Specification, Supreme: Single-cylinder, two-stroke, 197cc (59 × 72mm). Three-speed gearbox. 1954-57, 223cc, 11bhp/4,750rpm; 1957-58, 250cc, 15bhp/5,500rpm. Flywheel magneto. 2g petroil. Telescopic/plunger. Tyres, 3.25 × 18in. 260lb. 57mph.

Ambassador 197 Supreme, 1953, in chromium and grey.

Ambassador SS Supreme

Self-starters on motorcycles are not a Japanese invention. Ambassador had one of its two-strokes so equipped in 1953. The SS Supreme announced the fact that it had a self-starter pretty clearly, with an enormous enclosure for the vee-belt drive to the flywheel magneto that overwhelmed the rest of the engine. The battery was 6v, 47ah.

Ambassador SS Supreme, 1953, with extra luggage capacity.

ARIEL

Dating back to the very beginning of two-wheeling, Ariel was born in the pedal-cycle world around 1870, prospered, and took to the manufacture of motor-cycles during the last years of the 19th century with a tricycle having an engine mounted ahead of the rear wheel.

In 1905/6 Charles Sangster, the first of that family to take an interest in the new manufacturing, absorbed the motorcycle side into the car business at

Components Ltd, Selly Oak, with a White and Poppe-designed 4hp side-valve as mainstay of the two-wheelers. His son, Jack, who was to play a big part in motorcycle manufacture in the Midlands, took on the brilliant Val Page as designer; and from 1928 Page had the services, as apprentice designer, of Herbert Hopwood.

Though enlivened from 1931 by Edward Turner's Square Four, the Ariel range exerted its greatest appeal during a depressed decade with straightforward singles, sv and ohv, designed by Val Page. More horizontal than mere "sloper", the Page-style engine, in 500 and 550cc sizes, originated in 1926 in a strong, single-tube frame topped by a novel, handsome saddle tank. It gave the firm the basis of a best-selling programme for the early 30s. Even the side-valve – the 550 – was a good performer. Models that were quickly added had, variously, vertical engines and what the factory described as inclined engines; these latter set at approximately the angle pioneered by the BSA Sloper – ie, midway between the vertical and the earlier Page design.

While Page models were selling well, a more complex design was being developed at Selly Oak. The work of the young Edward Turner, the new ohc 500 had four cylinders disposed in a novel, square formation, the crankshafts being coupled by gears. It was the first of the famous Square Fours that were to be an enduring part of British motorcycling almost to 1960. The engine was light and smooth-running, so that only featherweight cycle parts were necessary. However, by the time the four was shown to the public at the 1930 Olympia show it was burdened with a frame and other ancillaries taken from the heavyweight end of the range. In this form its sales impact was less than had been anticipated. Through its various developments to 600cc, first as ohc, then as ohv, and on to 997cc, the Square Four had a "de-luxe" (meaning large and heavy) label. This was a disappointment for Turner, and something of a reversal of his original intentions.

In the Depression years of the 1930s, when Components Ltd. closed the Selly Oak factory, the highly developed *entrepreneur* side of Jack Sangster came to the fore. He stepped in, bought the firm at a knockdown price, and hand-picked a skeleton workforce to produce the Page-designed singles.

After the dust had settled, in 1931-32, by which time Page and many others had left, Edward Turner took a more commanding role. One of his first moves was to carry out a face-lift operation on the standard 500. With a new, bigger tank in red and chromium and a variety of tuning perks, it was transformed into the Red Hunter, the first of a range that was soon enlarged to include 350 and 250 versions and was to be a major factor in the restoration of Ariel (and Sangster) fortunes.

The Square Four, useful as a publicity vehicle, as top of the range, was something of a handicap in a practical sense to the struggling firm. Only when Turner

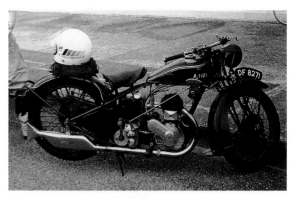

Ariel side-valve 350 of 1930.

introduced pushrods and vertical valves and dropped the original layout of Scott-style overhung cranks in favour of a more conventional assembly did Square Four sales pick up to a worthwhile level. As a biggish manufacturer, Ariel were able to rationalize production to some degree; hence, for example, the use of near-identical frames for 250, 350 and 500 singles and for the Square Fours. Later they did the same with crankcase design for the singles. Mr Sangster recouped his money and went on to make more; enough, finally, to enable him to buy the Triumph concern.

After the war, with Edward Turner long departed to Triumph, Val Page returned to Selly Oak. There, in 1948 (by which time Ariel was part of the BSA empire), he designed the 500 ohv twin, developed the Square Four through to its four-pipe style and, finally, evolved the 250 Leader which, mainly in later Arrow form, was to notch up the biggest sales of any Ariel.

In 1960 production was transferred from Selly Oak to the parent company's factories at Small Heath, where original Ariel design faltered and all but disappeared, surfacing only briefly in the form of the stillborn, Page-conceived 50cc Pixie. This was jettisoned in favour of a BSA design based on the Tiger Cub during the long rundown to final closure in 1967.

Ariel Square Four

The year was 1928 and Edward Turner was a year younger than the century when he arrived at Ariel, Selly Oak in search of a job. His pale hair was slicked down, his blue eyes were less poppy than they became in later years, and he was wearing an expensive suit. He was taken to see John Young Sangster, the proprietor. He emerged from the interview as chief development engineer. Technically, he wasn't much of a development engineer but he was every inch a chief. Mr Turner was on his way.

He was not merely ambitious, he had a mission. He was determined to wrench the motorcycle industry free of its obsession with the single-cylinder engine. And it just so happened – wouldn't you know! – that he had been working on a rather interesting design for a new four-cylinder. This was the Square Four, though it didn't have the name at that stage, and it was unique. Turner's drawings were not of the highest quality but that was of little importance. The idea was original, and audacious, and grabbed attention: it was an entirely fitting expression of the man.

A four *had* to be a better proposition than a single. It didn't need a Turner to point this out. There were, after all, plenty of four-cylinder cars on the road. But for motorcycle usage a multi in its usual form, as a "straight" four, had disadvantages. It could be fitted in only two ways – across the frame, or in line with it. In one case, the wheelbase would be uncomfortably long (and the final drive almost certainly would have to be by shaft, which was not acceptable). Set across the frame, the engine would touch down during cornering. So the idea of having the cylinders in a square formation, making the whole neither particularly long nor wide, really did have a touch of genius.

Ariel 500cc ohc Square Four, 1931.

Another advantage of Turner's design was that the layout – in effect, two parallel twins mounted in tandem – killed any secondary vibration, as the front cylinders drove one crankshaft and the rear pair another, with the two crankshafts geared together and thus contra-rotating, by means of a helically grooved flywheel. Both ends of the front crankshaft were overhung, as was the righthand throw of the rear shaft; on the other end it was extended to connect via chain with the gearbox. The cranks were phased to have diagonally opposed pistons moving in unison, giving excellent balance. Vertical valves – two per cylinder – were actuated by a single camshaft set across the one-piece iron head and driven by a Weller-tensioned chain running on the righthand side of the block from a half-speed gear on the forward crankshaft. Ignition was by a four-spark Lucas Magdyno.

Vibration was minimal and thus the lightweight engine could be accommodated in a frame ordinarily used for one of the company's 250 singles. Ariel testers loved riding the 500 four. It had a "zestful, zooming" exhaust note, and early development work subdued much of the characteristic rumble from the crankshaft coupling.

Ixion, of *The Motor Cycle*, borrowed a prototype and wrote about it in September 1930. More irritating than tantalizing in his veiled references to

technicalities ("my lips are largely sealed by solemn promises to the designer"), the erudite columnist prophesied that the experimental four would be the chief sensation at the Olympia show, two months hence, that it would sell in great numbers, and that it would prove a great success on the road in 1931. As things turned out, he scored only one – about the show sensation – out of three. Perhaps this should not be held against him. When the four did take to the road in production form it was a much more cumbersome package than the light, agile sportster – with its exhaust roar, when provoked, "reminiscent of a Baby Austin" – which Ixion had praised so warmly. The frame was massive, and performance had dwindled from outstanding to adequate. It was something of a flop, no matter what the weeklies chose to write about its brilliant design. And it was expensive, at £75.

Specification, Square Four 500 (1931): Four-cylinder, ohc, 497cc (51 × 61mm). Four-speed gearbox. 3g fuel. Tyres, 3.25 × 19in. 77mph. £75.

In the following year, when the engine was enlarged to 600cc, by boring out to 56mm, the frame was further strengthened. Rather more 600s than 500s were sold, but small Square Fours of either size remained a rarity on the road. The compiler recalls a 600 in daily use in his neighbourhood in the 40s. Among all the crackling singles, and barely quieter vertical twins, the Ariel was an object of wonder in its passage through a country town, clearly arriving in top gear within 20 yards from a standstill. It seemed, from the sidelines, to be a very de-luxe way to go motorcycling.

However the 600 had inherited shortcomings from the smaller four, not least a tendency for the rear cylinders to overheat and for gaskets to disintegrate. These were the misfortunes that dogged gallant Ben Bickell in his attempts to take a Square Four through 100 miles in the hour at Brooklands. He never managed to do so; the Ariel jibbed at the high running temperatures. On one occasion, though, he turned a lap at over 111mph, which was an almost unkind thing for fate to arrange, for it gave him the optimism to carry

Ariel 600cc ohc Square Four, 1936: a little faster than the 500 and much heavier.

A 600 Square Four with pushrod operated-valves: quieter, more oil-tight than the ohc models.

Ariel 1000 Square Four of 1939: 10 to 90mph in top gear.

on in what others could see was a hopeless endeavour. Years later, designer Herbert Hopwood (who was at Selly Oak until 1935) had kept his spectacles resolutely clear. His verdict on the fours is worth recording not merely for its frankness but because there appears to be some doubt whether all the Squariel variants are excoriated by him, or only the early ones. He has written ". . . [it had] the largest frame and wheels which were then in production. . . the result was a 'camel' of huge proportions with a shocking power-to-weight ratio and no performance. As a result the Square Four dribbled through years of minute production figures . . . I shall never understand why this machine was allowed to survive for so long and clutter the production lines".

The ohc 600 carried on until 1936; then for 1939 it appeared in pushrod ohv form, with different bore and stroke dimensions, when it enjoyed a brief, uneventful career in the shadow of the 4F.

Specification, Square Four 600 (1939): Four-cylinder, ohv, 599cc (50.4 × 75mm). Four-speed gearbox. 3¼g fuel. Tyres. 3.00 × 20in(fr), 3.25 × 19in.r). 80mph. £89.

The Square Four was extensively redesigned in 1935, mainly to introduce extra capacity, and power, to give substance to its arresting looks and still unfamiliar "multi" noises. At 65 × 75mm bore and stroke, the new dimensions produced 997cc and, as it turned out, 36bhp/5,800rpm, which amounted to a 10bhp increment over the 600's output. Overhung crank throws became a thing of the past, with plain bearing big-ends in place of the original roller type. Flywheels were bolted to the crankshafts and the coupling gears were moved to an oil-bath chamber on the side of the crankcase. The overhead camshaft, and drive, disappeared in favour of pushrods working from a somewhat whippy camshaft between the cylinders. The crankcase, having previously predated Japanese practice by 30 years in being horizontally split, was altered to conform to the traditional British pattern, with a vertical join. The front-facing Amal was changed for a car-type Solex mounted at the rear.

The 4F was offered in 1939 with a spring frame. It was the system devised by Frank Anstey – an amalgamation of ordinary plunger springing (as found

on the more expensive Nortons) and pivoting links to keep the rear chain in constant tension.

In looks, it suited the largish Squariel very well and its action, though limited, gave noticeable extra comfort. Fifty years on, with decades of easy-action springing and fat rear tyres setting high standards, commentators are inclined to give Mr Anstey's design a hard time. They say: ". . . it was not so clever for a Square Four over 100lb heavier [than the singles]" and ". . . the wheel movement was too restricted, apart from being undamped". All this may be true, and certainly is dismissive; above all, though, it rates as

Tank of a 1939 1000 Square Four: rear dial records oil pressure.

hindsight. See what a press tester of the day had to say: "The sprung rear wheel was found to be of great benefit. Not only did it eliminate all the jarring which becomes so tiring on a long run, but it was unnecessary to brace myself against road shocks, as on a rigid frame – on the Ariel, they never came." As for maintenance of the springing, the same tester cheerfully dismissed the chores: "The spring frame pivots and plungers added a few to the number of grease nipples, but they were all perfectly accessible."

Like all the Ariels of the time, a '39 600 Square Four had its clutch in a separate compartment, a rubber-mounted handle-bar, and an instrument panel set into the top of the fuel tank. It sold for £89 10s (and a 100mph speedometer was an extra, at £2 15s). Top speed was a shade over 80mph. In their final peacetime year the two girder-fork Square Fours, 600 and 1000, were almost indistinguishable. In performance, however, there were noticeable differences. Where the 600 made it to 80mph at 5,700 revs, the 1000 pulled a much higher top gear (4.5:1 compared to 5.4:1) to the same rpm level, to achieve almost 100mph … 98mph was the precise figure quoted by *Motor Cycling* in May 1939. There was much talk at the time of "10 to 100" – or was it 9 to 90? – "on top". The significant 0-60mph times were 12 seconds and 7½ seconds, and over the flying start quarter-mile the speed gap widened, at 78 compared with 97mph. The 1000 owner paid for extra performance, at the petrol pumps. The big bike's average consumption was no better than 50-55mpg whereas the 600 returned at least 70mpg. Time being short, and not having a slide rule to hand, the compiler will not attempt to estimate the extra financial burden implied for the 1000 rider in these figures. It would not have been unduly punitive, for top-grade (roughly 80 octane) petrol cost no more than 9d (4p) a gallon.

A keen motorcyclist could tell the models apart, of course. It helped if he was a reader of *The Motor Cycle*. The editor had a 1000 as his personal mount – the horsey analogy was much used in those innocent days – and seldom allowed an issue to pass without referring to, or picturing, the four. The big one had a valanced front mudguard and a wider saddle with a rear lip to it. The wheels showed an interesting variation, taking a 20 × 3.00in front tyre … Ariel's "sporting" practice … in the case of the 600; and a 19 × 3.25in and 18 × 4in, for the 1000.

In many ways the Square Four was technically more interesting than the few other 1000s of its time. And it was always more available to an average purse. But the penalties of an "ordinary" name on the tank and a relatively large production run mean that it did not survive into the new "classic" era with the appeal – or value, in strict financial terms – of the tattiest Brough Superior or Vincent Series A.

Specification, Square Four 4F 1000 (1939): Four-cylinder, ohv, 997cc (65 × 75mm). Four-speed gearbox. 3⅞g fuel. Tyres, 3.25 × 19in (fr), 4.00 × 18in(r). 98mph. £102.

1946 Square Four

In common with Ariel's less exalted models, the 997cc Square Four joined the immediate postwar range almost unchanged from 1939. With all-iron engine, the same rumbling gears coupling the crankshafts, and (as before) a tendency to overheat in the vicinity of the valves, the gentlemanly "Squariel" was good for 90mph, and when pressed could cover the "standing quarter", mostly in top gear, in a fraction over 16 seconds. In 1947 everything about the Square Four seemed big: engine, mudguards … even the Lycett saddle, which was set at no more than 28 inches from the ground. Perhaps it was on the low side in order to reassure new owners – legs weakened by wartime rationing? – who might doubt their ability to deal with the bike's 475lb dry weight, then considered prodigious.

Like other Ariels, it had a tank-top instrument panel and a separate clutch compartment. For an additional £15 it could be bought with the pre-war-pattern compensated-link rear suspension.

Square Four MkII

In 1948 the Square Four was extensively redesigned. Aluminium-alloy took the place of cast-iron as block and cylinder-head material, bringing a drop in overall weight of about 50lb, and cooler running, though no perceptible increase in top speed.

Ariel 1000 4G with all-alloy engine, the first major redesign postwar.

Main bearings remained unaltered, with rollers on the drive side and white metal on the timing side, for both crankshafts. Frame and suspension were as before. But the lower weight and more sprightly acceleration meant that for the first time the big Ariel could be seriously considered for solo use instead of being relegated, as in the past, to second-class status as a sidecar hauler.

A.B. Bourne, editor of *The Motor Cycle*, rode a new Four when reporting the 1948 International Six Days Trial in Italy, and pronounced himself well pleased with it. Years later a colleague, George Wilson, secured one as his editorial hack and loaned it on occasion to the compiler, who found the combination of zestful performance and roly-poly handling diverting and, on the whole, congenial.

Square Four MkII (four pipe)

The last major engine changes to the production Square Four occurred in 1953/54, when an effort was made to cure the overheating problems which had persisted, though in less severe form, into the early Mk II alloy series. A bigger head casting was evolved, with bolt-on manifolds for four separate pipes. At the same time various strengthening measures were undertaken, and the compression ratio was raised, to boost power to a level more in keeping with swept volume. The result was acceleration and top speed that hoisted the Mk II very firmly into a mid-1950s "superbike" bracket. Handling, which may have been pleasingly "roly-poly" when coping with the relatively mild power output of a 1951 engine, was less appealing when up to 50bhp was on tap. Not that this appeared to worry speedy Vic Willoughby, who had exchanged a racer's life for that of a writer on one of the weekly magazines. In 1955 – pre-motor-

Healey Special used the Ariel engine as part of the frame structure.

way days – he used a road test Mk II Square Four for a dash to Scotland during which he covered 140 miles in two hours on the A1.

It should be mentioned that the 1954 Mk II overheated too . . .

Specification, Mark II: Four-cylinder, ohv, 997cc (65 × 75mm). 45bhp/5,500rpm. Four-speed gearbox. Coil ign/dynamo. 5g petrol, 6pt oil; dry sump. Telescopic/plunger. Tyres, 3.25 × 19in(fr), 4.00 × 18in(r). 465lb. 105mph.

Ariel Mk 2 four-pipe Square Four, 1954: bigger, heavier and faster.

Healey 1000/4 with Ariel four-pipe engine in 1972.

Ariel Ex-WD350

When I was a lad (writes the compiler) and "had charge" . . . the circumstances behind this careful phrase being too complicated to go into. . . of a spring-frame 497cc Red Hunter Ariel, I looked askance at the ex-WD 350 of the same make that I encountered most days: it was undeniably poor stuff compared with the Red Hunter.

The London dealers Naylor and Root sold the ex-WD Ariel. It was in many respects merely a drab, cheaper version of the NG model that was coming through to the showrooms in late 1945. Both were barely changed from 1939. The one-time military bike had girder forks, of course, a 2½ gallon tank, perhaps an inch or two extra ground clearance (derived from a frame once used in trials), flexible rear panniers slung over a tubular framework, and one or two penny-pinching features, such as canvas handlebar grips. Top speed was 65mph and the price around £100.

Ariel 500 Red Hunter (pre-war)

The best all-round Ariel of the 30s was the 1939 497cc Red Hunter single. This judgement takes account of the more expensive Square Four, which was less frugal (all that weight) than the Red Hunter, more fussy (all those pistons and associated parts in frenzied motion) and very little faster, though more accelerative. The compiler's experience of a 1939 Red Hunter, with rear springing, was obtained courtesy of its one-time owner, a native German (turned Briton) with the suave grooming of a Conrad Veidt. In wartime (1939-45) he was the manager of a *kursaal* in a small seaside town and then, in the dark economy of the late 40s, turned to greengrocery in a city 25 miles away. This entailed high-speed commuting, mostly on the Red Hunter, sometimes on a rigid-frame International Norton (of which there will be more, in an appropriate place).

Ariel 497cc Red Hunter in 1938. Top speed was about 84mph.

Price of the 1939 Red Hunter was £68 10s; pillion equipment cost extra.

The Red Hunter engine, simultaneously refined (for the showroom) and toughened (for sporting use) since its inception in 1932, was never better than in 1939. Long of stroke, but not grotesquely so, at 95mm, and with plenty of "flywheel", it produced usable power from low revs and would soar to well over 5,000rpm while pulling a high, 4.7 to 1 top gear. Earlier criticisms of excessive noise and oiliness from the valve gear had been met by a comprehensive enclosure.

Speedometer and oil gauge were set in the top of a wide fuel tank panelled in red on chromium. The saddle was large, as were the oil tank (6 pints capacity), the headlamp (8in diameter), and the rear mudguard, which had valances and a neat rear-light which was semi-streamlined and a distinct improvement on the usual "bicycle"-size fitting in the top righthand corner of the number plate. The front wheel carried a 20 × 3.25in tyre, in customary Red Hunter style; the rear had a 19 × 3.50in.

As for the rear suspension, it was new for 1939 and was that odd combination of coil springing in vertical barrels with link action that was to be seen on Ariels until 1954, when it gave way to a full pivoted fork. Total movement was no more than 3 inches. The multiplicity of pivots meant that early wear allowed wheel movement to stray from the strictly up-and-down. This, however, was no particular handicap in the context of 90mph performance. The comfort and road adhesion conferred by the modest springing were considered a worthwile bonus, paid for by an occasional shimmy on bumpy bends. The *kursaal* manager-turned-greengrocer had much to say of the Ariel's advantages on the badly maintained country roads of the 40s. He was able to save several minutes by Ariel on his 25-mile commuter run compared with his times on the potentially faster International Norton.

Specification, 500 Red Hunter (1939): single-cylinder, ohv, 497cc (81.8 × 95mm). Four-speed gearbox. 3½g fuel. Tyres. 3.25 × 20in(fr), 3.50 × 19in(r). 84mph £81.

Ariel Red Hunter (postwar)

The Red Hunter was resurrected after the war virtually unchanged, telescopic fork excepted, from 1939 specification.

With a common piston stroke of 85mm, the 348 and 497cc Red Hunters were renowned as straightforward two-valve, pushrod-operated ohv singles capable of producing a surprising amount of fuss-free power. The 500, having a frame which was no heavier than the smaller machine's, was always a much better performer.

As noted earlier, the 500 Red Hunter was available even before the war with link-type plunger rear springing. It was little changed until the early 1950s when, in successive years, a duplex-pattern frame

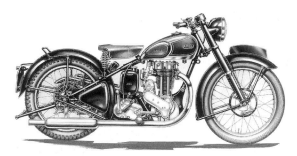

Ariel 348cc Red Hunter in 1951 displayed few engine differences from the late 1930s.

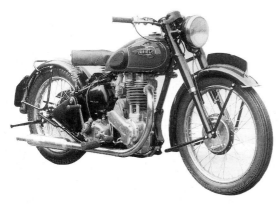

By 1952 the Red Hunter YHA had an all alloy engine with finning shrouding pushrod tunnels.

Ariel VB600 598cc side-valve, 1936: more usually seen in company with a sidecar.

The 350 Ariel of 1967, with rear-chain enclosure.

Ariel side-valve VB600 of 1953 had an alloy cylinder head.

was adopted with pivoted-fork rear springing, and the engine was fitted with a light-alloy cylinder head, with pushrod tunnels incorporated, and mainly hidden, in the finning. Other new fittings included full-width light-alloy wheel hubs, optional enclosure for the rear chain, and a cowl for the headlamp. At the same time the claret-coloured fuel tank acquired chrome-plated fluting.

Specification, NH(350)/VH (500): Single-cylinder, ohv, 348/497cc (72 × 85mm/ 81.8 × 85mm). 19/26bhp. Four-speed gearbox. Magneto/dynamo. 3¾g petrol (later 4½g), 6pt oil; dry sump. Telescopic/plunger/pf. Tyres, 3.25 × 19in. 365/375lb. 75/82mph.

Ariel VB 600

The side-valve, whose virtues as a slogger made it ideal for sidecar hauling, was a valued part of British motorcycling in the early postwar years. Ariel's contribution was the VB. Differing only in minor respects from corresponding models on offer from BSA and Norton, it was bought not on account of any technical superiority over the others but simply because it was . . . an Ariel.

Like the Norton it had something of a speed pedigree. In the 1930s a Hartley-tuned example was ridden by Jock West at over 90mph. But after the war the VB settled firmly into the BSA M21 mould and was seldom seen other than manacled to a dreadnought of a sidecar.

Based on a Val Page design of the 1920s, the VB arrived at its final engine dimensions of 86.4 × 102mm, giving 598cc, in 1936. Cylinder-head modifications, mainly to the fixing studs, were carried out at a later date. The original cast-iron head was exchanged for a light-alloy one in 1951, when it was confidently predicted that a long-standing overheating problem would become a thing of the past. It did not; but the affliction never was terminal.

With a move to a pivoted-fork frame and full-width hubs, in line with similar changes to other models in the Ariel range, the VB barked on into the 1960s towards its and the company's demise in 1967.

Specification, VB600: Single-cylinder, sv, 598cc (86.4 × 102mm). Four-speed gearbox. 16bhp/ 4,400rpm. Magneto/dynamo. 4g petrol, 6pt oil; dry sump. Tyres, 3.25 × 19in. 370lb. 65mph.

Ariel KH Twin

Val Page's Ariel twin was announced in September 1948, as similar news about new 500 twins was coming from other British makers anxious to share a market successfully exploited originally by Triumph and then by BSA.

A restrained-looking design, without extravagant finning, the Ariel engine used cast-iron for barrel and one-piece head, with air spaces in the cylinder block between the bores. A one-piece chrome-molybdenum crankshaft carried a cast-iron flywheel. Connecting rods were in light alloy, with steel-backed white-metal big-end bearings. A duplex chain drive was employed in the large timing chest and the magneto was equipped with automatic advance.

Running on a 6.8:1 compression ratio, the engine turned out 25½bhp at a shade under 6,000rpm – enough to propel this 414lb bike at up to 78mph. *The Motor Cycle* said that success was assured for the newcomer but spoilt this optimistic send-off by reporting that 0-30mph took 18 seconds, which may be taken charitably as a misprint.

Ariel 650 Huntmaster, 1958.

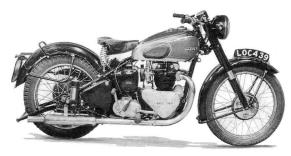

Ariel KH 498cc twin of 1951 with pre-war pattern rear springing.

Sound and reliable, the KH fared little better than Page's earlier 650 as a sales competitor against Edward Turner's Speed Twin. In 1954 it was fitted with a light-alloy cylinder head and housed in a new duplex, pivoted-fork frame, thence to canter on to meet the catalogue fate of all moderate-to-poor sellers – the fateful word "Discontinued" – in August 1957.

Specification, KH: Twin-cylinder, ohv, 498cc (63 × 80mm). 25bhp. Four-speed gearbox. Magneto/dynamo. 4g petrol, 6pt oil; dry sump. Telescopic/rigid/plunger; pf in 1954. Tyres, 3.00 × 20in(fr), 3.25 × 19in(r). 414lb. 80mph.

Ariel Huntmaster

In 1954, somewhat later than BSA and Triumph, Ariel got round to marketing a 650 version of their 500 vertical twin. It was in fact not an enlargement of the 498 KH500 but a crib of the parent factory's Golden Flash. There were some changes to the BSA-based unit, mainly in the timing chest and valve enclosure, an entirely new Burman gearbox, and of course the

Ariel 646cc Huntmaster used BSA A10 engine, with subtly altered timing chest.

distinctive Ariel frame and tank to mask affinities between the two. The average Huntmaster owner probably had no inkling that his engine shared capacity and bore and stroke measurements – 646cc, 70 × 84mm – with BSA's A10. If he had known, he would have said that it was a coincidence and that the Huntmaster was twice the bike the Golden Flash was.

Even more than the BSA, the Huntmaster was used for sidecar work. In 1954 C.E. "Titch" Allen took a Huntmaster outfit, with long-suffering ACU observer John McNulty in the sidecar, on a 10-day 3,600 mile round-Britain trip, finishing with a flat-out 500-mile solo stint at Silverstone. He said the Huntmaster was the best of the bikes available for the job. Having been outrun while attempting, on a 500 solo, to keep station with Allen-McNulty, the compiler is inclined to agree.

Specification, Huntmaster: Twin-cylinder, ohv, 646cc (70 × 84mm). 35bhp. Four-speed gearbox. Magneto/dynamo. 4g petrol, 6pt oil; dry sump. Telescopic/pf. Tyres, 3.25 × 19in(fr), 3.50 × 19in(r). 365lb. 100mph.

Ariel Leader

When Ariel settled to the business of making a two-stroke engine they had the good sense to take a long, hard look in advance at a German design, much as BSA had done ten years earlier when designing the Bantam. In the case of Selly Oak, the model was provided by the Adler twin. The Birmingham-made two-stroke eventually appeared in 1958, installed in the 250 Leader.

The engine was not the most striking part of the Leader. It was the total concept of the new machine that was important, striking a fresh note in British motorcycling. The work of a team directed by long-serving Ariel designer Val Page, the Leader was a bold attempt to break the stereotype of the motorcycle in the 1950s as sporting vehicle or, alternatively, cheap (and generally nasty) runabout. The Leader aimed to combine agile handling and a fair turn of speed with clean, quiet convenience.

Ariel 249cc Leader, 1958: one of the very few new designs to come from Britain postwar.

The latter consideration was served by having presswork in place of a conventional frame. A beam-type chassis carried panelling which enveloped the engine and much of the rear wheel, extending forward by way of a fake "petrol tank" (in reality a useful storage unit) to a point where in-built shielding swept up, protecting the rider's legs, ahead of the handlebars, where it was carried round as a half-moon segment to form a simple control panel. The fuel tank was a painted pressed-steel box tucked out of sight under the seat.

The three-main-bearing engine with integral four-speed gearbox was slung from main-frame brackets and drove the rear wheel via a fully enclosed chain. Twin exhausts silenced the 18bhp engine very effectively. Though the Leader was intended for mythical Everyman, its handling and general road behaviour were so good that even hardened motorcyclists took to it with enthusiasm; years later, it is

these aspects, rather than the luggage-carrying facility, rider protection and general convenience, that are chiefly remembered.

A host of accessories was available to the Leader owner: lockable pannier cases, chromed rear bumper, prop stand, eight-day clock, winkers, a telescopic jack . . . the list seemed endless. Investing in all the extras would have meant a sizeable outlay on top of the £210 charged for the bike alone.

Specification, Leader: Twin-cylinder, two-stroke, 249cc (54 × 54mm). 18bhp. Four-speed gearbox. Coil ign/alternator. 2½g petrol. Trailing link/pf. Tyres, 3.25 × 18in. 360lb. 70mph.

Ariel Arrow

The sensible folk who bought Leaders were pleasantly surprised to find that their Mr Everyman's bike – bodywork, screen, luggage boxes and all – actually handled very well. The engine was good too. The Leader encouraged enthusiastic riding.

Bob Currie on a 1964 Ariel Arrow.

Ariel Arrow developed up to 20bhp.

Super sports version was known as the Golden Arrow because of its light-colour finish.

BAC Lilliput of 1958: it died within two years.

Ariel responded to this enthusiasm, and in 1959 introduced the Arrow, which was the Leader sans legshields, dashboard and side panels. Later, in 1960, the Arrow was tuned a trifle, to justify a further variant with a "sports" tag. The compression ratio was raised to 10:1 from 8.25:1, and a bigger-bore (1¹⁄₁₆in) Amal was fitted, the result being 20bhp at 6,000rpm. The name Golden Arrow related to the particularly attractive finish in gold and white, plus whitewall tyres.

Specification, Arrow: Twin-cylinder, two-stroke, 249cc (54 × 54mm). 16-20bhp. Four-speed gearbox. Coil ign/alternator. 3g petroil. Trailing link/pf. Tyres, 3.25 × 18in(fr), 3.25 × 18in(r). 300lb. 78mph.

Ariel Three

It would be pure charity to say that Ariel's ending, as enacted in the brief career of the Ariel Three, amounted even to a whimper.

Years after the closing of Selly Oak, when production of the Arrow had petered out, the parent company heaped final indignity on the Ariel name in 1966 by using it for an oddly styled tricycle in which the single wheel at the front flopped ... banked ... through turns. It was certain, explained BSA, to attract housewives and any others who might have forgotten, or had never leaned, how to ride a bicycle.

The engine was a 50cc two-stroke made in Holland. Very few were sold. It was, as indicated, the last vehicle to bear the Ariel name.

BAC

Lilliput

The BAC Lilliput came on the market in 1958, and expired two years later. It had a 98cc Villiers engine, plus two-speed gearbox, set rather airily in a loopy, all-welded frame having a telescopic front fork. Wheelbase was 45in, saddle height 25½in, and the finish polychromatic bronze. At less than £70 it ranked as inexpensive but not cheap; for the same price you

could buy a 125 from one of the big firms such as Francis Barnett or James. Did BAC (Bond Aircraft and Engineering) have plans for a Brobdingnag? There is no record ...

BAUGHAN

Baughan motorcycles were assembled in H.P. Baughan's home town of Stroud, Glos, to guidelines laid down by that veteran organizer of the one-day sporting trial.

Surprisingly agile, of indeterminate though evidently advanced years, Mr Harry Baughan in the 1950s was lean and stooping, and usually wore a beret. He was invariably – or so it seemed – flanked during his forays into the Gloucestershire countryside on sporting occasions by a couple of elderly ladies carrying vacuum flasks and clipboards. They were his assistants and, as the years passed, among the few to recall the Baughan trials machines that had enjoyed much success in the 1930s. Competition Baughans were more or less bespoke; customers chose the engine they wanted, though it usually turned out to be a JAP. There is little to record about the bikes other than that Mr Baughan liked, customer willing (or unknowing), to include a qd rear wheel in the specification. The bolts holding the wheel were fragile, and prone to shear. Designers have their foibles.

Baughan Model 0 of 1933 had a Sturmey Archer (Raleigh) 348cc ohv engine.

BOWN

In 1950 Bown lifted their sights from the autocycle to the light motorcycle. The difference, when it is realized that the engine, the 98cc Villiers, was much the same in both cases, was largely in a lack of pedals and the provision of an extra gear ratio, on the more up-market version. The frame was of twin-tube cradle type, rigid of course, with front springing by a link-pattern fork with tubular legs.

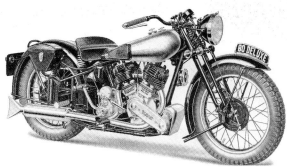

Brough Superior SS80 in 1939 with Matchless side-valve engine: "the most charming thing . . ." said George Brough.

Brough Superior 11-50 Special, 1939: a favourite with police forces.

Bown with two-speed 98cc Villiers engine-gear unit in 1951.

BROUGH SUPERIOR

The Brough Superior was, quite simply, always the motorcycle that George Brough himself wanted to own and ride. It was never, in any of its numerous incarnations, designed to follow a fashion; G.B. had to be *determined* to produce it – if necessary against all odds, and certainly at all times with scant regard for any objections, reasoned or otherwise, voiced by his long-suffering associates at the Haydn Road works in Nottingham. By the 1930s it was clear that his tastes had changed. No longer was he intent on turning out the fastest motorcycle in the world.

Brough Superior 500 model of 1931: one of nine manufactured.

Brough-Austin 4

One could hardly say that a production run of 10 is significant in the annals of 1930s motorcycling. However, as the motorcycles in question were made by George Brough and powered by a watercooled four-cylinder engine never previously seen in a single-track vehicle, no further reason will be offered for presenting some account of them in these pages. What better than to start with a personal story from the owner of the first such Brough Superior to be sold. Mr Tony Branson, at that time resident in Sevenoaks, Kent, has described the events that changed his life – if only temporarily. "At the motorcycle show [in 1931] I saw the Brough four with sidecar. I had on a most ancient green leather coat, almost of horseless carriage days, belonging to my grandfather. I was admiring the four when George Brough asked me to move off the stand.

Noel Pope and Brough Superior at derelict postwar Brooklands.

When I came back it was to find that Hubert Chantrey [riding partner of George Brough and one of the inner circle of Brough enthusiasts] had been warned to keep me clear. But I told Chantrey I wanted to buy a four – and of course George had gone off for a drink. Chantrey was interested, and asked me to have a drink, but I played it casual and told him I might drop back. When I did so, George was there, all smiles.

"I told him I wanted the machine solo and we had quite an argy-bargy. He said it was not a solo model, and that I could take it or leave it. I said I'd leave it, so George and Chantrey started working on me again, and finally Chantrey took me out on the Great West Road on a four with sidecar to a quietish spot where he removed the sidecar and told me to go off on the solo.

"I went off very gingerly in second gear, absolutely terrified. Then the camber of the road and the tricycle effect took me and the bike into the gutter, and nothing I could do would make it steer out again, and there I stayed, still upright, quite still, clutch out, in second gear.

"After 15 minutes I got off, turned the bike round, and went off in second gear till the camber and the three wheels again affected me and I shot across the road and landed up alongside Chantrey, still in second

Four-cylinder (Austin) Brough Superior of 1931: 10 were made.

Tony Branson on his solo Brough Austin 4 in 1933.

gear. He was very impressed. He had never seen riding like it.

"Putting a bold face on things, I said I would definitely have a solo four. Chantrey reported my riding in glowing terms to George Brough. In due course the machine arrived."

Mr Branson – obviously no ordinary man – went on to develop an enviably carefree riding style on his Brough Superior. On boat race night in 1933 he went the "wrong way" round Piccadilly Circus. A policeman told him to go back, which he did by putting the four into reverse and riding backwards round Eros.

What was this machine, that thrilled the motorcycle world at the Olympia exhibition of 1931? C.E. Allen has researched the genealogy of the four . . . After building two prototype fours (one a vee-four, the other a straight four, both sv and air-cooled), which did not measure up to expectations, Brough had become convinced that a watercooled unit was the only sensible answer. The most suitable engine of this type being the one fitted in the Austin Seven, he went to Herbert Austin and persuaded that usually unco-operative man to supply the Haydn Road works with engines – slightly bored and tuned, mind – complete with gearboxes, as and when G.B. should send in an order. The prototypes had been equipped with final bevel and chain-drive, but for the Austin-engined version Brough elected to maintain the car connection by using *two* back wheels, but very close together, and running the propellor shaft between them. This meant – *pace* Mr Branson – that the new four was unlikely to appeal as a solo. For the sidecar man an advantage was that the wheels were qd. In the event of a puncture in one tyre, one could carry on with the other wheel, as a get-home expedient. Other outstanding features were self-starting, a lefthand throttle twistgrip, a foot clutch giving engagement fully as sudden (with approximately ½in travel at the pedal) as anything experienced in Austin Sevens, and a gearbox that introduced the phenomenon of the "crash change", hitherto known only to the motorist, into motor-cycling circles.

Performance of the Brough-Austin was rather less than was to be had from the Austin car. The outfit, while being at least as heavy as the four-wheeler, presented additional, and oddly shaped, bulk to the wind and there was some power-sapping tyre scrub through sidecar toe-in. It would be exaggerating to suggest 55mph as maximum. Overheating was a problem, too, despite an alloy head and water pump.

Altogether, 10 sales in two to three years stands as a respectable showing for a machine that, even by Brough Superior standards, departed rather too drastically, both in specification and price, from the cosy paths of motorcycling to appeal to an appreciable number of potential buyers.

Specification, Straight Four (1932): Four-cylinder, sv, 800cc (57.9 × 76mm). Three-speed gearbox. 4½g fuel. Tyres, 3.00 × 19in(fr), 3.00 × 19(×2)in(r). 55mph. £188.

Brough Superior SS100

A late 30s SS100 was a very different motorcycle from the earlier big twins that had made Brough Superior a byword for power, noise and often anti-social behaviour on the road. It was still as exclusive as ever – its high price, nearly twice the figure asked for an Ariel Square Four, ensured that – but with the passing of the years George Brough's interest in out-and-out performance was fading. There were, too, occasional hiccups in his relations with J.A. Prestwich, suppliers of the archetypal vee-twin for the BS. By 1937 the SS100 had a Matchless engine which, though equipped with hairpin valve springs and other aids to quick motoring, was more notable for a superbly slow, even tickover, quiet mechanicals and wooffly exhaust note than outrageous performance. At Plumstead, Matchless (AMC) had instituted exhaustive studies into quiet-running following acquisition of the Sunbeam, with its industry-old reputation for quality. Their conclusions pointed to the need for improved lubrication. Naturally the vee-twins came in for treatment. The result was a considerable diminution in internal din, as the oil supply was stepped up.

Mindful of his name for speed and exclusivity, however, Brough continued to advertise the SS100 as the fastest motorcycle on the road. He should have been thankful that the young Philip Vincent, experimenting with his prototype Series A at Stevenage, was either too busy or too timid to litigate. Never one to do things by halves, G.B. went on to advertise the standard SS100 as able to lap Brooklands at 100mph. Nobody, apparently, was brave enough to put this claim to the test – more likely, nobody doubted George Brough's word.

The enormous fuel tank – surely the most memorable in motorcycling history – was as

Bob Berry with the Brough Superior he was to ride in speed-record attempts at Pendine in 1949.

impressive as ever. The Matchless engine was at least as well finned as its rorty predecessor. In any case, to the lay world it remained a "Brough Superior" engine, with cast-in lettering dotted about the place to prove paternity. The gearbox was anonymous but well-tried, being of Norton manufacture, with any name to indicate Norton or Sturmey origins ground off at Mr Brough's behest.

If it was not "the world's fastest motorcycle", perhaps the SS100 by the late 1930s was more deserving of the other legend favoured by George Brough in his advertising material . . . "The Rolls Royce of motorcycles".

Specification, SS100 (1937): Vee-twin cylinder, ohv, 990cc (85.5×85.5mm). Four-speed gearbox. 4¼g fuel. Tyres, 3.50×19in(fr), 4.00×19in(r). 100mph. £140.

Brough Superior Golden Dream

The story of the Austin-engined four has been told. It was merely one manifestation of George Brough's obsession with fours. First there had been an in-line vee-four, then a straight four, then the watercooled Austin venture (possibly the most successful of all, on a production count, with 10 models finding customers); finally, in 1938, G.B. came up with the horizontally opposed Dream. All were the result (according to C.E. Allen, who got to know the great man well in the autumn of his life) of recurring dreams in which G.B. was forever searching for the formula for the ultimate motorcycle. Forty years before Mr Honda's 750 of 1968 made headlines, Brough was convinced that, for acceptance by the public at large, a new-style motorcycle should have the good manners – the quietness, the smoothness – of a car; and that to this end it would have to be a four, probably with shaft drive.

As manufacturer of the Brough Superior and leader of the cult that claimed it as the world's foremost motorcycle (wasn't it, after all, the Rolls Royce among motorcycles?), he felt it was incumbent on him to point the way. Hence the Golden Dream – last and, fleshed

Brough Superior SS100 of 1938, with Matchless engine.

Brough Superior "Dream", 1939: a 996cc ho flat four.

out, most expensive of all George Brough's dreams. It was shown at Earls Court in 1938.

It was the fruit of intense labour by G.B., who received much help along the way from his friends. H.J. Hatch, once Blackburne's designer, assisted in design work; Freddie Dixon came in on development. Producing two prototypes was staggeringly expensive but the result was a machine having all the hallmarks of luxury and success – more than sufficient to bring fresh meaning to that "RR" tag.

But the success that looked so certain did not materialize. The Dream proved a costly disappointment for reasons beyond the control of its sponsor and chief begetter. Best – briefly – described as a pair of flat-twins mounted one on top of the other, the engine was served by one carburettor for each bank of cylinders, giving rise to uneven running. And there was some early trouble with heating-up of the rear pots.

In homage to the forward thinking and extravagant imagination that directed the Dream's advance from design board to prototype in less than 15 months, it is fitting that the potential world-beater should be described in greater detail. C.E. Allen has written: "The crankshafts were geared together and the drive taken from the lower one. The serpentine crankshaft and subsequent complex of the normal flat-twin with two crank throws and pistons moving in opposition was obviated by running each 'engine's' connecting rods on a common crankpin, one rod being forked. In consequence, the crankshafts were short and immensely rigid, being more truthfully two half shafts with integral crank cheeks, one formed with a 1¾in crankpin to which the other cheek was bolted after the connecting rods had been assembled. Gear rings bolted to the rear crank cheeks coupled the shafts, being timed so that all four pistons moved in the same direction at any time. . . all the theoretical implications of this unexpected feature are beyond me, though I can see that the out-of-balance forces of one 'engine' would be cancelled out by its mate.

"The first dimensions, of 71mm bore and 63mm stroke, were surprisingly 'oversquare' for the period, the alloy connecting rods, running directly on gudgeon and crankpin, impressively massive and

short. Cylinder-blocks of light-alloy with cast-in liners were topped each side with heads cast in one. The exhaust valves were operated by pushrods in a tunnel at the rear, where a single carburettor fed two inlets through a bolted-on manifold.

"The result was a most compact power pack, total width just over 26in. Developed to the performance of two Triumph twins on a common crankcase, there should have been over 50 smooth horses, with more to come, because the transverse layout offered ideal cooling . . . with heads and their hot exhausts in the perfect position to catch the breeze. Again using the Triumph twin yardstick, one can imagine a 'hot' version producing enough power for a world-record-breaker.

"The rest of the machine was in keeping with G.B.'s avowed intention to produce the perfect motorcycle. Although the prototypes had a conventional gearbox, with positive-stop footchange and a kickstart, there was talk of a hush-hush four-speed box so secret that it was never described, and a hand lever starter. Final drive was by worm wheel and underslung worm, to allow a low bevel drive shaft.

"Accessibility had been studied. The rear wheel and drive could be detached from the plunger suspension in a couple of minutes. Detail work was superb.

"Teething troubles began with uneven carburation. One pot was updraught, the other downdraught, on each side. When a single central instrument was tried, the long manifolds iced up. As the power was stepped up there was trouble with the connecting rods. Seizures snapped the massive rods like carrots. Some said it was because the stroke was too short . . . too much angularity. More likely it was the use of plain alloy connecting rods before the technique had been mastered.

"But flat-fours are notoriously packed with gremlins. G.B. and his men had only a few months to sort out the problems before the war called a halt."

Forced to shelve the Dream project during the war years, George Brough returned to it in 1945 with plans for separate side-valve cylinders, to achieve a longer stroke. But power was down, with this layout. G.B. lost interest. The Dream was allowed to die.

Specification, Golden Dream (1938): Four-cylinder, ohv, 996cc (71 × 63mm). Four-speed gearbox. 4½g fuel. Tyres, 3.50 × 19in(fr), 4.00 × 19in(r). £185.

BSA

For almost all its 60 years as a motorcycle maker BSA had the distinction of being the biggest in Britain, and on occasion in the world. From far-off beginnings in the 19th century as the Birmingham Small Arms Company, formed to supply munitions for Britain's sorties into Empire building, the Small Heath concern had by the early 1900s developed an interest in road vehicles. The first all-BSA motorcycle, a 3½hp single, appeared in 1910, at the same time that the company took over manufacture of Daimler cars.

Small Heath was expanded to cope with the burgeoning motorcycle business. At the beginning of the First World War it had the vast sprawl of buildings and the thousands of workers that were to give BSA, alone of motorcycle firms, stature to compare with the car giants.

By 1913 all chain drive, with a two-speed transmission, was a feature of the Model H side-valve, which was followed by the enlarged, three-speed Model K. After the remunerative years of the First World War the first of the vee-twins, a 6-7hp model, appeared at the 1919 Olympia Show.

In the 1920s BSA consolidated its leading position in the industry with popular ride-to-work side-valves and the ohv models that were to be the mainstay of the company's sporting activities. These were never (despite a few entries in pre-war TTs) angled towards road or track, but rather at trials and scrambling.

At this time came BSA's first dalliance with a two-stroke (repeated 20 years later with the post-Second World War Bantam, almost certainly Small Heath's most successful model).

Production in the 1930s was centred on the Herbert Perkins-designed Blue Star of 1931, which diversified into the Empire Star (so called in tribute to King George's Silver Jubilee) and later, after radical redesigning by Valentine Page, into the 90+mph Gold Star.

The Blue – Empire – Gold Star line was notable for emphasis on sporting prowess. From the outset the

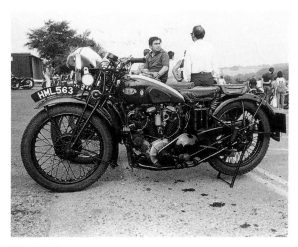

The J12 500cc vee-twin.

specification of these handsome vertical singles included, either as standard equipment or as readily available extras, such essentials to high performance as a high-comp. piston, double-coil valve springs, special cams and a four-speed, foot-controlled gearbox. Equally desirable in the early years, though of less proven worth, were the high-level exhaust pipes featured on the Blue Stars. With help from David Munro and Val Page, in 1936 the 500 Blue Star gained its new name of Empire Star and lost some 3cc, to 496cc, on dimension changes to 82 × 94mm bore and stroke, with a resiting of the Magdyno to a front-of-engine position. When Page had sole charge of rearrangements, a year or two later, he put the electrics back behind the engine, did away with the sump oil reservoir and smartened up the offside of the barrel with a single, large aluminium tower for the pushrods, in place of twin chromed tubes.

They were, in all forms, highly successful motorcycles. Produced in prodigious numbers, and with a well-organised service backup, they put the parent company in an unchallenged position; not merely on home ground but in what were then the colonial territories.

Other notable designs presented by BSA included a short-lived range of high-camshaft engines based on a layout originated for a 500 ohv vee-twin to be supplied to the War Office. It was turned down as being too complicated and expensive. Undismayed, BSA adapted the top half of the would-be WD unit, with its single pushrods tube, for use on a single. The idea was to cash in on its resemblance to the cammy engines currently in vogue. Not enough people were fooled, or impressed, to make the project worthwhile. BSA, having plenty of funds, could afford this sort of experiment.

Their three-wheeler should not be forgotten, either; with twin-cylinder engines, then fours, they provided better value for money than Morgan or Raleigh.

Mrs Miriam Anning (left) and Miss Marjorie Cottle at the 1938 International Six Days Trial in Wales. The BSA is a 250 Empire Star.

And so into the Second World War, during which BSA made by far the biggest contribution of Britain's factories to the Allied stock of military motorcycles, chiefly in the form of the redoubtable M20 side-valve single. Then, in peacetime, the company launched a three-pronged assault on world markets with models from Ariel (taken over in 1944), four BSAs, and the new in-line twins made by Sunbeam, another wartime acquisition.

A run of wins in trials, scrambles and Isle of Man Clubman's events helped to secure big sales of BSA's B-series ohv singles. Technical status was maintained with new parallel twins, first in 500cc form, later as 650s.

The 1950s were heady years for BSA. The order books were full, and money flowed in. The Triumph concern was purchased. Daytona races in the USA fell to BSA twins; the scooter market was tackled with high-speed 250s. Profits doubled. It would have required a wiser man than chairman Sir Bernard Docker, consort of flamboyant Norah, to question the euphoric thinking of an industry that saw successive events as confirming the age-old right of the British, and BSA in particular, to lead world motorcycling.

The 1960s opened with record profits of more than £9 million, a new chief executive (later chairman) in one-time accountant Eric Turner, a new range of single-cylinder models, Queen's Awards for Industry, and the setting up of a vast, expensive research centre.

But the signs, despite apparent success, were not good. The Japanese were encroaching into BSA's traditional markets – most painfully in the USA, for long the richest ground for motorcycle makers. British buyers too were beginning to find the native product long in the tooth, lagging behind the smoothly styled, ultra-reliable, high-performing models from the Far East. The much-heralded 750 triples were upstaged in 1968 by the more advanced, but no more expensive, Honda CB750-4. By the end of the decade BSA sales were in decline.

Profits turned to calamitous loss. In 1971 the group's shortfall amounted to £8 million. The competitions department was closed. A year later there were further losses. Bankruptcy loomed. Dennis Poore, head of the Norton Villiers concern, the only other large-scale remnant of the British industry left by the marauding Japanese, was prevailed on to take over BSA/Triumph and form a Government-financed national motorcycle combine. Within a couple of years the Small Heath works had been sold and demolished, and the last all-BSA motorcycle sold.

BSA Sloper

Some years ago the motorcycling journals often wrote of their testers, and other folk, taking a motorcycle out

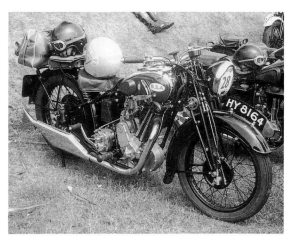

The BSA Sloper in 1931 form, with four-speed gear box.

BSA 500cc Sloper circa 1932.

for a "spin". It was an expression little used in real life. The compiler can recall only one occasion when he was invited to take a bike for a spin. The offer came from someone who, pipe smoking and serious, probably saw himself and his elderly BSA Sloper as characters in the motorcycling world discussed (and probably largely created) by the weeklies. It gave the compiler some satisfaction during the course of his spin to discover a fourth (top) gear among the Sloper's rackety hand selection, and to pass on news of this to the owner, who had based his *three*-speed motorcycling on a reading of a test report dashed off by one of the press experts. It said much for the Sloper's stamina that it had been able to cruise at 50-55mph, often two-up, without apparent strain in third gear.

BSA initiated the Sloper craze in 1927 with an overhead-valve 500 that bore the catalogue identification "S": whether the initial stood for sloper, or speed, or silence – or something quite different – is not possible to establish.

What is certain is that the Sloper was handsome, fast and quiet-running, and so successful that it figured, with yearly updates, among the company's offerings for the next 10 years.

It began as a 493cc (80 × 98mm) single with single-port cylinder head carrying a cast-aluminium enclosure for the rockers alongside exposed valve springs. Long plated tubes covered the pushrods. Gentle cam contours and wide-base tappets diminished valve clack and contributed to the Sloper's early and long-lasting reputation as one of the quietest of sporting 500s. The crankcase was large, accommodating a separate oil container feeding a gear-type pump controlled by hand meter. Early models had a duplex-tube frame and three-speed gearbox. Later the top tube was replaced by an I-section forging carried forward to support the steering head; in 1932 the gearbox became a four-speed. By 1929-30 the single-port head had been dropped in favour of twin ports, and the ohv model joined by a side-valve version (which was never to usurp the Sloper name in any popular sense).

Heavy flywheels gave the Slopers a ponderous tickover, and there was a mellifluous exhaust note at near-zero rpm through large fish-tail silencers. Cruising speed could be up to 55mph, and top speed on the standard model with low-compression piston was around 75mph, when exhaust noise was still comparatively subdued. A race kit, available during most years of the Sloper's life, offered for under £10 a high-comp. piston and special valves and springs and a racing plug; there were few buyers for these for the Sloper's well-mannered image, so quickly established, frightened off the 30s tearaways. The Sloper ended its run in 1935.

Specification, Sloper S32 (1932): Single-cylinder, ohv, 493cc (80 × 98mm). Four-speed gearbox. 2¾g fuel. Tyres, 3.25 × 19in. 68mph. £71.

BSA Special

Neither Blue nor Empire Star, and certainly no Gold Star, the 499cc Special, introduced for 1933, really did have something special about it. The inlet tract was inclined, when most BSAs were resolutely horizontal in that area, and the carburettor was a TT Amal; the

piston was of racing type, and the cams had a rather "sudden" profile. The spark plug was 14mm instead of the still-common 18mm. All these gave the overhead-valve Special 80mph performance and a heavy fuel consumption – around 55mpg at a cruising speed of 60mph – which helped to convince owners that they were paying the time-honoured price for extra power.

Oil was carried in a small container just ahead of the crankcase, which left the Lucas battery to fill the space below the (adjustable) saddle and above the four-speed, foot-change gearbox. Other features considered essential in a sporting motorcycle were the narrow front tyre, of 3in section, and twin exhausts which probably *diminished* performance, because of their extra weight compared with that of the entirely adequate single-pipe layout of lesser models in the range.

The finish was traditional BSA green and chrome for the tank, which was fitted with a dial to show oil pressure, and there was plenty of plating elsewhere. Altogether, the Special was fully a match as a mile-eater for more exalted and more expensive models from rival manufacturers.

Specification, Special 500 (1933): Single-cylinder, ohv, 499cc (85 × 88mm). Four-speed gearbox. 3g fuel. Tyres, 3.25 × 19in. 90mph, £68.

BSA C11 (pre-war)

When a large engineering company concentrates on a particular product or area of manufacture, the result probably will outclass anything turned out by competitors of lesser stature. That is the probability; it cannot, of course, be taken as a certainty. BSA demonstrated some aspects of this proposition in 1938 with their new 250, the C11, which while it never acquired the style of something like the Excelsior Manxman had virtues appealing to a far larger public than ever fell for the eccentric charms of an ohc sports bike.

The C11 started life on the drawing board under the constraint of a specification restricting the final price to £40. It was essentially a utility motorcycle but (because BSA management was shrewd and experienced, with some knowledge of the motorcyclist's capacity for self-deception) it had to have a fair turn of speed, to support any fantasies of TT wizardry on the part of ride-to-work owners. Further, it had to be reliable because

The 1934 499cc Special: as fast as a Norton.

BSA C11 250 of 1939 was good for 65mph.

it would be maintained by people of widely varying competence. It was a demanding outline for a £39 15s motorcycle. For a start, BSA's chief engineer, David Munro, laid down a properly thought-out coil ignition system with a half-speed contact-breaker skew-driven from the camshaft, car-style. It worked with automatic advance and retard, relieving riders of the necessity for fiddling with a manual control and almost certainly ensuring better starting. With a C11 there was a good, fat spark, never a kickback, and thus usually a start at the first attempt; when the ignition was switched on, that is, which for some owners took a while to get used to after the always "on" condition of a magneto. C11 owners learned to ignore the forebodings of the magneto school who spoke gloomily of flat batteries. Running on a modest compression ratio, and having these excellent starting arrangements, the C11 was able to dispense not only with the usual handlebar lever controlling the sparks but also the pull-up trigger to raise the exhaust valve, otherwise considered essential.

Munro believed that the auto advance, set by the factory to vary for optimum effect at certain rpm, would relieve valves and sparking plug of much of the detrimental heating-up that could result from an owner's control of the spark. Probably he was right. Another unusual feature was the crossover layout of the pushrods for the overhead valves, adopted to avoid side thrust on valve guides and rocker bearings. The valve cover, too, showed new thinking in being a rigid light-alloy casting. Other makers tended to make do with flimsy – thus seldom oil-tight – pressings sitting over valve gear which only a year or two before had been open to the breeze.

The C11 developed 11bhp at 5,000rpm. Weighing no more than 240lb, it had a top speed of over 60mph. Testers of the day – men of monumental patience – rode the C11 for hours at a steady 40mph on the new arterial roads and came up with fuel-consumption figures of around 110mpg. Away from the flat, one C11 showed the benefit of its sensitive auto-advance ignition (and, perhaps, a tankful of special ethyl fuel) by climbing 1-in-5 Pebblecombe Hill in Surrey in second gear (9.8 to 1) without pinking. The compiler rode a post-war C11. It was precisely as per the 1939 model apart from a change in front fork, from girders to telescopics, a more ordinary angle for the exhaust pipe, and a cleaned-up cover for the gearbox. The engine did everything Mr Munro had claimed for it.

Specification, C11 (1939): Single-cylinder, ohv, 249cc (63 × 80mm). Three-speed gearbox. 2g fuel. Tyres, 3.00 × 20in. 66mph. £39 15s.

BSA C11 (postwar)

High performer in the C range, the post-war C11 overhead-valve 250 had a 10mph margin over the side-valve C10's 55mph, lower fuel consumption and, generally, a little more zip to it. Not enough, though, to make 250 BSAs much of a power in the land in the 1940s and 1950s.

With various modifications, the C11 lasted until 1954 at which time it gained a "G" to its name and an ac generator and a built-in contact-breaker. By the end of 1954 it had a pivoted-fork frame and 7in front brake.

Specification, C11: Single-cylinder, ohv, 249cc (63 × 80mm). 11bhp/5,000rpm. Three-speed gearbox; four-speed in 1954. Coil ignition; ac generator on C11G. 2¾g petrol, 4pt oil. Telescopic/rigid/plunger; pf from 1954. Tyres, 3.00 × 20in. 280lb. 65mph.

BSA Empire Star/Gold Star

The 1921 Senior TT was important for BSA. Six entries marked the company's return to Isle of Man racing. All six fell out in the course of the first lap, victims of an assortment of valve and piston troubles.

It was failure on the grand scale. The effect on BSA's racing policy was traumatic. Thereafter, in fact, there was *no* racing policy. From 1921 until after World War II, and their Clubman TT-winning exploits, the country's largest motorcycle manufacturer steered clear of big-time racing.

Keeping out of racing did not have any noticeable effect on sales. BSAs continued to be revered, and bought, for their down-to-earth design, reliability, good finish and value-for-money. Norton and Velocette might steal the limelight with race-bred specials but BSAs outsold all other roadsters on the market. But why, enquired some of the people at Armoury Road, didn't the firm go racing . . .? One very good reason, apart from the management's refusal to give the go-ahead, was lack of a model in the 1930s range that lent itself to race development. Until 1936, that is, when D.W. Munro's improved Blue Star made its appearance. The new model was shown at Olympia with a stiffer flywheel assembly and a modified cylinder head. Bore and stroke were 82 × 94mm, to give 496cc, against the previous year's 499cc, and the engine had been subjected to a thorough r. and d. programme at track and factory. The result of all this ambitious development was seen when the new Empire Star circled Brooklands in faultless style to cover 500 miles at an average of 73.3mph.

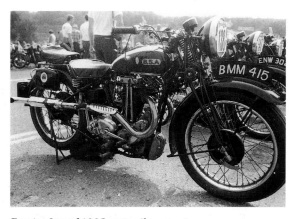

Empire Star of 1935; note oil reservoir sump.

By 1938 the Empire Star had taken this form, with revised enclosure for pushrods and timing case.

The 1939 Gold Star with Amal TT carburettor, all-alloy engine.

This success marked the beginning of the end of the company's 15-year moratorium on racing. The directors' growing confidence was given a further boost during the following year, 1937, on the introduction of Val Page's reworking of the Empire Star. Page had made the cylinder head a single-port (though insuring against the public's wayward tastes by keeping the two-port head as an option) and had turned the crankcase over to the dry-sump principle.

The Magdyno had gone to the rear and the valve gear was enclosed in a strikingly different way. For the first time the pushrods went into a single tube, the aluminium tower which was to be a familiar feature of BSA's ohv singles for many years; and – also for the first time – the rockers and valves were decently, indeed totally, covered. The crankcase was strengthened, with two driveside main bearings, and the very handsome power unit was bolted into a revised, brazed-up frame having a tube top member in place of the previous forged backbone. It was this model that became known as the Gold Star.

BSA director J.W. Bryan had allowed himself to be pressganged, not too unwillingly, into approving an Empire Star entry in the June 30 1937 handicap meeting at Brooklands. The rider was to be Walter

Handley, out of racing since his retirement in '36. The bike was prepared by replacing the Magdyno with a race magneto, and raising the compression ratio to 13:1 with a special piston, to give a power output of 34bhp. There could have been more power had it not been for track regulations which called for use of the so-called Brooklands can in the exhaust system. Impressive to look at, and moderately useful as a noise inhibitor to pacify the litigious non-motorcycling residents of nearby Weybridge, the Brooklands can was above all supremely efficient in diminishing power.

Several BSA men were involved in the Brooklands affair, which had all the ingredients of a ripping yarn. There were the chums of the Remove (Perrigo, Page, Munro, Perkins)... supportive stinks master (Bryan) ... dour headmaster (BSA chairman) ... dashing ace (Handley). Then the race... victory... congratulations all round ... the Beak won over. Handley finished first, at 102.27mph, with a best lap at 107.57mph, to take a Brooklands Gold Star with ease. And that, of course, was the name given to the M24 production version of Handley's racer, when it was listed in BSA brochures the following year. By then it was equipped with an aluminium head and barrel, and Elektron gearbox shell, TT carburettor and a qd rear wheel.

The price was £82 10s.

Specification, Empire Star (1936): Single-cylinder, ohv, 496cc (82 × 94mm). Four-speed gearbox. 3¾g fuel. Tyres, 3.00 × 20in(fr), 3.25 × 19in(r). 77mph, £65.

M24 Gold Star (1938): Single-cylinder, ohv, 496cc (82 × 94mm). Four-speed gearbox. 3g fuel. Tyres, 3.00 × 20in(fr), 3.25 × 19in(r). 92mph. £82 10s.

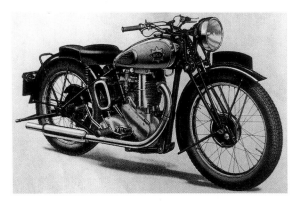

BSA Gold Star in 1938, when it was listed officially as Model M24.

BSA Gold Star (postwar)

The postwar Gold Star, Goldie to fan and detractor alike, apotheosis of the traditional British sporting single, was in reality little more than the punter's B31/33 tuned up to provide more urge than the ohc sportsters turned out by Norton and Velocette.

In 1947, the first postwar Gold Star was a 350, designated B32GS, having the bore and stroke measurements of the B31/32 series but with a choice of cams, gearing and pistons to give differing states of tune for scrambling, trials or road-racing. Later, when the B32/34 models were fitted with alloy engines, there was added confusion. The "competition" machines, used mainly in trials, were sometimes taken to be Gold Stars. Doubts, said BSA, could be easily settled by reference to engine numbers, which in the case of a true-blue Goldie always included the letters GS.

By 1949, when a plunger-sprung 500 Gold Star had joined the line-up, the 350 was producing 25bhp at 6,000rpm on a straight through pipe (compared with the standard B31's 18bhp/5,000rpm). The 500 was acclaimed following a fine showing in the 1949 ISDT, but for the time being it was the 350 that took the limelight, with its first victory in that year's Clubman's TT, at over 75mph.

Eddie Dow on a 1953 500 Gold Star in the Manx Grand Prix.

BSA 499cc Gold Star, 1954.

BSA 500 Gold Star scrambler.

For more than 10 years the Gold Star, in variations encompassing changes to frame, brakes, engine finning and carburation, and with code names running from ZB (1949-52), through BB (1953), CB (1953-55) and DB (1955-56) to DBD (1957-63), was outstanding in motocross, trials and road-racing. Its record in the Clubman's races in the Isle of Man is unbeatable, with 12 wins over the years from 1949 to 1956, when the bike's popularity stood so high that no fewer than 63 among 68 starters were mounted on Gold Stars.

The Gold Star sold best in its "racer" spec. In this form, harsh, noisy and intractable, it was seldom seen on the track, but was much favoured for use on the open road by besotted owners. Now Goldies are museum pieces, with an inflated value.

Specification, Gold Star: Single-cylinder, ohv, 348cc (71 × 88mm); 499cc (85 × 88mm). Varying power outputs: from 26bhp (350) to 40bhp (500). Four-speed gearbox. Magneto, dynamo optional, 4g petrol, 6pt oil; dry sump. Telescopic/plunger/pf. Tyres, 3.25 × 19in (fr), 3.50 × 19in(r); or 3.00 × 21in(f), 4.00 × 19n(r); or to suit. Road trim (with silencer), 90mph (350), 110mph (500).

BSA Fluid-flywheel 500

When a veteran reporter such as R.R. Holliday, for many years editor of one of the weekly journals, writes to the effect that such and such a model was short-lived, and very few examples survived, it may be assumed that only one saw the light of day and that it exists no longer. (Long-serving writers tend to be cautious. "Very few" is less categorical – is safer – than "none".)

The fluid-flywheel BSA was announced in November 1933 and appeared at Olympia during that month. Perhaps it came as no particular surprise, for the mighty BSA company included in its car division both Daimler and Lanchester, famed exponents of clutch-less drive. In its motorcycle application, the transmission was in harness with a mainly conventional 499cc ohv twin-port single. The major difference occurred in the leftside flywheel which, in an enlarged crankcase, was wider than normal and hollowed out to accommodate the driven member of the fluid flywheel. An "exchange of momentum" was achieved by a system of vanes picking up fluid thrown up by centrifugal force, with the driven member serving a sprocket and thence, by chain, the gearbox shaft. No mechanical cut in drive was called for, the fluid flywheel performing the function of a clutch, disengaging the drive at a predetermined, low-revs level. A bolted-up gearbox having three ratios operating on the epicyclic (Wilson) principle was controlled from a handlebar lever working in conjunction with a foot lever on the right side, to permit pre-selection.

Fluid flywheel-transmission 499cc ohv BSA: ingenious and expensive.

bikes were still equipped with forks of pre-war girder pattern, pending development of new telescopics.)

For the rest, the B31 was a rehash – admittedly a stylish rehash – of older components, including a basically pre-war Silver Star engine, cleaned up in some details, with a cast-iron barrel and head, tappet adjustment at the lower end of the pushrods, and a separate, four-speed gearbox. It had a nicely shaped petrol tank in silver and chrome carrying a Smiths 85mph speedometer.

During its 15-year life the B31 came in for regular facelifts, primarily plunger rear springing, then a duplex all-welded frame with rear pivot-fork, and a new-shape tank, together with many minor changes such as a hint of valancing for the mudguards. But as the engine remained virtually untouched, the effect of the changes was to make the B31 a heavier, though better-handling, motorcycle that became progressively slower over the years.

BSA 348cc B31 in 1945: a "stylish rehash" of the pre-war 350.

Because of the fluid flywheel a kickstarter operating in normal fashion through the gearbox was out of the question. Instead, kickstarter motion was taken to the main shaft through a chain of gears mounted in a rearward extension of the timing case.

Emitting the distinctive whine associated with the system in car usage, the BSA's new transmission also depressed performance in much the way that had become commonplace with "fluid-flywheel" four-wheelers.

The 500cc overhead-valve BSA, in standard form a sprightly performer, became bland to the point of tedium when equipped with Mr Lanchester's ingenious transmission.

BSA B31, with pivoted-fork rear springing and enclosed drive, in 1956.

A few months after the '33 show BSA were able to announce a tremendous upturn in sales. The £70 fluid-flywheel model played no part in this change of fortune.

Specification, FF500 (1933): Single-cylinder, ohv, 499cc (85 × 88mm. Three-speed (epicyclic) gearbox. 2¾g fuel. Tyres, 3.25 × 19in. 64mph. £70.

BSA B31

The first BSA to make an impact after the war was the B31, in 1945. It was a trim ohv 350 with plenty of performance and good handling conferred by long-movement telescopic forks which gave it a distinct advantage over much of the "opposition". (Most other

BSA B40 343cc WD model was equipped with "trials" tyres.

In 1960 it was replaced by the short-stroke B40 350 Star of 343cc (79 × 70mm), which was patterned on the C15 250.

Specification, B31: Single-cylinder, ohv, 348cc (71 × 88mm). 16bhp. Four-speed gearbox. Magneto/dynamo. 3g petrol, 4pt oil; dry sump. Telescopic/rigid/plunger; pf available 1954. Tyres, 3.25 × 19in. 340lb. 73mph.

BSA B32

The B32, a competitions version of the B31, came along in early 1946. It was marginally lighter than the roadster, and flashier, with chrome-plated mudguards and brake plates, and a high-level exhaust. More telling practical differences included a wide-ratio gearbox and increased ground clearance through the use of a bigger (21in) front wheel and 4in section rear tyre.

Specification, B32: As B31 but with high-level exhaust pipe, wide-ratio gears. Tyres, 3.00 × 21in(fr), 4.00 × 19in(r). 300lb. Alloy cylinder and head from 1953.

BSA 348cc B32, 1947: big wheels, high-level exhaust, chrome-plated mudguards.

BSA B33

In 1947, a couple of years after the B31 made its debut, the long-anticipated 500 version was added to BSA lists. In all important respects save one – an 85mm bore in place of 71mm – near identical with the 350, the B33 was capable of 80mph, in good conditions 85. Somehow it failed to pick up the sort of following that had made the smaller bike a success.

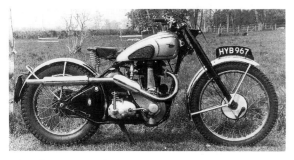

BSA 499cc B33, 1947: slightly faster and heavier than the 350 B31.

BSA M33

The announcement of the M33 500 for 1948 indicates the importance attached to the sidecar market in pre-Mini days. Though it carried on till the late 1950s, few examples were seen. It was an odd mixture of M (for side-valve) and B33.

The forks were girders, the gearbox was a heavyweight, the oil tank more angular than on the "B" 500. Brakes were smaller – which may not seem over-sensible, if they were to slow a bike *plus* perhaps 400lb of laden sidecar – and the mudguards were wider. The M33 was a throw-back to a pre-war line, even to the name. The likelihood is that it was a means of using old stock. The selling price, surprisingly, was the same as for the B33.

Specification, B33/M33: As for the B31 apart from 85mm bore giving a 499cc capacity, 23bhp/5,500rpm, 3.50 × 19in rear tyre; girder fork, cradle frame on M33.

BSA 499cc B33, 1951: mainly for sidecar hauling.

BSA A7

Originally a Val Page design, very quiet, very distinctively "BSA", the A7 was among the second wave of BSA offerings that appeared late in 1946. With an unfamiliar "500" capacity of 495cc, this overhead-valve twin had a cast-iron block and head, with a single camshaft behind the cylinders operating pushrods in an angled tunnel. A short duplex chain drove to the close, bolted-up gearbox – a semi-unit-construction layout, with slipper tensioners, that did away with adjustment for the primary chain, customary in most

BSA 495cc A7 twin, 1947: challenging Edward Turner's Triumphs.

BSA A7 500 in 1959, still with separate, though bolted-up, gearbox.

BSA A7 Star Twin, 1952 (above) and Star Twin engine (below).

Even faster than the Lightning: the BSA Spitfire with race cams and two Grand Prix carburettors.

other designs. The gearbox being small, and set so close to the crankcase, the total effect was rather unbalanced, with the bulk of the engine/gearbox apparently far forward, leaving an impression of wide open space to the rear.

Quickly detachable and interchangeable wheels, and an ingenious but unreliable (soon abandoned) arrangement, with ratchet, to put the bike on its centre stand were other features that gave the duplex-frame A7 some distinction, compared with the Triumph Speed-Twin, the established vertical twin of the day.

Specification, A7: Parallel twin, ohv, 495cc (62 × 82mm). 26bhp. From 1955, 497cc (66 × 72.5mm). Four-speed gearbox. Magneto/dynamo. 3½g petrol, 5pt oil; dry sump. Telescopic/rigid/plunger; pf available 1954. Tyres, 3.25 × 19in(fr), 3.50 × 19in(r). 375lb. 85mph.

BSA A7 Shooting Star

BSA's answers to the Tiger 100, Triumph's sporting 500, were first the Star Twin and then, in 1952, the A7SS, the letters standing for Shooting Star. A 1957 example in pale green differed very little from the first of the line. The original single-side hubs had become full-width, the light-alloy cylinder head and inlet manifold were cast integrally: these were the major changes.

A 1961 500 Shooting Star twin.

One of the most appealing features of the SS was the full enclosure for the rear chain, a commonsense fitting as rare in the 1950s as it is in the 1990s. This BSA was a nicely contoured bike, as fully suited as the Tiger 100 to high-speed cruising. But it lacked the glamour – or perhaps merely the reputation – of the Triumph, and not many were sold.

BSA A10 Golden Flash

In 1950 the A7 grew by 150cc, as part of an industry-wide move to boost the staple British 500 twin's power and speed, mainly to satisfy American requirements. As Triumph enlarged the Speed Twin to 650 Thunderbird dimensions, so BSA went the same way, and called their bike Golden Flash. Though the "golden" colour

BSA A10 646cc Golden Flash, 1951, with plunger rear

BSA A10 Golden Flash in 1960, with duplex-tube frame and pivoted-fork springing.

BSA 650 Lightning, with 53bhp engine.

was more accurately beige, the title had something of the glamour associated with the Gold Star name and soon became part of the motorcyclist's vocabulary. Available at first only with a rigid frame, the archetypical Golden Flash, code-name A10, was plunger sprung by 1951.

The 70 × 84mm engine, outwardly very similar to the A7 power unit, was essentially a new design by Bert Hopwood. The rocker box, for example, was manufactured as a one-piece casting in light-alloy, in place of the separate boxes of the 500.

Power was restricted in the beginning to less than 40bhp. There was plenty of torque, for hauling a sidecar.

When the Golden Flash was equipped with a

pivoted-fork frame in 1953, it gained an abbreviated nacelle, or cowling, for the headlamp, speedo and lights switch. Though more handsome than the plunger-frame A10, and a better handler, the later 650 had problems with uneven carburation that beset it well into its first year and helped to depreciate the reputation of the big BSAs. The early A10 is the one sought by collectors.

Specification, A10: Parallel twin, ohv, 646cc (70 × 84mm). 35-39bhp. Four-speed gearbox. Magneto/dynamo. 4½g petrol, 4-5½pt oil; dry sump. Telescopic/rigid/plunger; pf. Tyres, 3.25 × 19in(fr), 3.50 × 19in(r). 409lb. 95mph.

BSA Rocket Gold Star

The Rocket Gold Star of 1962, not to be confused with the Super Rocket (which as a model name might be said to border on overkill), was a very quick hybrid consisting in the main of a tuned A10 engine and gearbox inserted into a Gold Star frame.

Among BSA twins in the 1950s and 1960s Rockets, Stars and Spitfires abounded, some of them Royal, others merely Super. In 1956 the A10 Golden Flash was joined by the Super Flash which, fitted with high-compression pistons and Amal TT carburettor, was claimed to turn out 42bhp, giving the new model a performance suitable for hard-riding – perhaps only hard-talking – Americans. This model was forerunner to the RGS.

Specification, RGS: As A10 apart from 46bhp engine, 115mph top speed.

BSA Rocket Gold Star: 650 engine, separate gearbox.

BSA A65 Star

By 1962/63 the A10 was ageing unacceptably, and BSA replaced it with the A65 (companion to the similarly styled A50 500). Sweeping changes were evident in the

BSA A50 500 twin, 1962.

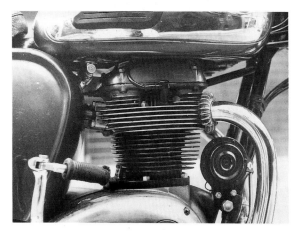

BSA A65R: plenty of performance, and vibration.

adoption of full unit construction for the engine/gearbox, an integral rocker box, and coil ignition plus alternator. With a stroke of 74mm (for both 500 and 650), a bore of 75mm gave the A65 a capacity of 654cc.

A single carburettor bolted to an alloy manifold fed the engine via parallel inlets, while the exhaust ports were splayed in Norton twin fashion. A modest compression ratio of 7.5:1 helped to restrict peak power of the first production 654 to 38bhp/5,800rpm.

The design brief had been to achieve a smooth line and rounded contours. Contributing to this were the ovoid crankcase/gearbox halves, with the gear internals behind the righthand casing. On the left, at the front, the casing concealed an alternator rotor. The light-alloy cylinder head was large, rounded, and topped by the unbroken dome of the rocker cover. The mudguards were valanced, the headlamp had an embryo cowl. Twin casings, one to each side, covered oil tank and carburettor air filter on the right, and battery and rectifier on the left.

The 650 A10 in 1958.

With the new duplex frame and smaller diameter wheels, the total effect was undeniably smooth – perhaps too smooth, even bland.

Known at first as a Star, the A65 handled well but was hardly a match in performance for a good A10.
Specification, A65: Twin-cylinder, ohv, 654cc (75 × 74mm). 38bhp. Later variants had tuned engines of up to 56bhp. Four-speed gearbox. Coil ign/alternator. 4g petrol, 5½pt oil; dry sump. Tyres, 3.25 × 18in(fr), 3.50 × 18in(r). 407lb. 97mph.

BSA Bantam

The Bantam was BSA's most popular model. Over the years it was consistently lowest priced of all the bikes turned out by Britain's principal motorcycle manufacturer.

Introduced in June 1946, the first Bantam, code named D1, bore a close resemblance to a pre-war German DKW. This, however, was apparent only to those with first-hand experience of the DKW. The connection, a matter of war reparations, was never officially disclosed.

Potential owners were grateful to see a newcomer among the lightweight hordes. Rigid-framed, with

Sheep farmers in Australia used Bantams.

A 125cc Bantam, with rear springing, in early 1950s.

Last of the line: 175 Bantam in 1968.

The Bantam engine was a favourite for lightweight trials specials.

telescopic forks and unit construction for the three-speed gearbox, the £60 125cc Bantam was painted pale green and was better looking than any of the small machines relying on Villiers power. It was also a better performer, in speed (at 50-plus mph) and in handling.

In 1954 the 125 Bantam was followed by the 146cc (57 × 58mm) D5, which soon acquired pivoted-fork rear springing in place of the plungers available for some years on de-luxe versions. Then in 1960 came the

Don Cameron on a Walsh-tuned Bantam in Australia, 1957.

D5, of 175cc, named Bantam Super. All models were running concurrently in early 1960.

A few months later the 150 was dropped. As the new decade went on and BSA fortunes declined, so various other offshoots of the line – Standard, De-luxe, Major and most of the Supers – were whittled away until, around 1968, only one remained, the 175 D14 Super.

Specification, Bantam: Single-cylinder, two-stroke, 123cc (52 × 58mm). Three-speed gearbox. Coil ign/alternator. 1¾g petroil. Telescopic/rigid/plunger. Tyres, 2.75 × 19in. 170lb. 148cc (57 × 58mm) introduced in 1953; pf from 1955. 173cc (61.5 × 58mm) introduced in 1957. 53mph (125) to 65mph (175).

BSA M20/21

For some years following the war the major manufacturers offered side valve engines. When the engines were big, the understanding was that the bikes they powered were for the "sidecar man". This was a species occupying a distinctive place in the motor-cycling hierarchy.

The image evoked by "sidecar man", a term much used in motorcycle literature of the time, was clear though seldom spelled out. He was a man of indeterminate size enveloped in stormcoat and

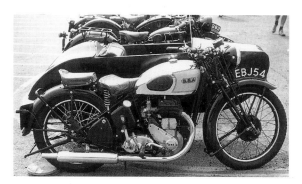

Side-valve 500 M20 in 1939.

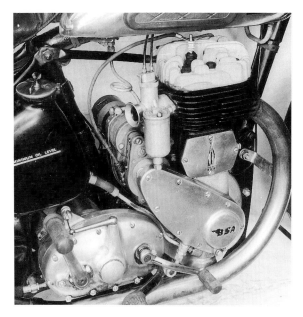

Alloy-head M20 in 1951.

BSA 249cc C15, 1959, with "unit" construction of engine and gearbox.

BSA C15T trials model, 1960.

waders . Like some latterday dinosaur he was capable of only slow, faltering movement when dismounted. He displayed two main, conflicting emotions: pleasure in his solitary life in the saddle, distanced from sidecar-bound wife and children; and some understandable resentment in being restricted to sub-50mph cruising because of the low power of his side-valve motor.

BSA's models intended for sidecar hauling were the 500cc M20, a carry-over from the military bike, and a bored-out relation,the 600 M21.

Equipped from September 1946 with a telescopic fork, the M20 was joined within nine months by the M21, which outlived the smaller bike by a year in lasting until 1958, when both it and the "sidecar man" disappeared virtually overnight, respectively slaughtered and seduced by the new £600 Mini.

Specification, M20/21: Single-cylinder, sv, 496cc (82 × 94mm) 13bhp/591cc (82 × 112mm) 15bhp. Four-speed gearbox. Magneto. 3g petrol, 5pt oil; dry sump. Telescopic/rigid/plunger. Tyres, 3.25 × 19in (M20); 3.25 × 19in(fr), 3.50 × 19in(r) (M21). 370lb. 63mph.

BSA C15

When BSA trials bikes, being too big, too heavy, and indeed too powerful, were shown to have outlived their day, Small Heath found the necessary incentive to come up with the C15 250, in 1958. It had a short-stroke, semi-high-camshaft motor in unit with a four-speed gearbox, an ac generator and a power output of around 15bhp.

An obvious improvement, as a road-going bike, over the C11/12 series, which was then dropped from the range, the C15 metamorphosed within a year into the C15T and C15S, for trials and scrambles respectively. In these forms, with power upped to 20bhp, it was

ridden with great success by, among others, BSA competitions manager Brian Martin, Jeff Smith and John Draper.

Specification, C15: Single-cylinder, ohv, 249cc (67 × 70mm). 15bhp. Four-speed gearbox. Coil ign/ac generator. 2½g petrol, 3pt oil. Telescopic/pf. Tyres, 3.00 × 17in. 290lb. 68mph.

BSA C25

Perhaps following some obscure law of arithmetical progression, the code name for the successor to the C15 was C25. Known in the USA as Barracuda or

Two BSA C25s; the 1968 Barracuda (above) and the 1969 Starfire (top of next page); developments include a large tls front brake for the Starfire.

Starfire, this late-1960s 250 was the fastest bike of that capacity turned out by BSA. With a square-finned, light-alloy cylinder barrel, it had what BSA described as a "sculptured" petrol tank; this and the nearside panel and the oil tank were made in glass-fibre.

The extra performance, compared with the C15, was the product of a higher compression ratio, at 9.5:1, sports camshaft, large inlet valves with heavy-duty springs, and development in the "breathing" department. Other changes were to the crankshaft, now formed as a one-piece forged-steel unit, with bolted-up flywheels. A plain big-end bearing took the place of the C15's roller bearing, and the connecting rod was in duralumin.

BSA B50SS

Product of the Umberslade Hall think tank and (to the disgust of Goldie adherents) given the name of Gold Star 500, the B50SS of 1970 shared the major distinguishing feature of most designs emanating from Umberslade – a ludicrously high riding position resulting from the use of a frame with a large-diameter top tube doubling as oil reservoir.

Following general criticism, efforts were made to reduce seat height, in the main by the uncomfortable expedient of thinning the seat padding.

BSA B50SS of 1970 was designed at Umberslade Hall. Main feature is the high riding position.

BSA Sunbeam Scooter

The compiler rode a BSA Sunbeam scooter for 5,000 miles, and liked it. But scooter-minded people were not impressed. They found the BSA's 70mph and fine handling either irrelevant or a deterrent. Instead of being a sales asset, the Sunbeam's superior performance evoked the alien world of motorcycling, which to any right-thinking citizen planning to become a scooterist seemed to be peopled exclusively by speed-mad dropouts.

The Sunbeam was announced in late 1958, in company with the lookalike Triumph Tigress. The 249cc engine, a Turner-inspired parallel twin, was built in unit with a four-speed gearbox and had a single light-alloy head incorporating in-line valves.

The low-mounted camshaft was set at the rear of the block and operated the valves via flat-base tappets and pushrods. A plunger-type oil pump was driven from one end of the camshaft, with a contact-breaker at the other.

A 1962 BSA Sunbeam scooter in 1962 fitted with BSA accessories.

The engine/gear unit was mounted upright in a tubular frame which supported a flat floor and a subsidiary frame for the seat. Final drive was by duplex chain in a casing doubling as swing arm for the rear wheel. The front wheel was attached by a stub axle to a telescopic arm.

The bodywork, in pressed-steel panels, was graceful but suffered from "over-engineering" in being secured by a multitude of nuts and bolts.

Production of this speedy, reliable scooter ended in 1964. As a big-seller it was stillborn through its failure to meet the scooterist's requirements and because of a little matter of bad timing on the part of the management. Instead of coming in on the new wave of scootering, in the mid-1950s, it arrived three years late, on the ebb tide. Two handicaps too many.

Specification, Sunbeam/Tigress scooter: Twin cylinder, ohv, 249cc (56 × 50.6mm) 10bhp/6,000rpm. Four-speed gearbox. Coil ign/alternator. 1g petrol. 2½pt oil; wet sump. Telescopic/swing arm. Tyres, 3.50 × 10in. 245lb. 68mph.

BSA Beagle

Mr Edward Turner, emperor at BSA (and hence at Triumph and BSA), relaxed from his executive chores in 1961 to return to the drawing board, whence he shortly gave to the world the 75cc Beagle.

Having a pressed-steel chassis with pivoted fork at the rear and leading-link front suspension, the Beagle was aimed at the commuter market then being wooed by Honda and Suzuki. However, it was handicapped by an ohv engine that vibrated like a road drill. It never caught on.

BSA 75cc Beagle, 1963: a failure.

BSA A75 Rocket 3

The Rocket 3 of 1968, more soberly called A75, represented BSA's bid to hold the USA market in face of ever-increasing competition from the Japanese. The work of Bert Hopwood, assisted by Doug Hele and Jack Wicks of Triumph, Meriden, the Rocket 3 was, in brief, a Triumph twin plus a cylinder – an all-alloy 740cc (67 × 70mm) engine having 120° firing intervals. A vertically split crankcase carried two camshafts, fore and aft, in traditional Triumph style, with tube-encased pushrods, and there were three Amal Concentric carburettors.

It was in almost all respects a double of the Triumph Trident 750. Where it differed was in having its engine inclined at a small angle (whereas the Trident was vertical) and in the use of a twin-down-tube frame instead of the Meriden version's single-tube layout. For the rest, there was little between them. Both produced, in early models, 58bhp at 7,250rpm and had a top speed close to 120mph. Racing versions did very well in the UK and, in 1971, at Daytona, where 200-mile winner Dick Mann rode a Rocket 3 to establish a record lap of 104.7mph.

In later years it has become a truism to cite BSA's bad luck/timing/management (choice to taste) in marketing the 750-3 at the same time as Honda came forward with an ohc 750 four.

One point, at least, was made by the clash, though perhaps it was not appreciated at the time. In all those qualities which motorcyclists are supposed to hold dear in their machines – good handling, the simplicity that invites tinkering, and "character", however you define that term – the three was a clear winner. The

BSA Rocket 3 750, 1969: beaten by Honda's new 750-4.

Honda, by comparison, was frighteningly complicated, did not handle as well, and was extremely short on "character". And in racing, always said to be crucial for sales, its record was nothing to write home to Tokyo about.

But the Honda sold in overwhelming numbers, while the BSA tottered into the shadows. Never believe the customers until they have put their money on the table . . .

Specification, A75: Three-cylinder, ohv, 740cc (67 × 70mm). 58bhp/7,250rpm. Four-speed (later five-speed) gearbox. Coil or capacitor ign/alternator. 4¾g petrol, 6pt oil; dry sump. Telescopic/pf. Tyres, 3.25/4.10 × 19in(fr). 4.10 × 19in(r). 470lb. 115mph.

BSA Fury

In the Autumn of 1970 the Fury received much publicity but did not go into production. A 350 dohc parallel twin, it was designed by Edward Turner,

Edward Turner's 350cc ohc Fury SS was intended for 1972 production.

retired from BSA/Triumph and working in a freelance capacity.

With its engine claimed to produce 34bhp at 9,000rpm, the Fury was intended to head the BSA range in 1972. But by then the company was in financial disarray and there was no question of large-scale production.

The design incorporated a forged crankshaft with integral flywheel set for 180° firing and running in two main bearings (ball race on the right, rollers on the left), with light-alloy connecting rods carrying three-ring pistons which gave a compression ratio of 9.5:1 in shallow combustion chambers. Contrary to Japanese practice, Turner kept to the old British style of vertically split crankcase.

Light-alloy was used for cylinder block and one-piece head, with inbuilt posts to support chain-driven camshafts running directly in the head. An electric starter, sited above the five-speed gearbox, was to be an optional extra.

The engine was carried at an inclination of 20° in a duplex frame having pivoted-fork rear suspension and exposed-stanchion front forks. The drum brakes were in Umberslade Hall-inspired conical hubs incorporating, on the front one, a large racing-style air-intake.

A 1935 Ivory Calthorpe with enclosed gear valve.

CALTHORPE

A small manufacturer, Calthorpe turned out motorcycles which were in many cases superior to those produced by big league names. They were undervalued by all except their owners, who had a high opinion of the Calthorpe's straightforward design and quality finish. Early in the 30s the costly 500 ohc models (dating from 1927-28) had been abandoned; in their place came a simple two-model range of 350 and 500cc ohv singles. The engines, well-developed slopers, were made "in house" by Calthorpe. In their final form, as fitted to machines sold at low, low prices by Pride & Clarke, they had total valve-gear enclosure. An endearing characteristic of all Calthorpe engines was good slogging power that made top gear usable from 15mph.

Ivory Calthorpe

The Ivory Calthorpe came along in the late 20s and lasted for a decade. The descriptive part of the name is soon explained. Ivory was the colour chosen for the tank and mudguards of a range that began with an ohv 350 and finally boasted a 72mph 500 known as the Ivory Major.

With five years between them, a 1930 350 and a '35 500 shared a broad sweep of similar design features. The engines were twin-port-head slopers, following the BSA pattern, fitted in full cradle duplex frames that held the crankcase a little to the rear of an integrally formed oil chamber. The gearbox, in both cases, was a bought-out Burman, a three-speed with tankside hand change for the earlier model and a four-speed foot-change (though a hand control was available) on the 500. Pushrods were close together in a single tube that ran up to the rocker box in vertical-shaft style, simulating overhead-camshaft operation; where the 350's valve springs were exposed, the later machine had all its valve gear tucked away in a larger rocker box. In both cases a BTH magneto was mounted to the rear of the cylinder. The 350 had its Amal's mixing chamber vertical. The taller 500 engine, housed in what appeared to be a duplicate of the earlier model's frame, was found to have too little space around its upper reaches; so the mixing chamber was swivelled to the horizontal.

The tallish steering head, allied to a low saddle, promoted in both a characteristic "sit-in" riding style; experience of the earlier machine caused one tester to opt for a more vivid description – "sack-of-potatoes slump".

Strangely, top speed of the 500, at 72mph, showed little benefit of the extra capacity and the intervening years, for the 350 was good for 70 or thereabouts; and the price, again, was much the same, at £47. But this was mainly attributable to the forceful policies of the London dealers, Pride and Clarke, who had been asked to take over sales of the Ivory line.

Stipulating a cut price, P & C duly added Ivory Calthorpes to their list of postal bargains and from 1935 to the outbreak of World War II cleared a fair number of these handsome motorcycles. Handsome; but in conventional retailing from the manufacturer's Birmingham base, the Calthorpes of the 30s had clearly shown they lacked any particular appeal that might single them out from their competitors.

Landing up in Pride and Clarke's garish emporia was an appropriate, even charitable, conclusion to the story of a line of motorcycles that dared, to its cost, to challenge tradition by showing off in a flashy paint job while neglecting the back-up of TT-style performance.
Specification, Ivory Major (1936): Single-cylinder, ohv, 493cc (85 × 86mm). Four-speed gearbox. 2¾g fuel. Tyres, 3.25 × 19in(fr), 4.00 × 19in(r). 68mph. £47.

CHATER-LEA

As the 1930s began, the sands were running out for this pioneer firm which had, it seemed, supplied most of the cycle parts used at one time or another by at least half the British motorcycle industry. Tucked away in the leafy enclaves of Letchworth Garden City, far from the grimy setting of a mainly Midlands-based industry, Chater-Lea may have thought themselves insulated from the commercial pressures affecting other manufacturers. If so, they were wrong. When it came to making their own machines, Chater-Lea felt obliged to excel. Quality, therefore, was of the highest ... resulting, quite properly, in above-average retail prices.

This might not have mattered in the palmy days of the 20s, or even later on as World War II approached. But high pricing during the early 30s was an almost certain recipe for commercial disaster. Production ended in 1936.

CORGI

Corgi was the postwar name coined for the military Welbike used by parachute troops in Allied landings in Europe. It was powered by an 89cc Excelsior Spryt engine. After the release of a few bolts at salient points, it could be folded to no more than 53in × 20in × 13in and placed in a holdall. In a civilian context, there was some uncertainty as to who or what should carry this package, weighing at least 100lb. The compiler recalls heaving a Corgi over a lowish hedge (to enjoy some wild Spryt-powered cross-country riding) and finding it no easy task.

Nobody was known to mourn the Corgi's passing, in the Autumn of 1956.
Specification, Corgi: Single-cylinder, two-stroke, 98cc (50 × 50mm) 2.8bhp/4,000rpm. Flywheel magneto/direct lighting. 1¼g petroil. Unsprung front fork replaced by springing Nov. 1951; telescopic saddle tube. Tyres, 2.50 × 12in. 100lb.

Corgi MkIV of 1953 would go in a (big) car boot.

COTTON

The founder of the firm was Frank Willoughby Cotton who trained for the law but gave it up when he became interested in motorcycling. Before-the-war Cottons are chiefly remembered for two things: their TT win, in 1923, when the young Stanley Woods rode a Blackburne-powered model to score the first of his 10 IoM victories; and the patented triangulated frame that Cotton devised even before he went into motorcycle manufacture full-time in 1918. The engines were ordinary (though often good) proprietory units turned out by the hundred by JAP and Blackburne and Rudge-Whitworth. But Mr Cotton's rakish frame was unique. It was, geometrically, possibly the best ever produced by a British concern. His "Principle of Design" stipulated that all the tubes should be straight, subject only to compression or tension forces, and laid out in full triangulation, stress being concentrated at the apex of any triangle. Thus the steering head was strongly, and visibly, supported by twin sets of duplex tubes running back, from top and bottom of the head, to the rear wheel spindle. It amounted to an unbeatable formula for superb handling. And thanks to the designer's legal expertise, it was retained exclusively for Cottons despite a number of "poaching" attempts by other makers.

Woods' Junior win put Cottons on the map, generating sales through the 1920s and even into the straitened 1930s when the range was reduced chiefly to JAP-powered singles.

F.R.W. England rides a 250 Cotton with Rudge engine to second place in the 1936 Manx Grand Prix.

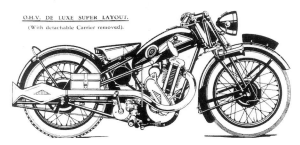

O.H.V. DE LUXE SUPER LAYOUT.
(With detachable Carrier removed).

Super De Luxe Cotton of 1929 with JAP engine and Druid front forks.

Cotton in the 1970s, with a 125 Minarelli engine.

Still in their home town of Gloucester, but in smaller premises, Cottons after the war were without F.W. – Bill – Cotton but acquired instead new directors in sporting enthusiasts Monty Denley and Pat Onions. As was the case with so many of the small firms in the industry, Cottons had to rely on Villiers for power.

There was little to distinguish the firm's products from any rival bikes – certainly nothing as eye-catching, or as provenly superior, as the original triangulated frame, which had been put to one side on the outbreak of the Second World War.

F.J. Williams on a 500 Blackburne-engine Cotton in the 1951 Cirencester speed trials.

In the 1960s and 1970s Cotton were mainly engaged in producing trials bikes, often in kit form, and 250 racers used by riders of the calibre of Derek Minter.

Cotton-Blackburne 250

In the mid-30s Cottons were eking out a precarious existence. Orders were few; competition for dealers' business was intense. Like others in the industry, Cottons were grateful for the helping hand held out by the government with road-tax concessions on machines weighing under 224lb and, soon after, on those with engines of less than 150cc. Building "tax-dodgers" and sending them off to be sold at rock-bottom prices by the "manufacturer's friend", Pride and Clarke, in London, kept many of the smaller firms going in circumstances when commonsense – or hard-headed shareholders – might have dictated closure.

So it was with Cottons; and years later F.W. Cotton, the founder, was moved to express his feelings about Pride and Clarke, a firm not universally loved in the 30s, or after. He was unexpectedly enthusiastic, and grateful. There was no question of Pride and Clarke stocking up with inferior Cottons, he said. The secret of the low price asked for his bikes, which gave sufficient sales to keep his company in business, was that P&C took only £1 profit on each machine, relying on hp interest and part-exchange deals to make up a reasonable margin. When times were particularly hard, Mr Cotton recalled, they would take a railway container of any dozen machines he might have available, without insisting on particular models.

One of the bargain-basement Cottons qualifying for the tax concession was a 1936 model with a 250ohv Blackburne engine that appeared to have been assembled from components left over from the early 20s. Somewhat lost in the straight-tube frame, it had pushrods which chattered busily, and in full view, between cam and open valve gear set on top of an inclined cylinder having a single exhaust-port head. A handy Best and Lloyd unit on – not in – the timing chest pumped lubricant here and there, but not as far as the rockers, which required an occasional greasing. And there was coil ignition of a rudimentary kind, with the contact-breaker chain driven from the engine sprocket.

Pride and Clarke's best efforts, allied to an advertised price of under £35, failed to shift many of these rare machines.

Specification, 6/JB (1936): Single-cylinder, ohv, 249cc (62 × 80mm). Three-speed gearbox. 2g fuel. Tyres, 3.25 × 19in. 63mph. £34 15s.

Cotton with sloper JAP engine, 1933.

Cotton 500

Blackburne engines, long favoured by Cottons, were in short supply by 1936; the antique ohv 250 previously described may well have been a scraping from the Blackburne barrel. Rudge Python engines were hard to come by. Cottons had little choice but to fit JAPs in their bigger machines – though there could have been little to quarrel with in the single that JAP made available in 1938. With high, chain-driven camshafts, short pushrods covered by a single tube, and an enveloping aluminium lid over the valve gear, this was a handsome engine with a strong suggestion – intended? – of "overhead camshaft" about it. Adding to the sporting look, finning on the cylinder head was numerous and deep. The engine was mounted vertically.

How many Cottons with this engine were sold? No reliable information is available, unfortunately – and much the same applies in the case of the final machine in this "pre-war" section . . .

In 1939 another JAP engine, this one designed by Dougal Marchant, made an appearance in F.W. Cotton's unique frame. Like the 1938 version, it was arranged vertically, but visually was less impressive, having pushrod passages cast in cylinder and head, meagre finning on both, and an insignificant rocker box partly hidden by the petrol tank. The effect, if not quite of a tallish two-stroke, was of something eccentrically, though not interestingly, new – like a Cross, say, or an Aspin rotary.

Mr Marchant had come up with one or two out-of-the-ordinary ideas. Inspired perhaps by Phil Vincent's efforts to reshape the traditional form of ohv geometry, he designed the valve gear on this new 500 to take a ball in cups formed at the extremities of pushrods and rockers; at the other end of the rockers was a roller to bear on the valve stem. He was determined, it seemed, to eliminate side thrust, though this could hardly have been the objective in his final novelty, in which both valves shared one pair of cantilever springs rocking on a centre pin, with the extended legs of the springs hooked under the valve collars.

Tested in the Spring of 1939, the Cotton attracted praise from *The Motor Cycle* (what motorcycle did not?). It was, they said, a machine with an excellent all-round performance capable not only of high speeds – 76.3mph was achieved over a timed quarter-mile – but having a tickover and slogging powers more like those of a gas engine than a normal motorcycle. Was Mr Marchant pleased by this tribute? Had he been aiming for a gas-engine likeness? Nobody can now say.

As for the "well-proved Cotton triangulated frame . . . with Druid central-spring front fork", there could be no doubting the magazine's approval. "The result of these features", it declared, "and no doubt the weight distribution . . . is steering, roadholding and cornering that are as good as probably have ever been attained with a 500cc machine other than with rear springing." For *The Motor Cycle*, whose praise of manufacturers and their wares, though unremitting, tended to be rather low key, this rated as near-hysteria. (Familiarity, however, with *The Motor Cycle's* locutions reveals the careful qualifications embedded in that passage.)

A sequel to the story of these gas-turbine-like Cottons is that some were fitted with commercial sidecars and supplied to the Gloucester County Council, running for upwards of 50,000 miles, and hauling loads of up to 10cwt until pensioned off in favour of light vans in the early 1950s.

Specification, 500 de Luxe (1939): Single-cylinder, ohv, 490cc (85 × 88mm). Four-speed gearbox. 3g fuel. Tyres, 3.25 × 19in. 76mph. £58.

Cotton 247 Conquest

In October 1981 the Castle Coombe circuit was used for motorcycle racing for the first time in many years. It was there, 16 years before, that the Cotton Conquest had made news in the two-wheeler world by scoring a 250-class victory, in the hands of Derek Minter and Peter Inchley.

The 1965 Conquest's engine was the Bernard Hooper-designed Villiers Starmaker two-stroke single. A light-alloy barrel and head, two phased carburettors and other features helped in producing about 25bhp at 6,500rpm – more than enough to put this latest Villiers well ahead of the earlier competitions unit, the 34H.

In the Conquest, the Starmaker had a compression ratio of 10:1. Top speed was around 85mph, with 1³⁄₁₆in

Cotton 250 Conquest, 1965.

Monoblocs fitted, and an expansion-type exhaust system. A short-wheelbase, duplex-tube frame with an Armstrong leading-link front fork and pivoted-fork rear springing gave a smooth ride. Very few Conquests were used on the road, for the Starmaker's power characteristics were more suited to track than urban going.

Specification, Conquest: Single-cylinder, two-stroke, 247cc (68 × 68mm). 25bhp. Four-speed gearbox. Flywheel magneto/alternator. 5g petroil. Tyres, 2.75 × 19in(fr), 3.25 × 19in(r). 230lb. 85-90mph.

Cotton Corsair

The Cotton Corsair of 1962 was fitted with Villiers' 31A 246cc two-stroke single and listed as a sports machine. Supporting this claim were some streamlining around the headlamp, an impressively strutted leading-link front fork, and a generally sporting appearance. Performance, however, did not match looks, and top speed worked out at no more than 65mph.

The engine, producing 12bhp at 4,500rpm, was not remotely in the sports category – understandably, for it had been designed to power the newly popular three-wheelers of the day. The other limiting factor was Cotton's policy of keeping to the same top-gear ratio for all their models, irrespective of engine size. For the

Cotton Corsair, 1962: 246cc Villiers engine, leading-link front fork.

250 a ratio of 6.2:1 meant under-gearing; even 65mph entailed 1,000rpm in excess of peak-power revs.

Handling, though, was good. If one could overlook certain anomalies, such as the provision of an invitingly long, comfortable duel seat, with the absence of pillion footrests, the Corsair impressed as a good example of the motorcycles turned out by the small English factories after the war.

Specification, Corsair: Single-cylinder, two-stroke, 246cc (66 × 72mm). 12bhp/4,500rpm. Four-speed gearbox. Flywheel magneto/rectifier. 2¾g petroil. Leading-link/pf. Tyres, 3.00 × 19in(fr), 3.25 × 19in(r). 275lb. 63mph.

COVENTRY EAGLE

How did Coventry Eagle keep going in the 1930s? With origins dating back to the last decade of the 19th century, the firm offered little in its early 30s ranges for the hard-up motorcyclist wooed by dozens of other, more resourceful manufacturers. There were Villiers-engined lightweights, and biggish four-strokes from 300 to 500cc, the engines supplied by Sturmey-Archer (Raleigh) and JAP, but nothing about these lifted Coventry Eagle out of the ruck.

Coventry Eagle K3, with JAP engine in pressed-steel frame, in 1933.

By 1933 the choice had been cut to 150 and 250cc, two-stroke and four-stroke, and business was at a low ebb. It was at this stage that the company decided to follow an avant-garde line, and work was put in hand to design Coventry Eagle's stab at an "everyman" motorcycle that finally appeared in 1936. Fitted with either a Villiers two-stroke or a Blackburne four-stroke, both 250cc, the Pullman featured comprehensive enclosure, rear springing and pressed-steel forks; there was even an attempt at car-style streamlining, especially towards the rear. Press pundits predicted big sales for it (which – needless to say? – were not fulfilled).

Possibly the greatest claim to fame of the marque was that record-breaker Malcolm Campbell rode a Coventry Eagle; the reason might have been no more than friendship between Campbell and Percy Mayo of Coventry Eagle.

Coventry Eagle Pullman 250

In a motorcycle manufacturer's interpretation of the term the "man-in-the-street", that near-mythical creature is waiting in the rain for a bus and dreaming of a motorcycle – *anything* with powered wheels – to take him on his independent way. This remains a maker's fantasy long after the 1930s, which saw some interesting attempts to flesh out the dream. There were, for example, the Francis-Barnett Cruiser and the Royal Enfield Cycar, the first having the "dirty bits" partially enclosed, the other a 100 per cent cover-up. The Coventry Eagle Pullman belonged to the half-and-half persuasion, but was rather more interesting than either of the others.

Coventry Eagle Pullman 250, 1936: one of the more successful attempts at an "everyman" motorcycle.

The Motor Cycle said the Pullman was "a plucky attempt to break away from the commonplace". This possibly ranks as faint praise. The frame, which properly should be described as a chassis, had semi-elliptic springing for the rear wheel. Manufactured in pressed-steel, the chassis was like two sides of a (primitive) boat bolted to an upper tubular section carrying the steering head and the saddle support, with a conventional fuel tank running along a horizontal member between the two. The entire rear section of the bodywork comprised panelling to enclose the upper part of the rear wheel, with a pillion seat on top. Pillion rests were incorporated, as were legshields for the rider. A large cast-aluminium silencer box protruded to the front between the legshields.

A variety of engines was on offer for the Pullman, including Villiers (in two forms) and an ohv Blackburne with a four-speed footchange gearbox. "Built like a car, sprung like a car," declared Coventry Eagle advertising. Not many were made, and very few survive.

Specification, M11 (1936): Single-cylinder, two-stroke. 250cc (67 × 70mm). Four-speed gearbox. 3g fuel. Tyres, 3.25 × 19in. 58mph. £45.

DMW

DMW stands for Dawson's Motors Wolverhampton, a company formed by W.L. Dawson in the early years of the Second World War to make suspension systems for owners dissatisfied with their solid-frame machines.

But DMW as it existed until the 1970s was much more the creation of Harold Nock, who joined it in 1946, bringing a much-needed financial boost, and took over when Dawson left. Harold Nock was more interested in making lightweight motorcycles than rear springing. The first DMW was announced in late 1947. It was 122 Villiers-powered and had an undamped telescopic front fork.

As production picked up, more room was required. DMW moved from original Dawson premises in Wolverhampton to Nock's Metal Profiles factory, a one-time train depot in Sedgley, whence over the years a number of more than ordinarily interesting motor-cycles was despatched to selected dealers.

Trials were an early interest of the firm, underlined when Michael Riley, a keen competitions rider and no slouch on the technical side, joined Harold Nock as development engineer. Successes with Riley-designed DMWs were recorded in Scottish and International Six Days trials. As late as 1976/77, long after the Riley era, DMW trials bikes were winning Midlands events.

Distinctive marks of early DMWs included the use of square-section tubing, and a clever method of

DMW Trials, 1959, with Earles-type front fork.

Villiers 197cc power in a Mark 9; note square section frame.

adjusting the rear chain by snail-cam at the fork pivot (overcoming the difficulty of achieving parallel movement of the rear-wheel spindle, as experienced with more conventional layouts). This arrangement predated by several years the similar, much publicized device fitted to Jeff Smith's championship-winning BSA scrambler.

With bikes selling well, the "springing" side of the business was reactivated under the Metal Profiles banner. Over the years the Sedgley works supplied MP telescopic and leading-link front forks to many small concerns in the industry.

Throughout the 1950s Harold Nock, supported by his daughter on the accounts side of the business, turned out a series of models powered by Villiers two-strokes, with a brief interlude, around 1953/54, when DMWs were announced – but never produced – with French AMC ohc units of 170 and 250cc.

In the 1960s a heavyweight scooter, the Deemster, appeared. There was also some involvement in road-racing, using the newly released Villiers Starmaker 250 single to power a model known as the Hornet, which achieved a very creditable 10th place in the 1965 IoM

Lightweight TT in the hands of future world champion Jack Findlay.

The company's racing ambitions took the form of a 250 hybrid utilizing DMW and Royal Enfield components, and reached a peak with plans to produce a 500 two-stroke twin, the Typhoon, which was no more (or no less) than two 250 Starmakers coupled at the crankshafts by a Nock-devised method which was never explained. A prototype was built, but thereafter nothing was heard of the project.

With jigs and machine tools acquired from Villiers when that firm ceased engine production, DMW carried on to the late 1970s with a restricted programme of trials models. The firm's manager, Michael Parks, had a run of successes on light, MP-forked two-strokes.

DMW Cortina

DMW's Cortina of 1954 owed its attractive name to the inspiration of George Wilson, then assistant editor of *The Motor Cycle*. He had received a desperate call from Michael Riley, who was due to show the firm's new model at Earl's Court and was at a loss for a name for his brainchild.

The Cortina was chiefly interesting for its pressed-steel bodywork, which covered all the untidy electrical bits and pieces. The engine was the 225cc 1H Villiers with four-speed gearbox. Where pressed work was not in evidence, the frame was in DMW's customary square-section tubing.

DMW 224cc Cortina, 1955.

DMW's four-stroke Dolomite at the 1953 show; the rider, middle, is *Motor Cycling's* Norman Sharpe.

The DMW Typhoon 500 twin racer never took to the track.

DMW Deemster

On his way through rural parts in the 1970s the compiler of these notes often noticed an oldish DMW Deemster parked outside a policeman's house in Chelmsford, Essex. The Deemster was a hybrid devised by Michael Riley in 1961 which remained popular with the police long after it was dropped from production. Of limited value as a pursuit vehicle, its hard-pressed 15bhp Villiers having to propel more than 3cwt of bike, the twin-headlamp Deemster was favoured because its odd-looking construction, part scooter, part motorbike, provided better-than-average rider protection and ample storage for anything a country policeman might be obliged to carry on his daily round.

DMW Deemster: part motorcycle, part scooter, 1961.

Dot Mancunian, with 197cc Villiers, as produced 1958-60.

It should be said, though, that if it was no jet the Deemster still managed to out-perform many 250 motorcycles, and any scooter, because of its large wheels and well-engineered chassis.

Framework comprised a main 2½in-diameter tube in 14-gauge, having welded-on brackets to carry the pressed-steel body, arched fuel tank and in-built front legshields.

The front-wheel suspension was a pivot-fork (made of course by Metal Profiles) controlled by a single hydraulic unit. In de-luxe form the Deemster was fitted with a Siba 12-volt generator for coil ignition and electric starting.

The screen and carrier were fitted as standard equipment; the makers made a point of there being no extras to buy.

Specification, Deemster: Twin-cylinder, two-stroke, 249cc (50 × 63.5mm). 15bhp/5,500rpm. Four-speed gearbox. Coil ign/alternator. 3g petroil. Tyres, 4.00 × 12in. 350lb. 67mph.

DOT

Nobody now seems able to say with authority whether Dot stands for Devoid of Trouble, as was once popularly supposed, or merely signifies the dot that graced the tank of early models. The firm died, as far as motorcycles were concerned, in the same Ellesmere Street, Manchester, location where Harry Reed had opened his business 70 years before.

One among dozens of tiny firms turning out bone-shakers relying on proprietory power, Dot used French Peugeot engines and acquired early fame with a TT win, in the twin-cylinder class, in the 1908 Isle of Man races. This was enough to give Harry Reed a fixation on "sport" throughout his career as a manufacturer. With outings at Brooklands and the TT, he continued in business to the outbreak of the First

World War. Afterwards, as enthusiastic as ever, he returned to the Isle of Man with a Junior (350) entry, powered by an ohv JAP, which managed fifth place.

During the 1920s Dot, though hardly a household name (even in motorcycling households), continued to support racing, with JAP, Bradshaw and Blackburne engines, securing second places in the Sidecar and Junior TTs of 1924 and more lowly finishes in the following year's Island events. These last were effectively Harry Reed's sporting swansong as manufacturer. The firm had to seek outside help, and in the change to Dot (1926) Ltd. the founder left.

Road-racing was soon dropped. It was an expensive sideline for a struggling business, even if it did promote extra sales. Dot struggled through the depressed 1930s until the Second World War brought contract work.

After the war, with cash in the bank, Dot brought out a range of lightweights powered by Villiers and kept these in production through the 1950s. With plenty of hefty frame on view, a smallish tank, and a link-type front fork, retained long after others firms no bigger than Dot had MP telescopic forks, these bikes were, frankly, ugly.

The machines' toughness was shown to be real as well as apparent when Dot moved into the scrambles field in 1950s, challenging BSAs and other four-strokes. The up-to-250cc classes in national events became Dot benefits. In the UK the performance of the Dots, with their "breathed on" Villiers engines, paved the way for the eventual takeover, in all classes, by lightweight two-strokes from abroad.

Always unhappy to be one of the crowd, Dot introduced around 1956 an agricultural-looking front fork made in the foundry at Ellesmere Street. This was enormously strong and was fitted to the scramblers for many years.

When Villiers withdrew from engine manufacture, Dot were hard hit and had to turn to imports from Germany and Italy. At the same time Bultaco and others were moving in. Dot (for some years in the hands of B. Scott-Wade and Son) quietly petered out of the motorcycle business in 1973.

Dot 200 Scrambler

Dot's scrambler of the 1950s was a favourite with North of England sporting riders. As recounted previously, it achieved many successes, mainly in the hands of Bill Barough, at a time when scrambling, later moto-cross, was considered more properly the preserve of large, powerful four-strokes. The lightweight, comparatively low-powered 197cc Dot scored by virtue of its easy handling, which gave more scope to a rider's dash than his biceps. It may be seen as predating the Scandinavian and Japanese two-strokes which took over the sport in the 1970s.

The Scrambler's tuned engine was housed in a specially strengthened short-wheelbase frame (49½in as opposed to the standard road machine's 51in). An expansion chamber was set immediately ahead of the cylinder, leading into a normal exhaust pipe and silencer. When the bike was used in competition, silencer and tail pipe were removed and the outer part of the expansion chamber turned so that its exhaust-pipe stub pointed down to emit, without hindrance, plenty of gas and decibels.

Dot 197cc Standard of 1949 with spindly telescopic fork.

£5 cheaper, model. A spindly-looking but effective Metal Profiles telescopic front fork emphasized the all-British complexion of the Dots, and some play was made of a *faired* speedometer, the implication being that precious mph were gained thereby. This must rank as one of the more fanciful notions of the usually down-to-earth British motorcycle industry.

Dot Demon scrambler was immensely strong.

Dot Works Replica, 1960.

DOT Standard 197

For several years after the war, until 1951, the roadgoing Dot was the Standard, which came in two forms, each powered by the ubiquitous 197cc Villiers two-stroke unit linked to a three-speed gearbox but differing in provision of a battery rectifier set on one model, as opposed to the direct lighting of the other,

DOUGLAS

The Douglas, destined as the years pass to be recalled chiefly as a "British BMW", first saw the light of day in Bristol around 1907. It was a carry-over from a failed design by W.J. Barter, who had the good sense to take his ideas to Douglas Bros. of Kingswood, where he helped that company, at the time engaged in foundry work, to start in the motorcycling game.

Interestingly, the first Douglas was a horizontally opposed 350, and so was the last, 50 years on; other similarities were, of course, few.

Single-speed, then two-speed, with automatic inlet valves, early Douglas machines with "fore and aft" cylinders engaged in mildly sporting activities. In 1912, some bikes being enlarged to 600cc, with mechanical inlet valves and a four-speed gearbox, Douglas entered for the Isle of Man TT. They won the Junior, and took second and fourth places as well.

During the First World War thousands of Douglas bikes were turned out for military use. The company had expanded by the time it returned to civilian production. Overhead-valve engines were introduced in 1921, with all-chain drive, in new, low frames. This new breed attracted the attention of gifted engineer/riders such as Rex Judd and Freddie Dixon whose association with the flat-twins was to be life-long, the latter's best-remembered exploit being his win in the 1923 Sidecar TT on a unique banking outfit.

No motorcycle firm tried harder than Douglas between the great wars; no firm had to contend with more financial setbacks. Newish designs were teamed with successive changes in the oiling system (always a source of potential worry with fore-and-aft twins). But, such were the varied fortunes of the different proprietors, there never was enough time available for thorough evaluation of customer reaction. Simply,

Douglas never stuck long enough with a model to get it right.

Undoubtedly the most famous Douglas of the 1920s was the Cyril Pullin-inspired EW series which originated as a 200lb 350 side-valve and grew to 600cc. Douglas expert Jeff Clew has calculated that the firm produced no fewer than seven distinct model ranges during the years from 1920 to 1931. These were merely the basis of an unfathomed number of further variations – commonplace for Honda in the 1980s, perhaps, but a staggering achievement for a small West Country motorcycle manufacturer 60 years ago.

Douglas Motors (1932) was formed in the first years of the hungry 1930s, with outside financial interests taking over from the Douglas family. To no good end, however, for sluggish sales soon got the new firm into difficulties. One of the founding fathers had to come back to put the firm to rights.

Douglas competition model, 1951: few were made – consequently, it is a sought-after "classic" in the 1990s.

Anyone with a passing interest in motorcycling history would pick the Endeavour as the outstanding model to come out of Bristol in the 1930s. The Endeavour of 1934 had a 494cc engine, one of about eight options on offer. It was an in-line horizontally opposed twin, of course, but mounted *across* the frame, with alloy barrels and heads, and driving the rear wheel by shaft through a four-speed gearbox rearward of the clutch. It sold – in very small numbers – at little more than £70, and its high production costs undoubtedly helped to persuade the firm to accept another takeover offer, from the British Aircraft Company.

Providentially, another World War came along to boost Douglas fortunes with contract work for the Government. Afterwards, with new ohv 350s, Douglas motored on, never hoisting itself to a position among the big sellers but always being comfortably ahead of the two-stroke pack represented by such firms as DMW and Norman.

Updates on the 1945 T35 design, designated variously Mark 3, Sports, Mk 5, 80 Plus and Dragonfly, kept the design staff busy. In 1949 the company began to import Vespa scooters from Italy, and in 1951 produced them under licence at Bristol.

Motorcycle and scooter manufacture was brought to a halt in 1957 by Westinghouse, the American owners who had taken over four years earlier.

Douglas Aero 600

It was one of the recurrent financial crises bedevilling the Douglas concern that gave rise to the Aero models. In 1935 the British Aircraft Company formed Aero Engines Ltd to take over William Douglas (Bristol) and with it the interests of the Douglas family. The intention was to assemble aircraft engines with the motorcycle plant. But little came of the plan. The new owners had no choice other than to continue with motorcycles, albeit in a starkly reduced programme. For 1936 and '37 Douglas models carried the Aero prefix and were sold at cut prices, the unique transverse Endeavour, for example, having a price tag of £59 10s, compared with £72 in the 1935 season. The fore-and-aft 600 was available at under £40, a strikingly low figure even in those depressed days for a large twin-cylinder motorcycle.

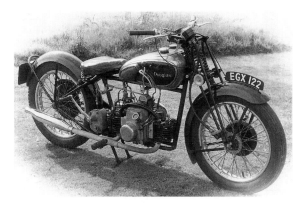

Douglas 600, 1935: a 60mph twin for less than £40.

Fore-and-aft Douglas had a top-mounted magneto: stray sparks – with adjacent carburettor – could be dangerous.

Bore and stroke of the 1936 Aero 600 were 68mm × 82mm, power output was under 20bhp, and top speed modest, about 62mph. Control for the four-speed gearbox was by hand, unusual at a time when the majority of manufacturers had turned to foot change but doubtless a factor in the low selling price. The brakes were impressively large but failed to live up to their looks. They worked on a semi-servo principle devised by famous Douglas charioteer Freddie Dixon which was complicated and largely ineffective. (It was unclear why Dixon, a man of legendary strength who anyway appeared to have little use for brakes, devoted time to this project.)

A three-pint oil supply from a separate tank was deployed in an apparently thorough manner in and around the crankshaft assembly and big-ends. But heating-up problems were not uncommon, though usually confined to the front cylinder, an anomaly explained by the crankshaft flinging oil to the rear and starving the well-ventilated front cylinder. The carburettor was an Amal feeding the combustion chambers via long plated induction tracts which were prone to condensation (and icing in cold weather).

Specification, Aero 600 (1936): Twin-cylinder, sv, 584cc (68 × 82mm). Four-speed gearbox. Tyres, 3.25 × 19in. 62mph. £39.

Douglas OW/OW1

In the early 30s a would-be Douglas owner had the choice of ohv sportsters at 500 and 600cc, and at least five side-valve models ranging from 248 to 750cc and identified – in the larger displacements – by names that were more idiosyncratic than logical. The sv 500, for instance, was the Bulldog, though it was lighter and scarcely slower than the 600 Greyhound, while the 750 was known as the Mastiff. Inspiration failed, apparently, with the smaller machines.

Douglas 494cc OW of 1934 featured totally enclosed ohv gear.

The division was clear. The overhead-valve machines were aimed at the man who might otherwise consider a Red Hunter Ariel or a sporty Velocette; the side-valvers were for ride-to-work people and for sidecar-hauling. Displaying clear links with record-breakers of the early 20s and the later speedway models, the ohv machines of 1934, known simply as OW (500) and OW1 (600), had totally enclosed valve gear on top of the cylinders and long induction pipes arranged in a graceful sweep from the offside-mounted carburettor. Many of the OW components were taken from the old speedway bikes. The relationship was strengthened by positioning the

gearbox above the rear cylinder, where it posed kickstarting problems for all but the athletic.

Specification, OW (1934): Twin-cylinder, ohv, 494cc (72 × 60mm). Four-speed gearbox. 3g fuel. Tyres, 3.25 × 19in. 65mph. £49 10s.

Douglas Endeavour

A few days before Olympia 1934 opened its doors, Douglas surprised trade and public – even, it was said, their employees – with their announcement in the weeklies of a flat-twin having its cylinders across the frame, heads in the breeze. This was the Endeavour of which, at the end of its run in 1937, it was reported that around 200 examples had been manufactured (though the figure has since been put as low as 50 by one authority). It was the first transverse-engine Douglas – a calculated move to focus attention on the positive aspects of the troubled firm's activities which for too long had been more widely reported in the financial press, in the wake of recurrent financial problems, than in the motorcycling journals.

Douglas Endeavour: transverse 500cc side-valve engine, shaft drive, in 1934.

The Endeavour was based on the new side-valve Blue Chief, itself barely a month older in conception than the ho twin and offering an innovation, for Douglas, in its aluminium-alloy cylinder barrels and heads. Inclined valves and seatings were carried in a cast-iron plate sandwiched between barrel and head, allowing easy and inexpensive replacement when need arose (which, as was subsequently, happily, discovered, seldom occurred). Flat-head three-ring alloy pistons topped steel connecting rods having caged-roller big-ends.

When Eddie Withers and Jack Clapham, of the Douglas experimental department, hatched their plan for a transverse-engined machine they had no further to look for a power unit than their own Blue Chief; and no need to go beyond Oxford, and Lord Nuffield's seasoned Morris Eight, when it came to the matter of suitable crown wheels and bevels for the shaft transmission to the rear wheel. It was all, apparently, carried out in three weeks, with most time being spent in fashioning a new frame that followed traditional Douglas lines only in its splayed front down tubes, which were joined to two under-engine rails running rearward and up to the rear-wheel spindle. What was new was the arrangement of twin upper rails, hidden by the tank, joining saddle tube and steering head. Cross members carried the engine, with lugs for the rear mounting of the unit four-speed gearbox from which ran, on the offside, the final-drive shaft, complete with rubber shock-absorber and universal joint. The bevel housing was carried on a large plate that functioned also as a junction piece for the offside chain and saddle stays. The rear wheel was qd, having a knock-out spindle that left the gear drive and brake drum undisturbed when the wheel was removed.

Priced at £72 10s when the similar – but three-speed – BMW was over £100, the Endeavour should have been a success for William Douglas and his reconstituted company. But the motorcycling public, capricious as ever, ignoring all the blandishments of the industry-led press, found no difficulty in restraining its enthusiasm for the new machine. The Douglas stand at Olympia was very popular, but of firmer interest thereafter, in dealers' showrooms, there was little sign; and of actual sales, virtually no evidence at all.

Specification, Endeavour (1935): Twin-cylinder, sv, 500cc (68 × 68mm). Four-speed gearbox. 3½g fuel. Tyres, 3.25 × 19in. 60mph.

Douglas T35

The first postwar Douglas, shown in September 1945, was a 350cc (60.8 × 60mm) horizontally opposed transverse twin that was to remain the basis of all the company's machines. The engine had been evolved from the unit employed in more than 20,000 wartime stationary generators, and therefore could be considered tried and proved. The factory name for the new model was T35, or 350 De Luxe. Interest centred not so much on the cast-iron engine, with its separate barrels and heads, car-type single-plate clutch and closely attached gearbox, as on the suspension, which struck a fresh note among the girders-turned-telescopics and solid rear frames of contemporary motorcycles.

Douglas 348cc T35 1947 with generous springing, front and rear.

The Douglas had generous springing at both ends. At the rear, torsion bars located within the lower frame tubes controlled wheel movement via linkages at the spindle. At the front was the ingenious Radiadraulic fork, which outwardly resembled a telescopic unit apart from small leading links at the bottom; these, restrained by long coil springs and comprehensive oil damping, allowed up to 6in of wheel travel and gave a low unsprung weight.

This wet-sump, 380lb newcomer, operating on a compression ratio of 6.1:1, was good for more than 70mph, covered the standing-start quarter in 18.8 seconds, and aroused much interest, if few firm orders.

Specification, T35: Horizontally opposed twin-cylinder, ohv, 348cc (60.8 × 60mm). 17-20bhp. Four-speed gearbox. Magneto/dynamo. 3⅜g petrol, 4pt oil. Leading-link/torsion-bar. Tyres, 3.25 × 19in. 380lb.

Douglas Mk 3

The Mark 3 Douglas of 1948/49 was a development of the 1945 T35. (For those of a precise turn of mind and concerned by the missing "marks" an explanation – probably fallacious – is that the very first postwar Douglas had torsion-bar *front*, as well as rear, suspension; in this form it was never offered for sale.)

A sports model with improved cylinder-head design, as introduced on the Mk 3, plus upswept exhaust pipes and large air-cleaner, was said to put out 22bhp. It was tested at 78mph, which enabled Douglas to claim it as the fastest standard 350.

Useful publicity during this period was provided by the writings of Cyril Quantrill, sports editor of *Motor Cycling*, who rode a 350 for some thousands of miles, usually flat out, and had very few complaints to make about it.

Specification Mk 3 As for T35 apart from higher-tune engine.

Douglas Mk 3, 1950: a 22bhp, 78mph sports three-fifty.

Douglas 90 Plus

The 90 Plus was the fastest Douglas and might have passed as the fastest 350 of all had it not been for the crushing superiority of BSA's B32 Gold Star in events such as the Clubman's TT in the Isle of Man.

Developed from the Mk 3 Sports, the 90 Plus displayed the most spectacular-looking front brake to be seen on a motorcycle in 1949. Of 9in diameter, and

Douglas 90 Plus, 1951: top speed was around 100mph.

1¼in wide, it had light-alloy cooling fins and a well-ribbed light-alloy backplate of fully floating design, with torque reaction being passed through an independent linkage to keep the front of the bike level during braking.

Alloy wheel rims, a rev-counter, TT carburettors and 21in front wheel were other striking departures from Mk 3 trim. Not so obvious were double-acting damping for the Radiadraulic front fork, an extra ball-race for the crankshaft, and a set of very "hot" cams. The clutch had been lightened (and strengthened) by use of an aluminium-alloy plate, and the gearbox was fitted with needle-roller bearings in place of the standard plain type.

The 90 Plus project was masterminded by Eddie Withers. He had entered a pilot version of the bike in the 1949 Clubman's and was sufficiently impressed to go ahead with a limited race programme. (Limited because Douglas was in the hands of the Official Receiver, who was known to frown on extra cash expenditure.)

The 90 Plus produced 25bhp at 6,500rpm and top speed was around 100mph.

The 90 was not the only Plus. When for any reason a potential 90 engine failed to come up with 25bhp, it was installed in an ordinary chassis, with a different tank colour, and the bike was sold as an 80 Plus. However, sufficient top-power engines were forthcoming to enable 250 90 Plus models to be assembled during the years to 1953, when production came to a halt.

Douglas Dragonfly

The Dragonfly first appeared at the 1954 Earls Court show. A mixture of 1952 500 prototype and Mk 3, the Dragonfly was intended as a motorcycle of integrated styling that was to distance Douglas from the bitty image of the earlier twins that had sold in fluctuating, mainly low, numbers for almost a decade after the war. A duplex frame carried an improved 350 engine having an ac generator and distributor and a light-alloy casing where once a Lucas Magdyno and other ancillaries had presented a nooks-and-crannies profile.

Internal improvements included stiffening of the crankcase, a bolt-through system for the cast-iron cylinders and heads, and duralumin pushrods. Suspension and "cosmetic" changes were radical. At the front the Radiadraulic fork was replaced by an Earles-type pivoted fork to match a similar layout at the rear, with control in both cases by Girling spring/damper units.

The lines of the large fuel tank were carried forward beyond the steering head in the form of a rather unlovely nacelle. Finish was in light grey, extending even to the frame. The Dragonfly appeared to be larger than the superseded series. In reality it was both larger and heavier – as was indicated by a road test top speed of only 70mph. Another disappointment was the considerable mechanical din (which had been quite acceptable in the old 350).

Prototype Douglas named first Dart, then Dragonfly, was introduced at the 1954 motorcycle show, London.

Production Dragonfly: was this a brave new look?

EMC

Vienna-born Dr Josef Ehrlich is the archetypical boffin. He has piercing eyes, a mane of hair and a tendency to transpose v's and w's when speaking rapidly. He was the man behind EMC motorcycles.

His first complete bike was announced in 1946. It was made in London and had the twin-piston layout, with single articulated connecting rod, that was to be an EMC trademark for many years.

Despite supply difficulties EMC appeared at Earls Court in the early 1950s with a range of 350cc double-piston two-strokes backed by a cantilever-frame 125 having a JAP engine. The latter did not go into production. Disappointed, Ehrlich left the motorcycle world for a time, moving to Austin cars and, later, to the De Havilland aircraft company.

In the 1960s he had De Havilland support for 125cc watercooled racers that rose to runner-up position in the World Championship. Producing 30bhp at the rear wheel, these machines were among the very fastest of their time. When running well – not often enough, for transmission troubles let them down – they were more than a match for rivals from East Germany and Japan.

When De Havilland lost interest in motorcycling, Dr Ehrlich set up a company of his own, in 1967.

EMC 350

Dr Ehrlich's 350cc double-single two-stroke of 1947 followed pre-war Puch and TWN designs. The pistons were carried on a forked connecting rod and had a common combustion chamber. There were three transfer ports, three exhaust ports, two inlets. The crankshaft was carried on ball and roller bearings.

This unusual engine was housed in an unusual frame employing an H-section top member in manganese-bronze. The front fork was a Dowty Oleomatic.

Performance was not startling. Top speed, about 72mph on a 4.25:1 top gear, was much the same as that

EMC 350 split-single, 1949. Gearbox is a Burman four-speed.

Ehrlich design of twin connecting rods on a single big end.

of a four-stroke single. Acceleration was sluggish and the exhaust note was not appealing, being hard yet flat. The price was £190, which was about £40 more than the going rate for four-stroke 350s. There seemed to be no particularly good reasons for buying an EMC, and few people did.

EMC 125

EMC's 125 two-stroke single of 1953 had a conventional engine in a frame that was startlingly unorthodox. A backbone running from the steering head to the rear of the fuel-tank ended in a pivot taking

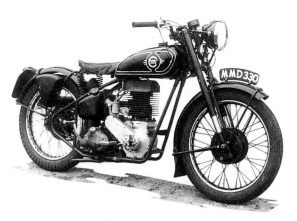

The EMC 350 of 1947 was a derivative of prewar German/Austrian designs.

EMC JAP 125-engined model T in 1953, with pivoting rear frame.

the forward apex of the rear-frame triangle. Rails from the base of the triangle supported the engine/gearbox, with a front-mounted spring going up to an attachment on the steering head. Thus rear-wheel deflection resulted in a disconcerting movement of the entire engine layout. Complicated, and of debatable efficiency, it reflected Dr Ehrlich's quest for innovation more than any effort to improve rider comfort or control.

EXCELSIOR

Excelsior had its roots as a motorcycle manufacturer in Coventry. There in the 1890s Bayliss Thomas and Co. turned out Minerva- and Werner- engined machines bearing the Excelsior trademark that are usually taken to be the first "British" motorcycles.

With regular advertisements in the new technical press, and support from satisfied owners, Excelsior picked up plenty of sales in the early 1900s. In 1910 the company dropped the Bayliss Thomas part of its name and became wholly "Excelsior".

After the First World War it passed into the hands of R. Walker and Sons, and motorcycle manufacture was transferred from Coventry to Tyseley in Birmingham. Excelsior supported road-racing. A win in the 1929 Isle of Man Lightweight TT was turned to good account when a replica of the winning bike, catalogued as B14, was turned out double-quick for sale to the sporting public. A wide range of roadsters, in which the B14 was the star, covered all sizes from 100 to 1,000cc, with a leaning towards enormous singles.

Despite reduced sales, the firm turned out memorable models in the years leading to the 1939-45 war. Chief among them were the Blackburne-made "Mechanical Marvel" which won the 1933 Lightweight

Harold Daniell on the 1932 Excelsior-JAP he rode to win a silver replica in the Junior Manx Grand Prix.

Excelsior 98cc Consort, 1959.

TT, and the Manxman racers, featuring a single overhead camshaft and (usually) a two-valve head, which were sold in 250 and 350cc forms to a large number of appreciative privateer racing men. One of these, Yorkshireman Denis Parkinson, was Manxman-mounted for more than one Lightweight MGP win.

During the war Excelsior brought out the Welbike for military use, and returned to the civilian market in 1946 with a programme of small two-strokes. Plans were made to re-introduce the ohc Manxman, but nothing came of them.

After the war Excelsior's chief claim to distinction was the Talisman, the first air-cooled twin-cylinder two-stroke. Smooth and reliable (when not afflicted with crankshaft troubles), the Talisman engine was later enlarged to 328cc for use in the Berkeley three-wheeler as well as in Excelsior's own machines. The twins were leaders of a range founded on low-capacity, low-price, two-stroke singles such as the 98cc Consort which, with two-speed gearbox and rudimentary suspension, was an undisputed big seller in a largely "ride-to work" market.

As the 1960s approached and, with the wide-spread slackening of interest in motorcycling, financial difficulties began to intrude, the firm made the apparently mandatory move into scootering. The 148cc Monarch was nicely styled, but too heavy.

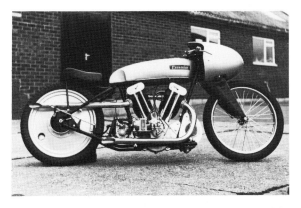

In 1931 Excelsior built the Silver Comet, a supercharged 994cc JAP-engined vee twin with which it was hoped J. S. Wright would regain the world's speed record for solo machines. The engine produced 100bhp at 5,400rpm with 15psi boost pressure, and drove a Burman 2-speed gearbox. In October that year it reached a one-way speed of 163mph at Tat in Hungary, but problems with pistons and the supercharger precluded its further use.

Excelsior had no more success than others in the British motorcycle industry who turned to scooters too late, and with the wrong product, in an effort to restore their fortunes.

The end came for Excelsior in 1965 when the factory was sold to Britax.

Excelsior Manxman

The Excelsior Manxman owed its existence to a loss of nerve on the part of the factory. The crisis was precipitated by the success of the earlier racing Excelsior, dubbed "Mechanical Marvel" in deference to the engine's complexity. (Four valves were arranged radially and operated from independent camshafts, that for the inlet at the rear, the other across the front of the head, with rockers worked from pushrods ending in sliding members). The MM gave Sid Gleave a Lightweight TT win in 1933.

The result was an awakening of public interest in Excelsiors, and a demand for a replica racer. It was at this point that the loss of nerve occurred. Both Eric Walker of Excelsior and Ike Hatch of the Blackburne concern, which manufactured the four-valver, had become well acquainted with the foibles of a design requiring constant attention if it were to give of its considerable best. The thought of turning out replica Mechanical Marvels for ham-fisted clubmen sent the pair into a decline. They decided to scrap the Mechanical Marvel, and set up the drawing board afresh. Again, Ike Hatch was responsible for engine design. The new engine was to be a straightforward ohc single with a two-valve head, in the classic style originated by Norton and Velocette. The Manxman appeared on the Excelsior stand at Olympia in November 1934.

Simple, attractive and immensely strong – some thought it was "over-engineered" – the 250 Manxman went on to spawn clones at 350 and 500cc. It merits further description.

Excelsior (who tended to keep the Blackburne connection dark) said they were going to retain part of

Excelsior 250 Manxman, 1936: solid, reliable and quite fast.

the MM crankcase layout – but it would be improved – while devising an entirely new top half. They were as good as their word. The crankcase was a marvel of robust construction, larger and stronger than the earlier version in every area of potential stress. The two steel flywheels were made in one piece with their shafts, which were carried in 2¾in diameter Hoffman ball and roller bearings. Crankpin diameter was large for a 250 at 1¾in, with two rows of rollers carrying the big-end of a connecting rod fashioned in hiduminium alloy, which was claimed by Rolls Royce to be stronger than same-weight steel. The piston was domed and the fins of the cast-iron cylinder, fewer than usual, were very deep. To obviate "ring", the fins were joined by additional flanges, which also increased the overall stiffness of the barrel.

Exhaust and inlet ports were canted to the left, with the angled sparking plug set between them. The TT34 Amal carburettor had a 20° down draught. A compact combustion chamber had narrow-angle (50°) valves operated by rockers from a single camshaft. All the valve gear – camshaft, rockers and valves – was totally enclosed in an aluminium casting, a feature which represented at least one major advance over Norton, if not Velocette, practice.

The camshaft ran in two ball and one roller bearings with the cams secured on keyless tapers; thus it was an easy matter to ring the changes among a variety of cams. The vertical shaft was carried on ball and roller bearings, with bevels top and bottom, in the familiar Norton/Velocette manner. On the Manxman, however, a design idiosyncracy – plus the fact of the 250's short stroke – made the shaft noticeably shorter, and the cover for the Oldham coupling at the top rather larger, than was the case with the other makers' designs. Another more basic difference was the use of all-gear drive, instead of chain, for the rear-mounted magneto.

Ike Hatch had little faith in plain bearings. With the exception of their use for one of the magneto gears, the gudgeon pin and the camshaft rockers, they were absent from the new design which otherwise ran on balls and rollers, likely to survive any temporary oil starvation. Gear-type oil pumps high in the magneto gear train were supplied through short pipes from the under-saddle tank; all other feeds were via internal passages, giving a neat and usually oil-free exterior. Lubricant for the vital cambox area was taken through a cylinder drilling and maintained at a predetermined level by a weir, the surplus draining through the tube for the vertical shaft.

For many years the 250 Manxman, and to a lesser degree the 350 and 500, served clubman racers well, in addition to giving Excelsior's sales brochures an enviable gloss.

By 1936 the 250, in touring trim, was selling at £63. A racing version – which meant that the specification included a cylinder head in aluminium-bronze, special valves, a high-compression piston, and a gearbox of close-ratio type – was available for an additional £12.

Handsome, and a shade weighty at nearly 300lb, the

touring 250 Manxman, on a 7.4:1 compression ratio, was good for 73-74mph. The factory was in the habit of suggesting 80mph as the top speed. A while before Mr Turner similarly equipped his Tiger 100, the Manxman had a bogus megaphone exhaust. Like those on the 1939 Triumphs, it could be converted to race-readinesss on removal of detachable baffles. Another item predating Turner was a combined speedometer and rev-counter which could be fitted to the Manxman at extra cost.

Specification, F11 Manxman (1936): Single-cylinder, ohc, 250cc (63 × 79mm). Four-speed gearbox. 3g fuel. Tyres, 3.00 × 20in(fr), 3.25 × 19in(r). 72mph. £63.

Excelsior Viking

Enclosure, to varying degree, was something of a theme of motorcycle manufacturing in the early 30s. The most notable and longest-lived "enclosed" motorcycles came from Francis-Barnett and Coventry Eagle. Another firm which trod the same path was Excelsior, whose opportunity came on Villiers' introduction, in 1933, of a 250cc watercooled two-stroke engine. Having fitted this unit in their conventional D6 model, Excelsior went on to use it in an enclosed version, the D9, otherwise known as the Viking.

A watercooled engine had several obvious qualifications for use in an enclosed motorcycle. Running temperatures could be more easily controlled (with the aid, if need be, of a fan); the radiator could be merged unobtrusively into the bodywork; and mechanical noise was muffled at source, which was of some importance when there were large areas of panelling to magnify rattles of any description.

There were no half measures in Excelsior's treatment. Enclosure was complete. Both sides of the engine, from exhaust pipe to fuel tank level, were hidden by shields, removable on release of two wing nuts. The shields had apertures for access to the carburettor, and generous louvres for the inflow of air to the crankcase. Deep valances in the mudguard covered the rear wheel from spindle level up and carried twin toolboxes, one each side. As with the main shielding, the entire rear mudguard could be removed very easily; in this case, on release of three nuts, when the wheel was completely exposed.

Ingenuity was not restricted to enclosure. A new method of lubricating a vital part of the transmission, the primary chain, had been devised. It consisted of nothing more complicated than a sponge-rubber moulding, soaked in oil, surrounding and touching the chain throughout its run. Experiments at the factory had shown that lubricant was retained in the sponge almost indefinitely. A further benefit was the way in which the rubber absorbed most of the thrash associated with chain transmission, which contributed to the Viking's low mechanical noise.

As for exhaust noise, this was fairly muted, too, thanks to the cavernous chambers of the extra-large silencers.

Specification, D9 (1933): Single-cylinder, two-stroke. 249cc (63 × 80mm). Four-speed gearbox. 1¾g fuel. Tyres, 3.50 × 19in. 61mph. £45.

Excelsior Talisman

Long before Villiers got round to making a twin-cylinder two-stroke, Excelsior were selling the Talisman, powered by an "in-house" 244cc (50 × 62mm) 180° parallel twin. Announced in late 1949, the Talisman was the only example of its type on the market (apart from the bespoke water-cooled Scott).

The Talisman's engine had separate cast-iron cylinder barrels and light-alloy heads, with a built-up crankshaft supported on four ball bearings and one roller bearing. Light-alloy flat-top pistons gave a modest compression ratio and breathing was through a single Amal. A Wico-Pacy flywheel generator produced 36 watts. The four-speed Albion gearbox was bolted to the rear of the engine, and the combined unit was housed in a frame equipped with Excelsior's unusual rear-suspension system in which spring boxes moved on fixed rods to give minimal movement over the severest undulations. Telescopic forks of conventional design were fitted.

Excelsior Talisman twin two-stroke, 1952.

Excelsior Talisman Sports, 1953, with additional cylinder-head finning.

Excelsior Talisman twin in 1954, with pivoted-fork rear suspension.

The 328cc Special Talisman twin, in 1959. Part-enclosure was becoming popular.

The most interesting aspect of the Talisman, with its "four-cylinder" torque, was the exhaust note, which had a very different quality from that of most two-strokes on the road. Unfortunately, motorcyclists' interest in the thrum of a passing Talisman never translated into a useful number of sales. The Talisman remained a poor seller despite updating exercises which included a twin-Amal sports version, a pivoted-rear-fork frame (1953) and, a year or two after that, some revisions in cylinder-head design to boost power.

Specification, Talisman: Twin-cylinder, two-stroke, 244cc (50 × 62mm). 12bhp/4,000rpm. Four-speed gearbox. Flywheel magneto/generator. 2¾g petroil. Telescopic/plunger; pf introduced 1954. Tyres, 3.00 × 19in. 250lb 65mph.

FEDERAL

Entirely undistinguished, Federal (sometimes Federation) motorcycles are noted here because their

manufacture was funded by the Co-operative Wholesale Society. As money became scarce with the slump that began in 1929, the CWS gave thought to its mission to ease the lot of the urban working class. Their motorcycles were assembled in Tyseley, Birmingham, with proprietory (mainly four-stroke) engines ranging from 250 to 500cc. However, prices were not spectacularly low – with the exception of £19 19s for a 1933 150 two-stroke – though no doubt the legendary Co-op dividends were attractive.

FRANCIS-BARNETT

Francis-Barnett's reputation in the opening years of the 30s rested with the straight-tube, pin-jointed frame advertised as being "Built like a Bridge". Another claim was that it could be dismantled and packed into a golf bag. Anybody, golfer or otherwise, foolhardly enough to do this was faced with a time-consuming exercise on reassembly. It was essential for the amateur to make a preliminary sketch of the tubes as originally assembled in the frame. Though apparently identical, they differed one from another by fractions of an inch. (Works fitters could do a complete assembly job – frame, engine, wheels, everything – in less than 30 minutes.)

However, this was not the frame employed for the 250 Cruiser of 1933, that cleanly styled all-weather model which turned out to be the most enduring of the 1930s enclosed motorcycles designed in the hope of winning over the "man-in-the-street" to motorcycling. (A steel forging incorporating steering head and front down member was the principal feature of the Cruiser's frame.) Nothing manufactured by F-B later rivalled the fame achieved by the Cruiser.

Francis-Barnett Black Hawk

In the mid-1930s the best known feature of the Francis-Barnett range, the bolted-up, triangulated frame, had been in production for more than a decade. Lugless and immensely strong, this impressive structure deserved to partner something more interesting than Villiers two-strokes.

In 1934 the 196cc Francis-Barnett was known as the Black Hawk 36. Why 36? Nobody now can say. As to Black Hawk, names of this sort followed a fashion that was much favoured in 30s motorcycling. Confronted with a product as thoroughly undistinguished, despite its frame/chassis, as the 196 F-B, the publicists had no option other than to project glamour by means of a starry nomenclature. The guidelines they followed seem clear. A genuinely high performer would usually carry no more than – for example – a terse "CS1"; if there had to be a name, something like Ulster or International would do. Conversely, run-of-the-mill machinery got the extravagant "Black Hawk" treatment.

Francis-Barnett Black Hawk 36, 196cc, 1930, priced at £28.

Top speed of this Francis-Barnett was about 50mph and fuel (petroil) consumption varied between 70 and 90mpg. The gearbox had three speeds (four were available at extra cost) and control was by hand. The frame, running on straight-tube lines, determined the position of engine and gearbox, once the overall height of the machine had been settled. In practice this worked reasonably well although the seat, being low (27in), pushed the apex of the frame triangle forward and meant that the rear-brake pedal did *not* fall under the ball of anything less than a size 12 foot.

Specification, Black Hawk 36 (1934:) Single-cylinder, two-stroke. 196cc (61 × 67mm). Three-speed gearbox. 1⅝g fuel. Tyres, 3.00 × 19in. 48mph. £28.

Francis-Barnett Cruiser

From 1933 to 1939 Francis-Barnett did its well-intentioned best to capture the man-in-the-street for motorcycling . . . the man who normally would wait for that Clapham omnibus . . . the man who never would become a motorcycle *enthusiast* but might appreciate safe, sheltered, economical, unhurried transport on two wheels. For him, F-B made the Cruiser. It was a 250cc two-stroke dressed up in curvaceous panels, to cover the dirty transmission, with valances and legshields to ward off that infamous Clapham weather.

Though there was much press work involved in the body and mudguarding, the frame of the Cruiser was

Francis-Barnett Cruiser in 1939, the last year of production.

impressively robust, as befitted a product of the concern renowned for its "Forth Bridge" triangulated frames. The Cruiser had a channel-steel cradle, with an I-section forging as the front down member – all more than enough to engender confidence in any novice about to unleash the power of the 8bhp two-stroke towards a top road speed of around 45mph. The gearbox was a four-speed Albion with hand-change on the right side of the tank.

The lower bodywork, doing an efficient job of protecting the rider's clothes from oil and dirt, allowed F-B to economize in the matter of subsidiary covers. Once the big casings were removed, a stark arrangement of cogs and chains and plates came to light. This was not important, for the bike was not intended to be used without its coverings.

At some point in the Cruiser's six-year life a three-port Villiers was made available, at additional cost, with the complication of automatic oiling from a separate tank, pressurized from the crankcase. Sensible people kept to the petroil arrangements of the standard model.

Specification, Cruiser F45 (1936): Single-cylinder, two-stroke. 249cc (63 × 80mm). Four-speed gearbox, 2¼g fuel. Tyres, 3.25 × 19in. 54mph. £39.

Francis-Barnett 250 Stag

Well known through the years for two-stroke lightweights, and from 1933 enjoying unprecedented success with the 250 Villiers-powered, enclosed Cruiser, Francis-Barnett sprang a surprise for the 1935 season with a brand-new 250 four-stroke, listed as the Stag. The engine was made for F-B by Blackburne in Surrey, to a design by Blackburne's own H.J. Hatch. (Bob Currie some years ago broke with initials-only practice by springing "Harry J." on the reading public; subsequently, however, other researchers have clung to the earlier form.)

Neat and practical, the engine predated by half a decade BSA's adoption of crossover pushrods for the ohv 250 C11. Using angled pushrods appealed to Hatch as the simplest way of having straight valve rockers, with none of the pivots, angles and attendant stresses of a conventional layout. To this end the pushrods, of tubular steel, were inclined at approximately the angle of the valves. There were no tappet guides; instead the pushrods acted directly between upper and lower rockers, moving within a channel formed in the cylinder casting. The valve rockers pivoted on large-diameter bearings in separate aluminium castings equipped with removable caps for inspection purposes. Oil was fed under pressure to the rockers before draining through the pushrod tunnels to the timing chest and thence to the shallow but large-capacity (4½pt) sump bolted to the underside of the crankcase. The crankshaft was carried on ball bearings. Behind the engine, pivoting on rearward extensions of the sump, with push-pull adjustment at its attachment to the engine plates, was an Albion four-speed gearbox.

Francis-Barnett Stag 248cc ohv, 1935. Manufacturer claimed it was "an aristocrat from stem to stern".

Engine and gearbox were mounted in a new frame comprising a front down member of forged steel in H-section, carrying the steering head, and a variety of mainly conventional tubes, the two sections being linked under the sump by L-section rails.

On test the Stag received much praise, as might be expected from an indulgent press welcoming a convert to the four-stroke persuasion. "What little valve gear noise there was barely reached the rider's ears." And: "Idling in traffic was excellent and several times on the initial run the rider blipped the throttle in order to be sure that the engine was running." Anybody who at this stage is entertaining doubts as to the hearing of *The Motor Cycle*'s road-tester may be reassured by another sentence which declares that "slight piston slap was detectable immediately after a start had been made from cold, though at no other time."

Top speed was 60 – just – and average consumption of "No 1" petrol was 85-90mpg.

Specification, Stag (1936): Single-cylinder, ohv, 248cc (68 × 68mm). Four-speed gearbox. 3¼g fuel. Tyres, 3.25 × 19in. 60mph. £47.

Merlin

Circa 1948-49, the 122cc Merlin was the "bigger half" of the Francis-Barnett range. The engine was the twin-port 50 × 62mm Villiers, top speed just over 40mph. Finish was a dignified black, even to the wheel rims. The tank was particularly well shaped, and big for such a low-performance bike.

A thoughtful touch was the provision of a separate oil tank – not plumbed into the lubrication system, of course, but present as a reserve supply should the rider have difficulty in buying the right sort of oil to mix with his petrol.

Francis-Barnett Merlin-125.

Francis-Barnett Merlin 125 engine.

The front section of the frame was brazed, the rear arc-welded; the bike was in all ways well-made, yet curiously old fashioned. It proved no match as a sales-puller for the BSA Bantam when that bright, up-to-the-minute two-stroke appeared.

Specification, Merlin: Single-cylinder, two-stroke, 122cc (50 × 62mm). 4.9bhp/4,400rpm. Three-speed gearbox. Flywheel magneto/rectifier on de luxe version. Telescopic/rigid; pf in October 1951. 2½g petroil. Tyres, 3.00 × 19in. 190lb. 47mph.

Francis-Barnett Cruiser and Falcon

Elsewhere in this guide the late-1950s move to conceal the jumble of frame tubes and impedimenta at the rear of a motorcycle has been described as being little more than a cover-up job: there was nothing in the nature of a fundamental redesign, no attempt to do away with the offending items. At the time, every change in motorcycle fashion was hailed by the Press as an improvement. There was much talk of (for example) "sensible cleaning up achieved by concealing, in motor car style, essential but

The 1957 Francis-Barnett Cruiser 75, with 224cc engine.

Bike built for sidecar hauling
  (Strong Frame)
Sidecar brake.
Comfort tailored for me : ease of riding pos
Windshield / Fairing
Rr. Springing / Pan Saddle - no dualseat
Front fork links   or Girder?? / Wasp / Earles
  Rear Rigid or Teles for Combo work
Norton Big 4
BSA M21
Panther??
BMW R60
Triumph TRW
Ural ??

September 9th, 2003

Dear Sir

I am writing to invite you to become a Member of my Club because I think you would enjoy it as much as I do myself.

The aim of the Club is to give our Members the best of everything — at a more easily affordable price. Our panel of experts seek out the best deals they can find, and if we agree with their choice we then recommend them to our Members each month.

Rather to my surprise, this works so well that I now find myself using the Club all the time. I stay at our clubs and our hotels, I eat in our recommended restaurants, and enjoy weekends at our country-house hotels. I buy my wine, food and clothing through the Club, all at much lower prices than I paid previously.

So why not join me? The Club is fun and easy to use, yet immensely rewarding for its Members. A small brochure and invitation card are enclosed with this letter, and I would be delighted to welcome you as a fellow Member.

Yours truly

Willoughby le Broke.

The Rt Hon the Lord Willoughby de Broke, DL
Chairman
Country*Club*uk

ps You do not need to be in London; the Club operates nationally — and you can also visit us on www.countryclubuk.com

Francis-Barnett Sports Fulmer 90 with four-speed gearbox 1964. Colours were red and silver, with plenty of chrome-plate.

Francis-Barnett Falcon 58, with 197cc engine, 1953: a handsome lightweight offering 55-60mph top speed.

unaesthetic components". Thus F-B in 1954 filled in the rear-frame triangle of their 224cc Model 71 Cruiser and went on to make the entire bike, with its valanced mudguards, slab-sided seat, egg-shape engine castings and nacelled headlamp, a tribute to "aesthetics"

A couple of years later, in time for the 1957 season, the engine was changed to AMC's 249cc (66 × 72.8mm) single.

In 1953 F-B left the Cruiser alone and concentrated on the 197cc Falcon, which escaped the fill-in treatment but acquired instead large boxes, one each side, to carry battery, tools and spares. Structural changes occurred from time to time. A new frame was evolved for 1955 having a single-tube layout in 1½in-diameter, 14-gauge material brazed into malleable head and seat lugs and branching into a twin-tube triangle at the rear to support the suspension units for the pivot fork.

Few other changes of any sort took place until 1960, when the 197cc Villiers was pensioned off in favour of the AMC 199cc two-stroke and the tank was enlarged to 3¾ gallons; in this form the bike was known as the Falcon 87.

Specification, Cruiser 71: Single-cylinder, two-stroke, 224cc (63 × 72mm). 10bhp/4,500rpm. Four-speed gearbox. Flywheel magneto/rectifier. 3½g petroil. Telescopic/pf. Tyres, 3.00 × 19in. 280lb. 60mph.

Falcon 70: Single-cylinder, two-stroke, 197cc (59 × 73mm). 8.4bhp/4,000rpm. Three-speed gearbox; four-speed optional extra. Flywheel magneto/rectifier. 2¾g petroil. Telescopic/pf. Tyres, 3.00 × 19in. 245lb. 55mph.

GREEVES

Among a select group of septuagenarians, one-time captains of the British motorcycle industry, who meet from time to time for a dash through country lanes on borrowed (Japanese) bikes, none was more dashing – some of his companions say terrifying – than the silver-haired Bert Greeves.

He it was who in 1951 built the first Greeves motorcycle.

Bert Greeves had started the Invacar concern, to turn out invalid carriages, with his disabled cousin, Derry Preston Cobb, just after the war. The first bike was an interlude in more serious work. But then news was leaked to the Press, with details of the bike's unusual springing and other departures from accepted practice.

When the machine was eventually shown to the public at Earls Court in 1953 it had been modified a little but was still, by the standards of the time, strikingly unorthodox. Springing was by rubber in torsion. The front fork had leading links joined at the rear, for strength, and controlled by rubber blocks, with hand-adjustable friction dampers. At the rear the pivoted fork, with angled, fixed struts where spring units might have been expected, deflected on movement of an unobtrusive wedge of tensioned rubber. As if this were not enough to frighten off conservative motorcyclists, the front down tube of the frame was not a tube at all but an H-section light-alloy casting. All very unusual, in 1953.

Early models included three- and four-speed versions of a 197cc roadster and a 242cc (British Anzani) two-stroke twin.

Greeves prototype of 1951 with rubber-in-torsion front suspension.

The 1954 Greeves front fork.

Greeves 325 twin in 1956.

Greeves 249cc Sportsman 25, 1962: the designer was given his head . . .

A need for sales rather than column inches in the technical press soon tempered Bert Greeves' innovative zeal. Orthodox tubular-frame models, at both 197 and 242cc, were offered at a discount. A factory trials team was formed to popularize the name.

Top riders like Peter Hammond prevailed on Greeves to modify the springing arrangements. They finally got a strictly conventional rear pivoted fork and at the front a partly conventional, though outwardly unchanged, layout.

It was in moto-cross, however, that Greeves were destined to make their biggest impact, at first through the exploits of their 1956-appointed competitions manager, Brian Stonebridge (ex-BSA, ex-Matchless). He developed the 197 enormously and made it – especially when he himself was aboard – a match for any of the 40bhp four-stroke scramblers of the day. When Stonebridge was killed in a road accident, his protegé, Dave Bickers, took over and enjoyed a long run of success, culminating in a European championship in 1960.

Greeves Hawkstone Scrambler.

Greeves Silverstone 24RAS racer.

The scrambler on sale to the public had been named Hawkstone, after an outstanding performance by Stonebridge at that circuit, and enlarged from 197 to 246cc, with a Greeves-designed, big-finned cylinder.

A multitude of awards was collected by Greeves-backed riders such as Mike Jackson and Don Smith, who were reaping the benefits of further weight-saving as the frame departed more and more from the original. In trials too Greeves was becoming a dominant name – certainly among the lightweights.

Finally road-racers were catered for with the Silverstone model, which had a Greeves-developed power unit based on a Villiers Mk34A bottom end, was good for about 110mph, and turned out to be reliable and easy to maintain. The climax of the Silverstone's career was a 250 Manx Grand Prix win, Gordon Keith riding, in 1964.

In the late 1960s Greeves became ever more self-reliant, building their own 30bhp Challenger engine for use in the competitions machines and even, eventually, their own gearbox. . . all of which was just as well, in view of the impending run-down of supplies from Villiers. Road machines tended to be edged into the background in the 1970s though contracts with several rural police forces kept production ticking over. On both competition and road bikes the former distinguishing features of a Greeves were finally abandoned as telescopic forks and all-tubular frames took over.

By 1977 both Bert Greeves and Derry Preston Cobb had retired, and the firm, hard-hit by new invalid-carriage legislation and the influx of foreign-born bikes, was earning its day-to-day income as a factoring agent in the motor trade.

GRINDLAY PEERLESS

After brief fame in 1928 when Bill Lacey captured the world hour record by covering over 100 miles in the hour at Brooklands on a J.A. Prestwich-engined model, Grindlay Peerless struggled through the early 30s with JAP and Villiers engines, and finally Rudge engines, until they gave up the struggle for good in 1934. Among an always stylish range, the 250 Rudge-engined model, called the Tiger Club (pre-dating Triumph), was particularly attractive.

Brooklands record-breakers: Bill Lacey and Grindlay Peerless.

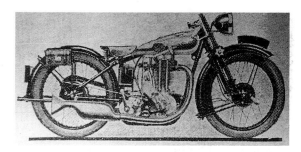

Grindlay Peerless 500, 1930, with ohv JAP engine.

HESKETH

Having established his credentials as an engineering entrepreneur in F1 car racing, Lord Alexander Hesketh graduated to motorcycling. In 1978 he announced that plans were well advanced to produce a top-quality British two-wheeler.

The first public showing of his vee-twin took place in 1980 at a garden-party occasion at Easton Neston, the Hesketh family's country house near Silverstone. Fashioned to revive memories of the hallowed Vincent, and trading on the excellent showing of later examples of the vee-twin turned out by Ducati, Morini and Guzzi, the Hesketh V1000 was unashamedly a snob vehicle. It was largely handbuilt, the gleaming light-alloy dohc engine, with generous finning and massive crankcase, a snug fit in an impeccably welded frame of Reynolds 531 tubing. It was of conventional design, with little other than a hydraulically operated clutch to lend design distinction; in this respect it cannot, of course, be fairly compared with the Vincent Rapide, which in the mid-1940s struck a fresh note in British motorcycling.

Fitted with such imported essentials as Italian Marzocchi suspension, Japanese Nippon Denso instruments and German Bosch lighting, the £5,000 Hesketh was scheduled to go into production at a new factory at Daventry in September, 1981. However, last-minute snags discovered in the transmission caused a

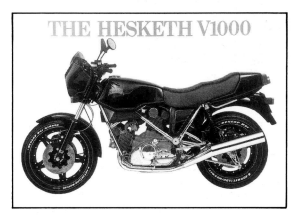

Hesketh V1000, 1980-82.

postponement; the first Heskeths became available in March 1982.

Specification, V1000: Vee-twin-cylinder, dohc, 992cc (95 × 72mm). 85bhp/6,500rpm. Five-speed gearbox. Electronic ign/alternator. 5g petrol, 6pt oil; wet sump. Telescopic/pf. Tyres, 4.10 × 19in(fr). 5.10 × 17(r). 500lb.

JAMES

In the postwar years James came to mean two-strokes, and small two-strokes, at that. There was about the "Jimmy James" nothing of the glamour that went with British manufacturers such as Norton and even BSA. Yet James was one of the oldest firms in the industry and long ago its two-strokes were merely supporting players to the big single and vee-twin four-strokes, overhead-valve and side-valve, that took star billing in the range.

Harry James, a Birmingham engineer, began making pedal cycles in 1880: James Cycle Co. was to be the name of the firm until the end in 1970. In 1897, after a decade of prosperous trading, James went public, still making and selling only muscle-powered two-wheelers.

It was not until Fred Kimberley joined the company just after the turn of the century, when it was controlled by Harry James' one-time partner, Charles Hyde, that the internal-combustion engine came into the picture. Kimberly became managing director before 1910 and held the job until well into the 1950s, at which time it was not unusual for him, then in his 70s, to take a new model round the Highlands or across a continent or two. Only in his last years with James did he compromise with old age and creaking joints by asking for a sidecar. Even then he was able to turn necessity to advantage by pointing out the power and versatility of whatever sidecar-burdened 125 or 200 he was driving and publicizing.

In the motorcycle shows of the early 1900s Minerva-, then FN-engined machines appeared. The first James with "own" engine was exhibited in 1908. It had other new features as well, such as wheel mounting by stub axle, and internal-expanding brakes. The latter caught on – they were possibly the first to be used in the motorcycle industry – but not the new wheel-mounting scheme. Despite all manner of advantages, not least ease of wheel removal, the stub axle had to wait for the coming of the scooter. (It is interesting that as late as 1980 even the respected engineers of the Bayerische Motoren Werke were unable totally to convince the motorcycling public that a stub axle, as employed on the new BMW GS/80, was a good thing. Mechanically – theoretically – it could be justified: visually, it seemed all wrong.)

In 1913 the first James two-stroke was sold with the spiky, interrupted finning that was to remain a design trademark for many years. Through the 1920s a succession of new models appeared, some of them two-strokes, others as diverse as a 7hp side-valve twin for sidecar hauling, an ohv 500cc twin and, in 1928, at the birth of speedway in England, a lightweight vee-twin four-stroke which, though it rarely disputed a winning place with the favourites from Douglas and Harley-Davidson, added a welcome interest to the dirt-track scene.

Around 1930 the company flirted with Villiers two-stroke engines, but within a couple of years reverted to units of their own making. The time with Villiers was more than an experiment, however. Maintaining a foundry for engine production was a costly business for James, and in the 1930s cost-cutting became increasingly important. In 1931 the firm took over the Baker company founded by Frank Baker, which produced exclusively two-stroke powered light-weights: undoubtedly this figured in the decision to return to Villiers, who were able to supply engines in a variety of sizes up to 250cc at absurdly low prices.

As the Second World War began James were turning out the ride-to-work 98cc Autocycle and others such as the 125, to be known as ML, that was used in company with Royal Enfield's "Flying Flea" during air- and sea-borne invasion landings.

In 1946 it was a two-strokes-only policy again for James, with power by Villiers. In 1951 the company passed into control of the AMC group, which was the signal for phasing-out of the Villiers connection and the introduction of two-stroke units of AMC manufacture. By that time, however, Villiers had evolved their engines to a very satisfactory level: though they were always somewhat "agricultural" and even at their peak only a distant relation to later

A 1930s James ohv vee-twin.

James 197 in 1950 was rugged and inexpensive.

Japanese developments, they turned out plenty of power. The AMC designs, though better looking, hardly ranked as an improvement.

The compiler recalls a 1951 8E 197cc James which he used for some thousands of miles, with the throttle usually held against the stop. Though this represented at best no more than 60mph he ended his time with the James convinced that the age-old bugbear of the two-stroke, the dreaded seize-up, was largely over.

James went in for the trials game, maintaining a works team through to the 1960s. At first, link-fork 125s were used, with improbably high saddles. The star

James' venture into the scooter market was not a success.

rider was Norman Hooten. Later the firm turned to smoothly contrived, all-sprung 200s ... this at a time when trials were considered purely four-stroke territory, long before the advent of the "strokers" from Spain.

In 1959 James ventured into the scooter field – but too late, for by then scooters were in decline, and in any case the James was unappealing. The motorcycle range, very cleanly styled, with a clever use of panelling, and reasonable performance, dropped in popularity when the Japanese landed in Europe with their cheaper, faster lightweights.

Hasty boardroom discussion at AMC threw up the idea of "joining them" (any idea of "beating them" died, it appeared, at a very early stage). The result was the formation, in 1963, of a company headquartered at the rear of the James factory in Greet, Birmingham, to import Suzukis. This move was to prove largely irrelevant, however, as AMC got further into financial difficulties. When the crash came, James disappeared along with much else of the Woolwich-based empire.

Competition James 197 for 1952 market.

James Cadet 150, with pear-drop tank.

James Sports Captain 200, 1965, with AMC two-stroke single engine.

LEVIS

The compiler's personal experience of the Levis marque began (and ended, just about) with a machine belonging to that period in the company's history identified, on engine castings as well as in sales catalogues, by the legend "The Master Two-Stroke" (which replaced the previous, less emphatic "Light and Quick"). It was a mid-20s 247cc two stroke with a large outside flywheel, separate magneto and three-speed Burman gearbox. The flywheel occasionally unscrewed itself, when it would depart on a usually dangerous trajectory. Following a breakage, the chain to the magneto was exposed, a threat to flapping trousers. The gearbox was pretty well faultless. As to the engine, it was prone to seizure (probably the fault of an improvised petroil system) but not to a masterful performance.

Two-strokes, like this had won an enviable reputation, and a TT, for Levis. In the 30s the firm built another reputation with well engineered four-strokes,

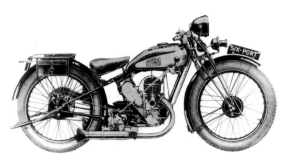

Levis 247cc six-port two-stroke, 1929.

Levis 350 side-valve, 1939.

mainly overhead-valve, of up to 600cc. These acquired a loyal following. There was a certain "handbuilt" quality about them; owners even learned to appreciate the benefits of the clean, fresh lubricant provided by the vintage-style constant-loss system although, because of the latitude allowed by hand control, it remained a matter of some skill to arrive at a balance between an over-generous setting – and an oiled plug – and a niggardly supply, when a seize-up was on the cards.

"Torrens", of *The Motor Cycle*, wrote in praise of the ohv Levis. An overhead-camshaft 250 appeared in 1934. It can be rated as a minor aberration on the part of this conservative firm. The Butterfield family, owners since the earliest days of Levis, had been tempted, as others were, to seek the renown enjoyed by Veloce with their ohc sportsters.

Levis ohc 250

Butterfield's overhead-camshaft 250 engine was introduced in late 1933. It appeared all set to challenge the best of established models in its class. Yet within a couple of years this excellent unit was reduced to the rank of an option . . . a £5 5s more expensive option . . . to the overhead-valve 250.

Roy Mason was one of the growing number of designers favouring chain drive for the camshaft, in contrast to the few, led by Norton's Arthur Carroll and the Goodmans at Veloce, who pinned their faith to a vertical shaft and couplings.

The new-for-1934 Levis had a vertically split crankcase and a crank assembly based very clearly on the practice followed in the existing Levis ohv units.

The mainshaft was carried on roller bearings, with a two-row version for the connecting rod big-end. A half-time shaft was driven from the mainshaft by a couple of gears, and it was to this shaft that the chain for the oh camshaft was attached, with a Weller tensioner on the front run of the chain. The camshaft, in a cast-aluminium box mounted on extensions to the cylinder head holding-down bolts, acted through adjustable rockers on exposed valves. Inlet and exhaust ports were canted to the right (off) side, and the intake had a pronounced down draught. A compression ratio of 8:1 contributed to the respectable power output.

The oiling arrangements were unusual. One half of a duplex Pilgrim pump drew lubricant from an under-saddle container and forced it through drillings in the mainshaft to the big-end bearing. The supply could be adjusted. From the big-end oil was splashed on to the cylinder wall and thence, via holes, into the timing case. From this point oil flow was controlled by the other half of the duplex pump.

Phosphor-bronze bearings supported the camshaft, with the rockers on pivot-pins; sales talk indicated that the ground surface on the outer diameter of the rockers formed such a precision fit in the rocker box that there could be no possibility of oil seepage. In theory, and in limited factory experiments with handbuilt prototypes, this may have been the case; on the road, after a few months in the hands of Mr Average, it was a different matter.

The camshaft drive was rather out of the ordinary in the matter of the chain-tensioning device, which *appeared* straightforward enough, as it was a Weller spring, but made claims to originality with an oil-filled dashpot behind the tension spring, oil pressure being maintained through a $\frac{1}{16}$in hole leading to a reservoir supplied by a double pump. Oil supply elsewhere was thorough. The camshaft, for example, was fed via internal drillings, with a bleed to the bearings and rocker heels . . . all of which, though laudable in the interest of a long life for the engine, made hopes of 100 per cent oil retention within the cambox pure fantasy.

Specification, 250OHC (1934): Single-cylinder, ohc, 248cc (67 × 70mm). Four-speed gearbox. 2½g fuel. Tyres, 3.00 × 19in. 69mph. £59 10s.

Levis ohc 250, 1934, selling at £59 10s.

MATCHLESS

Matchless steadily improved the quality of their motorcycles throughout the 1930s. No great shakes in the field of original design, the Collier brothers had the good sense, once they had recovered from the sales drubbing meted out to the "Silver" multis, both Arrow and Hawk (as explained in this section), to concentrate instead on making detail improvements, year by year, to the existing range of ohv and sv singles, and 990cc big-twins. Efficiency was stepped up with continued modifications to valve gear and crank assembly. But perhaps the most praiseworthy aspect of seasonal changes was the ever-increasing flow of oil that was directed at every bearing surface. The guiding principle seemed to be – if it moved, lubricate it; if it squeaked, flood it with oil. The result was that by the end of the 30s Matchless (and of course AJS) machines were the quietest on the market. And, because of paint-quality secrets learned on takeover of the Sunbeam concern, among the best-finished, too.

The Matchless big twin in 1938 form.

Matchless 1935 Clubman, with hairpin valve springs and horizontal carburettor.

Matchless 990 X4

Sweet natured and nicely made, a Matchless X4 990cc side-valve vee-twin of the mid-30s should have been a big seller to all those hard-up Dads who could not afford to run an Austin 7. Even linked to a Matchless sidecar it showed a saving, in initial cost and certainly thereafter in running expense, compared with any four-wheeler ... and, indeed, with many other big-twin motorcycles having an inflated, sometimes bogus, "pedigree". But, as C.E. Allen has pointed out, the Matchless lacked charisma. The compiler is doubtful

Matchless 990cc × 4 side-valve vee-twin in the early-1930s.

whether "charisma" should be expected of a 60mph side-valve. Lack of it, however, helps to explain the undistinguished sales life of this worthy motorcycle.

It was almost certainly a more pleasant motorcycle than the contemporary Brough Superior SS80, which employed the same engine, supplied by the friendly AMC management. It was lighter than the SS80, with a more appropriate tank to top the modest power plant, a neater if no stronger (Burman) gearbox, better brakes and sharper steering. It was also much cheaper. All of which helped not a jot in shaping public esteem, which forever rated it as a very obscure country cousin to the lordly Brough.

Specification, 990 X4: Twin-cylinder, sv, 990cc (85.5 × 85.5mm). Four-speed gearbox, 3g fuel. Tyres, 3.25 × 19in. 64mph. £60.

Matchless Silver Arrow

As 1930 dawned so Matchless, that motorcycling colossus set amid the traffic uproar of south-east London, began a polite war with Ariel to win the hearts, and open the purses, of all the two-wheeler enthusiasts who, both firms believed, were waiting for a chance to abandon their crackling singles and get aboard new-era multis. For Ariel – Mr Turner's 500cc Square Four. For Matchless – Mr Collier's Silver Arrow which, if scarcely entitled to fight in the same division as the Squariel, being no more than a 400lb twin-cylinder weakling, is dealt with here because of its kinship with the Silver Hawk four which was to appear in the Matchless corner within a year.

On the death of Harry Collier senior in 1925, design work became the prerogative of his second-born son, Charlie. He it was who designed most of the Silver Arrow. He should have known better. Whether the

Matchless Silver Arrow narrow-angle 400 vee-twin, 1931. It was not a success.

buying public was yearning, or even ready, for a multi is debatable. What is certain is that it was in no mind to spend hard-earned and increasingly scanty cash on a large, bland motorcycle having very little performance. It was technically interesting; but at the end of the day ... or perhaps even around breakfast time ... what a motorcycle enthusiast wanted was *speed*. The market was not big or diverse enough to provide the kind of riders – designers *manqué* – who might buy the Arrow and be content to marvel at its complexitities while clogging the nation's roads by their snail-like progress. The compiler claims to know what he is writing about at this point, after covering more than a few miles by Silver Arrow in Norfolk, a county reckoned by pedal cyclists to be inordinately flat. The Matchless found Norfolk hilly. Top speed was around 50mph and power was limited. Torque never rose beyond a gentle murmur.

This kind of criticism can be overdone, of course. The compiler has no time for the overheated style of some present-day observers, which purports to pass for reasoned evaluation. Contrary to anything these critics have suggested, there can be little doubt that, properly harnessed to the job and handled by an expert, a Silver Arrow on top form would have ripped the skin from any average-viscosity rice pudding. (A more revealing demo could have been one in which an Arrow in everyday condition, perhaps with a minor carburettor malfunction, was locked in combat with a week-old pud. That might have been a close-run thing.)

But to technicalities ... "Mr Charlie" had gone for the motor car look with his new twin, announced in the last months of 1929, for sale the following year. Before the Olympia show in December, the rumour was that the engine was a four. But it turned out to be a very narrow-angle (26°) 400cc vee-twin, cylinders in tandem, with side valves. The "car look" arose from the way in which the exhaust manifold went along the offside, giving the unit the appearance of a four-cylinder. It has been pointed out that horizontal lines predominated, and this may be so. The skew-driven camshaft, running on three bearings, was arranged longitudinally, of course, and operated vertical valves enclosed in an oil-tight chamber having a chromium-plated cover. The cylinders were cast together as one block, as were the heads, with copper and asbestos

gaskets forming the joint on pressure from no fewer than 12 screws. The exhaust manifold was formed as a separate casting, running through to a single rightside pipe terminating in a silencer of unlovely, turbot-like shape. Oil was carried in a tank bolted to the front of the crankcase, which meant there was no need for external piping in the dry-sump system. A single Amal carburettor was fitted on the nearside between the cylinder bores, feeding via an inlet pipe cored through the main casting of the block. Power (?) was taken to the rear wheel by chain via a Sturmey-Archer three-speed hand-change gearbox installed in a new frame having a triangulated rear section pivoting on Silentbloc bushes against twin barrel springs fitted between the rear apex and the top tube.

It was all rather tall, especially at the steering-head, for Mr Charlie had indulged himself with an instrument console on the handlebar. However, contemporary observers found the bike very attractive. Ixion had earlier written ecstatically about the new secret-list Squariel but impartially kicked off his Olympia review with a few lines about the Matchless. "Like so many people I made a bee-line for the Silver Arrow Matchless .... It is one of those machines which you cannot appreciate to the full till you have it outside, test its tickle-starting, listen to its baby's whisper tickover, and generally handle it on the road. But isn't it just a good-looker, if ever there was one?"

It was certainly comfortable. And, yes, it was quiet. But it never sold in worthwhile numbers, no matter what the columnists wrote. Hence in 1934 it was quietly ... of course ... withdrawn from the Matchless range. For a while the "multi" initiative, for the Colliers, was left to the more sprightly Silver Hawk four. (But by then the battle of the multis had been lost to Ariel and its 600, as will be made clear in the following entry.)

Specification, Silver Arrow (1931): Twin-cylinder, sv, 397cc (54 × 86mm). Four-speed gearbox. 2¾g fuel. Tyres, 3.25 × 19in. 56mph. £55.

Matchless Silver Hawk

Within a few months of the introduction of the Silver Arrow, the Colliers knew they had a failure on their hands. Glowing write-ups penned by head-in-the-clouds young men on the staff of the weekly journals were no compensation for empty order books. There was, they decided, only one thing to do: they would have to manufacture a true multi, something with a turn of speed. This time Mr Charlie was to stand aside, and let Mr Bert get to work on the drawing board. Mr Bert, youngest of the three Colliers, duly obliged – he was keen to do the job – and the result was the four-cylinder Silver Hawk, shown in November 1931 at Olympia, an aisle or two away from Edward Turner's new Square Four.

With a modicum of brotherly feeling, Mr Bert adopted some of the design features of Charlie's side-valve twin for the Hawk. Its block, for instance, was a

Matchless Silver Hawk 600cc ohc four, 1931.

one-piece casting. Essentially it was two 26° vee-twins mounted side by side. In other ways it paralleled design outlines followed by Turner with the Ariel four, in Selly Oak. Thus both engines had crankshafts set across the frame, avoiding a right-angle turn in the transmission; both had completely enclosed and lubricated valve mechanisms operated by a single camshaft, a central position for the carburettor, and all-chain drive, with an oil-bath case for the primary; and both relied on roller-bearing big-ends. The Hawk's built-up three bearing crankshaft had pairs of connecting rods mounted on the two throws, with weighty crank cheeks doubling as flywheels. The camshaft was driven by vertical shaft and bevel gearing on the right side, and the oil container was carried – like the Arrow's – at the front of the crankcase.

Rather bafflingly, at first glace the Hawk was often taken for an elaborately finned single or twin (whereas the sv Arrow twin appeared to impress bystanders as a four). If hard pressed for more than a few miles, it tended to overheat around the cylinder head, which was a problem also encountered on the Ariel in similar circumstances. Both fours had a top speed of around 80mph. On a Hawk, though, speeding was not the sometimes enjoyable experience it could be on an Ariel. Both were "fussy", with a fair amount of mechanical commotion making itself felt above 40mph. But with the Ariel this did not worsen as speed built up. Owners soon learned to live with it. By contrast, the Hawk seemed to become more frenzied with increasing speed.

"Torrens" entered the lists as staunch advocate for the Hawk in the columns of *The Motor Cycle*. To no avail, the public refused to buy. What four-cylinder sales there were went to the £5 cheaper Squariel. In 1935 the Hawk ended its run.

Specification, Silver Hawk (1932): Four-cylinder, ohc, 593cc (50.8 × 73mm). Four-speed gearbox. 3¼g fuel. Tyres, 3.25 × 19in. 81mph. £75.

Other Matchless models are dealt with in the AMC section.

MONTGOMERY

Once an exclusive make, turning out small numbers of well-finished machines, Montgomery was forced by the market requirements of the 30s to cheapen its products by the use of 10-a-penny proprietory engines, usually of JAP manufacture. The results did the firm some credit, because of the overall balance – even good looks – achieved; but there was nothing in the specification, and no spectacularly low prices, either, to tempt potential buyers Montgomery's way.

Montgomery Greyhound 500 (1935)

Small-scale manufacturers who were forced to fit proprietory engines identical to those employed by rival firms appeared at times to be busier coining grandiloquent model names than improving the product. Montgomery, for instance – and *there* was a fine name, to start with – labelled their 498cc JAP-powered single (and some others in the range) the Greyhound. As a canine analogy, Labrador might have been more fitting.

A 1935 example was sold at under £50 although, as usual, the price did not cover such items as pillion equipment, electric horn and speedometer. The well-proven JAP 85 × 88mm ohv engine had enclosed valves which could be adjusted on release of a finger nut securing a cover at the top of the twin pushrods. Lubrication was by dry sump, with the 4 pint tank mounted under the saddle, to the rear of the battery. The makers, constrained to follow fashion by inclining the JAP by about 15 degrees, decided there was too much open space between the fins and the seat stays; placing the battery in tandem with the oil tank, rather than alongside it, helped to fill the gap. Another, almost inevitable, result of canting the engine was that the carburettor was pushed close to the top tube and the fuel tank. Montgomery, like most others faced with this problem, chose to avoid major frame surgery and, instead, turned the mixing chamber of the carburettor to the horizontal.

For £48 6s the Greyhound owner had to tolerate hand-change for the four-speed Albion gearbox . . . a racing-style foot control would cost him a little extra . . . and the likelihood of oil leakage from a "pressed-tin" covering for the primary chain. A nicely made aluminium oil-bath case was available but pushed the total price through the critical £50 barrier.

In 1935, Montgomery still fitted a twin-strapped leather tool case to the Greyhound. Tucked into the vee between the leftside rear wheel stays, it soon lost natural oils through proximity to the silencer of the single, high-level exhaust system.

Specification, Greyhound 500 (1935): Single-cylinder, ohv, 498cc (85 × 88mm). Four-speed gearbox. 2½g fuel. Tyres, 3.25 × 19in. 73mph.

Montgomery 500 Greyhound (1939)

There was a brief period in 1939 (before the Cotton concern laid claim to them, to power the commercial outfits that were to delight Gloucester County Council) when Marchant-designed JAPs became available to the Montgomery concern.

No handsomer in a convential frame than when installed in a rakish, triangulated Cotton, the Marchant JAP produced a familiar spread of power, even prompting *The Motor Cycle's* tester to repeat his "gas-engine" analogy, first aired in a report on the similarly-engined Cotton.

New Hudson Bronze Wing in the early 30s, with enclosure of crankcase and primary transmission.

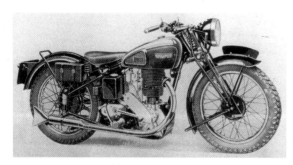

Montgomery 500 Greyhound, 1939. The engine was designed by Dougal Marchant.

The Montgomery in question was (of course) a Greyhound model, equipped with a spring frame of plunger pattern. Though simple, being no more than springs, more or less vertical, attached to the wheel spindle at either side and giving a movement perhaps of 1½in, this device greatly impressed the tester. He declared that it "smoothed out all roads – bumps . . . pot-holes, tramlines or stone setts could all be ridden over in absolute comfort." And no praise, apparently, could be too high for the steering and handling of this paragon: ". . . on the open road the comfort provided by the spring frame, coupled with the superb steering, tempted the rider to cruise in the 60s whenever conditions permitted."

Specification, Greyhound 500 (1939): Single-cylinder, ohv, 498cc (85 × 88mm). Four-speed gearbox. 2¾g fuel. Tyres, 3.25 × 19in. 78mph. £69.

NEW HUDSON

Publicity men have it as an article of faith that the word "new" must be invoked at some . . . usually critical . . . point in a consumer product's life. It is part of the advertising kiss of life that has to be administered when sales are going badly. But perhaps the word does not possess sales potency when used from the outset. New Hudson, one of the pioneer firms, with roots in the 1890s, had a last grand slam in the 30s with a range of handsome 346 and 493cc models that were part-enclosed by casings around the crankcase and primary

New Hudson Model 3, 493cc, 1932.

transmission. The engines, made by New Hudson, and slightly inclined in the contemporary fashion, were enclosed, too; at least the valve gear was, even to the springs. Four-speed gearboxes by Moss or Burman, automatic chain oilers, tank-top instruments and touring fitments ranging from an "all-weather" saddle and legshields, to travelling suitcases, added up to a specification that succeeded in frightening off the timid motorcyclist. Perhaps it was all too *avant garde*.

The firm hovered on the brink of financial disaster until it found a safe haven in making brakes for cars. Then New Hudson became Girling; and is, years later, in the process of living happily ever after.

NEW IMPERIAL

After enjoying a more or less normal vintage existence of sporting endeavour, New Imperial decided that its 1930s role was to lead the motorcycle world towards the bliss of unitary construction of engine and gearbox and universal rear springing. Such flouting of convention did not augur well; many enterprises of lesser invention had foundered in the deadly, placid waters of motorcycling apathy. But both features, as engineered by New Imperial, were well done and, surprisingly, well received.

A consistent money-spinner, however, was the least impressive bike in the new range, a rigid-frame (though unit-construction) 150 qualifying for the 1932 15s-a-year road tax that continued to be sold up to World War II. At the other end of the scale, in 1934 a 500cc GP vee-twin (more or less two racing 250s on a common crankcase) attracted plenty of column inches

New Imperial 250 racer ridden to second place by Charlie Dodson in the 1933 Lightweight TT.

New Imperial unit-construction 350 of 1937, with rear springing.

for New Imps in the weekly journals by its horrifying behaviour over Brooklands bumps as it was wrestled through 102.2 miles in the hour by "Ginger" Wood. It was the first British multi to cover more than 100 miles in the hour and *The Motor Cycle* presented a cup to commemorate the deed.

New Imperial 350 Blue Prince

A very fair example of an unremarkable, seldom encountered motorcycle from a small 1930s manufacturer would be . . . let's think . . a 346cc Blue Prince New Imperial of around 1933.

New Imperial Blue Prince 350 in 1930: a "thoroughly good motorcycle".

New Imperial 350 GP replica of 1934.

Massively built, with a full duplex cradle frame – modelled on the one fitted to their road-racing bikes, said New Imperial – and a twin-port, 74 × 80mm overhead-valve engine, the Blue Prince was good for 75mph at 4,900rpm on its 5.45:1 top gear. Plenty of finning, mainly vertical around the rocker box, and a hefty crankcase ensured adequate stamina: there was never any complaint from this bike when cruised within 5mph of its maximum. The gearbox was a three-speed with tank-side control, and transmission was all chain. It was, in all respects, a thoroughly good motorcycle – even to the sensible position of the speedometer above the steering head.

Yet it was never a big seller.

Specification, 350 Blue Prince: Single-cylinder, ohv, 346cc (74 × 80mm). Three-speed gearbox. 2¾g fuel. Tyres, 3.25 × 19in. 73mph. £40.

New Imperial Unit Minor 150

In 1932, a year or so after moving to Hall Green in Birmingham, New Imperial began turning out unit-construction motorcycles. The first of these was an ohv 150 which came to be associated above all other New Imps with this neat conjunction of engine and gearbox, in which the primary drive comprised helical cut gears.

The new 150 was a "Snowdon" model, meaning that it could take advantage of Chancellor Snowdon's

New Imperial Unit Minor of 1938 was relatively unchanged from the 150 that ushered in the firm's "unit-construction" programme in 1932.

concession of a lower road tax, of 15s a year, for under-150cc machines. It was to remain in the New Imperial catalogue up to World War II. The engine was inclined, with enclosed pushrods; also enclosed . . . totally so, which was a notable advance on most competitors . . . was the valve gear, in a largish aluminium box. The gear train was on the left, with final drive by exposed chain. The three-speed gearbox, originally with a car-type control, ie, one in which the lever was without a "gate" on the tank to restrain its travel (frequently to the "wrong" gear), was operated by a conventional tank-side lever.

Specification, Unit Minor 150 (1933): Single-cylinder, ohv, 146cc (55 × 62.5mm). Three-speed gearbox. 1¾g fuel. Tyres, 3.00 × 18in. 43mph. £28.

New Imperial Unit Super 250

The success of the Unit 150 persuaded New Imperial to build a 250 on similar lines in 1933 (with additional bearings in the transmission to withstand the side thrust imposed by greater power). It provided the basis, admittedly at a considerable remove, for the 1935 racers turned out by Matt Wright and Ike Hatch for the factory's team in international grands prix. Bob "Fearless" Foster up, one of these won the 1936 IoM Lightweight TT at 74.28mph, a record average speed for the race. Foster's effort was also a record of another sort, for never again was the 250 TT to be won by an all-British motorcycle.

The helical drive, running in oil, was invested by New Imperial over the years with near-magical properties. It was praised for 100 per cent reliability, freedom from noise, smoothness (an engine-shaft shock absorber was added for '36), and the end it spelled to all the tedious chain-adjusting which was the lot of owners of more antiquated models. After Foster's win another advantage was found for unit construction, and very seriously propounded by a press tester who had managed to borrow the TT-winning machine for a test run at Donington. Wrote "Cyclops", after describing several enjoyable laps of the manufacturers' circuit: "The acceleration out of Starkey's appeared to be every bit as good as it was on

Overhead-valve 250 Model 90 New Imperial, selling for £57 in 1938.

the level at Coppice Lodge. The gradient might have been non-existent. Even before reaching any of the level ground heading into the Coppice turn, the New Imperial was calling for top gear, which not only surprised me but "Ginger" (Wood, TT rider) as well, because his particular model pulls a slightly higher gear than New Imperials with separate gearboxes."

"We discussed this problem afterwards and came to the conclusion that it was the unit-construction which enabled the engine to pull so lustily. With unit-construction, friction in the drive is said to be less than with the normal all-chain method and it is also possible to get a drive that is in perfect alignment – two factors which must help considerably."

The racing New Imp had a much larger crankcase than the standard model, ribbed from front to back, to below the gearbox housing; the cylinder was vertical, where the road version's was inclined, following the style set by the remainder of the range; and there were other sporting aids, such as hairpin valve springs, a TT carburettor and a rocking-pedal foot-change. Nonetheless, the family connection between racer and roadster was clear, and the latter received high praise in an October '36 test report for its 60mph top speed, allied to fuel consumption of almost 100mpg.

Specification, Unit 250 (1935): Single-cylinder, ohv, 247cc (67 × 70mm). Four-speed gearbox. 2¾g fuel. Tyres, 3.25 × 19in. 61mph. £47.

New Imperial Model 110

Two examples in 1932; three the following year; by 1936 no fewer than 17 in a range of 23; finally, in 1938, a near-total changeover to the system . . . this was the record of advancing popularity for unit-construction in New Imperial's catalogues of the times.

A unit-construction 500 – with sv or ohv power – was introduced in 1935. With its hefty duplex frame and, puzzlingly, hand-change four-speed gearbox (slower, smaller models could be obtained with foot-change), the new 500s exemplified the kind of motorcycling that the makers claimed, in advertisements, was unobtainable with any other machine. The exclusive advantages of unit-construction were listed as: "no primary chain breakages; no sprockets to wear out or replace; no chain-adjustment worries; no whip between engine and gearbox; the whole unit

New Imperial Clubman 250, 1936.

continually running in oil." In 1939 the final unit-construction 500 was said to be "representative of a good modern motorcycle", which undoubtedly it was. Quite a few people thought that it merited a more full-blooded commendation, for it was as fast as, for example, a Norton 500, while being cheaper and quieter. It probably was better-looking, too, though judgement here can only be subjective. What made the engine so striking was its remarkably deep finning, suggesting a competition pedigree. In fact, the bike was no slouch, though less than a racer. One was ridden by a member of *Motor Cycling's* staff in a long-distance exercise to outface a motoring colleague who had been unwise enough to suggest that a motorcyclist would have to give best to a car driver on any run over 200 miles. The press man covered 388 miles ... "An hour was taken in Windermere, and a further 1½ hours were spent on business in the same town." Then ... "a call in Liverpool on the way home occupied eight minutes, and a further stop of 38 minutes was taken for tea outside Chester. The actual running time, not deducting refuelling stops, came to eight hours 54 minutes, which is an average speed of 43.6mph. A little under two pints of oil and 6.2 gallons of fuel were used, giving consumption figures of 1,648mpg and 62.5mpg respectively. These results were obtained without even exceeding 65mph, and paying due respect to the 30mph limits, which were only too numerous."

The clincher was provided in the concluding remark which told of "... the tester's ability to get straight off the New Imperial at the finish, enter his local and win three successive games of darts against the regular customers."

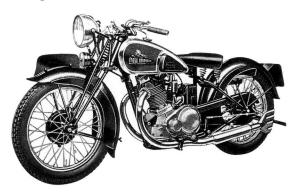

New Imperial twin-port 500 had enclosed valve gear.

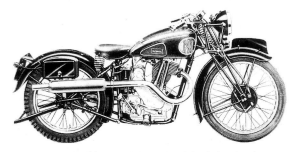

New Imperial 346cc Model 100, with high-level exhaust system.

As the man said – at £62 10s, complete with speedometer, the model 110 New Imperial offered wonderful value. A triangulated spring frame, rather in the Vincent fashion, was available at a mere £4 extra.

Specification, Model 110 (1939): Single-cylinder, ohv, 496cc (82 × 94mm). Four-speed gearbox. 3¼g fuel. Tyres, 3.00 × 20in. 82mph. £60.

NORMAN

People who did not have much time for Norman motorcycle nevertheless always looked out for the company's stand at Earls Court exhibitions in the 1950s, though not to see what was technically new. Whatever that might be, it could not in the circumstances be significantly different from anything else newly on offer from the other small firms relying on the Villiers Eng. Co. for engine supplies. No – the cynosure of all eyes, as they used to say in *The Motor Cycle*, was the vast, turreted facsimile of a Norman castle that, year after year, dominated much of Earls Court, dwarfing the presentations of more important manufacturers.

Norman TS250

Stranger in the everlasting night of Villiers-engined Normans was the Model TS of 1955-57, which had a two-stroke twin engine manufactured by British Anzani. Apart from not being a Villiers, it was notable too as the first over-200cc engine used by Norman. Other points of interest on the TS were the cantilever frame and a link-action front fork.

Specification, TS250: Twin-cylinder, two-stroke, 249cc (52 × 47mm). Four-speed gearbox. 10bhp/4,800rpm. Coil ign/alternator. 2½g petroil. Link-action/pf. Tyres, 3.00 × 19in. 260lb. 65mph.

Norman TS 250, 1957: engine was a British Anzani twin.

Norman B2S 197

Originality could be found on one or two Norman models of the early 1950s. The B2S appeared conventional enough in 1952, with its 197cc 6E Villiers engine and telescopic front fork. Where it differed was in having what the makers described as a cantilever frame, in which the rear fork was pivoted at the usual

Norman B2SC 197cc competition model, 1955.

place, just behind the gearbox, but moved against the pressure of two long – extremely long – telescopic struts that ran forward from the rear-wheel spindle to join the frame behind the fuel tank. Extra sensitivity was claimed for the layout, which was also featured on de-luxe versions of the B2S.

Specification, B2S 197: Single-cylinder, two-stroke, 197cc (59 × 72mm). Three-speed gearbox. Flywheel magneto/rectifier. 2½g petroil. Telescopic/pf. Tyres, 2.75 × 19in(fr), 3.00 × 19in(r), 250lb.

NORTON

Norton sales always owed a great deal to race success. In halcyon times for British motorcycling – periods in the 1920s and 1930s, and for 10 years beyond the Second World War – BSA, the biggest producer, were able to saturate the market with models fit for every application; they had no need for extra publicity. But Norton and other small firms, usually under-financed, had to make a name in sport.

Norton's first TT win occurred in the first TT race, when private owner Rem Fowler took his Peugeot-Norton over the 1907 course at 36.22mph (and 87mpg, fuel consumption being a consideration too at that date). Encouraged, James Lansdowne Norton set about producing his own engine. It turned out as the 82 × 120mm, 633cc side-valve that was called the Big Four and was to be on sale for nearly half a century.

J.L. Norton rode in TTs, but with no great success. He had the good sense to channel his energies into making racers for other people. One of them, D.R. O'Donovan, rode a smaller version of the Big Four in countless sprints and races. He went to Brooklands, where he was an even better tuner than rider. Some of the 490cc side-valves to receive his attentions were given the name BRS (for Brooklands Road Special) and a certificate to say they were good for 70mph. Single-speed, with belt-drive, these Nortons were marvels of flexibility, making light of 40-50mph averages on the open road, and coping with London's traffic.

In the early 1920s the first overhead-valve Norton, the Model 18, made an appearance at Brooklands and the IoM TT. In 1924 it won the Senior TT in the hands of Alec Bennett, which must have heartened 'Pa' Norton, by then ailing towards an early death in the April of 1925.

A faster Norton came on the stage in 1927. Designed by Walter Moore, this powerful ohc racer was ridden by Bennett to win the Senior of that year. When Moore left for Germany to work at NSU, the design was radically altered by Arthur Carroll, becoming the basis for the engine that brought so many road-race wins at home and abroad through the 1930s and into the postwar years. First as sohc and then, from the late 1930s, with twin camshafts, it was refined year by year by Norton's race chief, Belfastman Joe Craig, who counted himself blessed if he could drum up a further

Norton race shop. From left: Frank Sharratt, Joe Craig, Henry Laird, Gilbert Smith and Graham Walker.

Competition rider Vic Brittain with his 1937 ohc Norton.

horsepower or two after weeks, even months, of painstaking labour between race seasons.

With hindsight, Norton's supremacy in the road-racing field can be seen as being won at the expense of the roadsters. Edgar Franks' redesign of the ohv/sv models carried through in 1931 was not materially improved upon until after World War II, in 1947. Not that enthusiasts noticed at the time. They were happy to buy the dated, rather expensive roadsters whose only positive link with the ohc racers that bestrode the grand prix stage was the magic name on the tank. The man-in-the-street, on a roadster Norton, financed the firm's race programme. He did not realize he was doing so; and had he known, would not have complained.

In hindsight, too, it is possible to see that Norton's pre-eminence in the 30s owed very little to original research and much to the painstaking development of a limited design that was backed to the hilt by the very best that a thriving components industry could offer (no BTH magneto ever sparked like a BTH magneto earmarked for Joe Craig's use!); that, and a shrewd, even ruthless plundering of the best available riding talent.

Racing successes helped to sell Norton's ohv roadsters, which had little of the camshaft models' speed but, undeniably, something of their stamina.

In the early 1950s, when Craig's annual wizardry appeared to have fizzled out, leaving the racing Nortons stranded at 50-52bhp – no match for the four-cylinder Italians – the situation was saved, at least temporarily, by the McCandless brothers' pivot-fork frame. The Featherbed, with Norton engine installed, ran rings round the opposition for a year or more.

By then the roadster programme was leaning heavily on the 1948-designed 497cc twin Dominator, enlarged over the years to 600cc, then to 650, finally to 750cc. In 1953 Norton Motors was taken over by AMC, and in the early 1960s production was transferred from Birmingham to the Matchless/AJS plant in London. There some part of the roadster line was dropped (along with racing), emphasis being placed on the smaller twins, the 250 Jubilee and 350 Navigator, introduced in the last years of the 1950s.

By 1966 AMC had fallen into financial trouble, and duly passed into the Manganese Bronze combine, which then organized a new roadster programme based on the Commando. It was this machine, which had the 750, later 850cc, engine isolated in the frame on rubber mounts, that kept Norton alive for almost a further decade, until the worsening situation of the parent company, aggravated by troubles at BSA/Triumph, dictated final closure.

Norton Model 18/ES2

Every now and again, in the 30s, Norton's management would shift its attention from road-racing and give some thought to improving the motorcycles produced for the ordinary paying customer. Any changes made

would be advertised as arising from the firm's involvement in racing. The truth of the matter was that falling sales periodically brought home the need to bring the specification of the "bread-and-butter" machines up to standards achieved by firms having little of Norton's sporting eminence.

For a few years around the middle of the decade the most noticeable changes in ohv Nortons were an increase in fuel-tank capacity, to 2¾ gallons, and some smoothing of the timing case; a really diligent investigator might have spotted that the method of securing the cylinder barrel and head was altered for '36, to a system of long through bolts to the crankcase.

In 1938 changes were of a more radical nature, in response to a more radical falling-off in sales. In company with ... more factually, rather later than ... most of the industry, Norton decided that it was time for the everyday motorcyclist to put aside his grease gun and have his clothing free of lubricant slung back on the wind from partly exposed valve gear. But, being Norton, the firm was determined to give the credit for any improvements to the experience accrued from all those thousands of road-racing miles. So passages such as the following appeared as preamble to descriptions of the changes for 1938: "When the Norton factory has satisfied itself beyond doubt that a certain component modification to a machine has proved 100 per cent in competition work, it is then handed on to production machines, and so the Man-in-the-Street can purchase his race-bred machine and enjoy the benefits of racing experience."

Norton 490cc Model 18 of 1938.

It was all very reverential: part of a journalistic kow-towing to the olympian wisdom of "Mr Manufacturer". There were, it appeared, few who might question such worthy sentiments – no one, no Bateman man, to point out the incongruity of the continuing exposure of racing valve-gear and the well-publicised cover-up of valve springs for the roadsters.

To be fair, the changes for 1938 represented a worthwhile advance in ohv specification. All the valve gear, including rockers and valves, was given total enclosure and positive lubrication. Oil was sent to the rocker bearings through two small holes in the box leading to the middle of the rocker shaft, which was reduced in diameter at that point, to form an oil chamber. Skew grooves formed in the rocker journals set up a pumping action to force the oil through the chamber and on to the valve tops. Changes were not restricted to the new enclosure, for the cam gear had been redesigned for a reduction – by about 30 per cent, it was claimed – in loading on the cam wheels, with the followers being altered to flat-face form, in place of the previous curved surface; this last in hope of a lessening of mechanical din in the area. Norton enthusiasts had been known – though seldom heard, were their engines running – to complain about the noise of the race-bred thoroughbreds. The cam gear was lubricated from the pressure supply, with oil being fed to the inner surface of the gear wheels. The pushrods, in chrome-plated tubes, were inclined inward at the top on entry to the rocker box, where valve-clearance adjustment was effected after removal of a screwed-on side cover. Minor improvements included taking away the raised line on the timing case, for a completely smooth exterior.

A short-lived but much publicized change concerned the exhaust system, which acquired an odd-looking, flattened silencer having twin 10in-long tubular outlets, one above the other. Great thought, apparently, had been given to the design of this component, and great were the claims made for it – mainly that it allowed exceptional power while subduing the exhaust note to a whisper. There was little doubt that it was quieter than previous silencers; but the principal effect of improvement in this direction was to throw into prominence the rattle still emanating, despite the best effects of Mr Franks and his design team, from the rocker box.

This din gave rise to the following comment, taken from a *Motor Cycling* report on an ES2: "About the only criticism we have to offer is that the valve gear was on the noisy side, no matter how accurately the valve clearances were set. On the other hand, the exhaust note was very reasonable on all throttle openings, and at all speeds, a point very much appreciated when travelling through built up areas and along roads where the banks were high." (Who appreciated the very reasonable exhaust note, one may ask: rider or passers-by?) The silencer was also, as mentioned, odd-looking, and by 1939 was on its way out, an ordinary tubular design being the replacement.

Norton 490cc ES2, 1936, with full cradle frame.

Plunger rear springing – an extra in 1938.

The major difference in 1938 between the 500cc ohv machines was that the front down tube of the cheaper Model 18 ended at a bolt-on point on the top-front of the crankcase, whereas the ES2 had a full cradle frame; in addition there was a seldom-seen Model 20 which was to Model 18 specification, with the exception of a two-port cylinder head. By 1939 a spring-frame, previously available at extra cost only on the ohc International, was listed as an option for the ES2, when it accounted for £7 10s in the total price of £81 10s.

A tester's 1939 evaluation of the Norton spring-frame makes interesting reading, both from a 90s standpoint and as illustrating the euphoria of manufacturers and the press. Remember that the Norton springing system comprised nothing more elaborate than a couple of vertical sliders, restrained by springs, holding the ends of the wheel spindle. Total movement was less than 1½ inches, though such activity was rarely in evidence unless the machine was taken over what pre-war testers used to call "colonial" terrain. In 1939 *Motor Cycling* said of an ES2 spring-frame ". . . with the exception of spring strengths, it is identical to that used on last year's race machines." For such a rudimentary device, the magazine's praise bordered on the ecstatic . . . "In country lanes, when traversing cross-gullies and and even when travelling across country" – fields? – "the way in which the machine remained in contact with the ground was

Norton Model 18 in 1949.

AMC company's factory in London, in 1962, several of the long-standing Norton models were dropped, or at best crossed with existing AJS/Matchless machinery to produce oddly named mutants, mainly for the US market. The ES2 was one of the casualties. In its place came the ES MkII, which was no more than an AMC-powered single with a Roadholder front fork and Norton name plates on the tank.

uncanny . . . bumpy main roads could be traversed in real comfort miles an hour faster than when riding a rigid-frame machine."

Press testers found much to admire even in a stationary Norton. The centre stand was so well arranged, one of them wrote, in a passage that adroitly managed something of a sex-switch, that the machine "could be man-handled on to it by a not-too-strong girl." The frailty of mere woman in a man's motor cycling world was underlined by the declaration, in the next line, that "in the case of a man, [using the stand] needed only the pressure which can be applied by the first finger."

Specification, ES2 (1939): Single-cylinder, ohv, 490cc (79 × 100mm). Four-speed gearbox. 2¾g fuel. Tyres, 3.25 × 19in. 82mph. £80.

Norton ES2, 1949, with plunger rear springing.

The Model 18 returned to the market in 1946 with 1939-style girder forks but improved by use of a full cradle frame, of ES2/International pattern, in place of its one-time open design in which the crankcase was a vital part.

The 1948 Model 18, equipped with telescopic forks, had its engine updated with new timing gear in which cam followers were dispensed with, leaving the pushrods operating direct on flat-base tappets, for advantages in quiet running. Flywheels of smaller diameter but greater width, a longer-skirt piston and shorter, thicker pushrods were other changes, together with stiffened rockers and improved oiling arrangements. The Model 18 lasted until 1954.

Specification, 18: Single-cylinder, ohv, 490cc (79 × 100mm). 22bhp. Four-speed gearbox. Magneto/dynamo. 3g petrol, 4pt oil; dry sump. Telescopic/rigid. Tyres, 3.25 × 19in. 360lb. 78mph.

Norton ES2 with Featherbed frame.

A de-luxe rear-sprung version of the Model 18, the ES2 was part of Norton's postwar programme for 17 years. From 1947 to 1953 it had plunger rear springing; then a pivoted rear fork was grafted on for a season or two. From 1957 it had a full duplex frame.

In 1949 the 370lb ES2 was good for around 80mph and gave 80mpg at a steady 40mph. Years later despite numerous changes to the specification – for example, substituting aluminium for cast-iron as cylinder-head material, and raising the compression ratio – top speed had not improved noticeably.

After Norton's move from Birmingham to the parent

Norton ES2, 1956: note Model 7-style frame.

As an aside in the matter of model designations, C.E. Allen's researches of the early 1960s into the significance of the ES2 title may be mentioned. He was offered three explanations. "The first and most popular (because it is the most romantic)," he wrote, "is that ES2 was chosen as a tribute to the undoubted skill of Norton tuner Ernest Searle, who completely dominated sprints for several years with 490 and 588 ohv models. So much so that he frequently wiped up the 1,000 class from top big-twin opposition. He twice finished 17th in the TT on Nortons (in 1925 and 1927)."

It was an attractive theory, but Allen dismissed it. Manufacturers, he thought, were seldom moved by gratitude in this way.

Explanation number two was put forward by John Hudson, who devoted much time to Norton history. He thought that ES2 stood for "Enclosed Spring", with 2 denoting the second model of the 18 line. (The ES2 comprised, in effect, a Model 18 490cc ohv engine in a CS1-style cradle frame.)

The final explanation came from Walter Moore, who was the designer of the model. His memory, said Allen, was not precise – he didn't bother his head with what the office people liked to call the machine. But Moore thought E was a costing department symbol, meaning more or less that the bike cost extra, that S stood for sports, and 2 indicated the second sports model, when the Model 18 was the first. Moore's was the likeliest explanation, decided Allen, for it made sense when applied to the JE model, which had the 350 ohv engine in the CJ 350 ohc frame (a little ES2, in fact): J for Junior and E for extra cost.

The symbols were a matter of convenience at the time. Allen: "It is we who look back on them and read into them more significance than was ever intended."

Norton International

Some years after the war a 1938 International Norton passed into my keeping (writes the compiler). It had belonged to a *kursaal* owner turned greengrocer ... the entry on the Ariel Red Hunter is explanatory ... who had tired of daily commuting by motorcycle. He said it was a good bike but was not as comfortable as the Red Hunter, which had a spring frame. He was right; but in my eyes the discomfort of the Norton was a virtue. It was a mark of breeding. Nobody, I thought, should expect thoroughbred transport, animate or otherwise, to provide comfort as well as speed.

At home the greengrocer was something of a dandy, with a weakness for velvet jackets. On or newly off the Norton, however, he was different. He appeared to have a film of oil over his clothes.

I soon knew why. Internationals throughout their long model life had open rockers. Much of the oil supply to the cambox found its way to the great outdoors, and to a rider's legs, by way of the rockers. This wasn't supposed to happen. Felt pads pressing on the rocker bosses were intended, Canute-like, to staunch the flow. They would do so for a few hundred miles, when brand new. Thereafter the sensible Inter

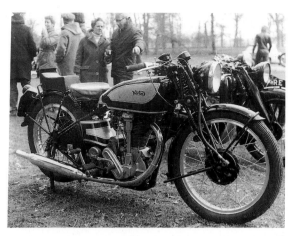

Norton International of 1936 with all-alloy engine and race-style oil tank.

Norton 1947 490cc ohc International Model 30.

rider resigned himself to an oily right leg. It was the same with cammy Velocettes before Veloce relented and enclosed all the valve gear. Nortons never got round to doing the same. This dereliction, if it be such, serves to reinforce the view that the Bracebridge Street crowd turned out some very "agricultural" machinery.

I thought a solution to the problem had been found with tough fibre bicycle brake blocks, to be used in place of the felt pads. I whittled a set to size and shape. When fitted, they bore so heavily on the rockers that it proved difficult to swing the kickstarter. For 50 miles the Inter was a shadow of its old, oily self. The novel oil retainers must have been absorbing several horsepower. Then they wore, and settled, and the first dribble of SAE50 appeared. It wasn't long before things were back to normal.

I began to ride the International at an impressionable age. It was a time when I saw my first Isle of Man race. After examining the Nortons in the enclosure at Douglas I bought a pair of 10in-long handlebar levers. They ran parallel to the Inter's handlebars and looked extremely racer-ish. With their restricted movement, however, they were of little use when it came to freeing the clutch or applying the front brake. The original levers were replaced – but not before I had sawn off the ends of the bar, by about 2in. This was a mistake. The sawn-off sections had held solid-brass plugs. A test ride showed extraordinary

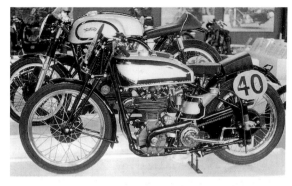

A 1939 Manx Norton in the National Motorcycle Museum.

Norton International petrol tank with bolt-through fixing.

the factory. They were valuable as kingpins of the range, available to well-off riders who fancied owning a "thoroughbred" akin to the racers which dominated Isle of Man racing during most of the 1930s.

Specification, Model 30 (1938): Single-cylinder, ohc, 490cc (79 × 100mm). Four-speed gearbox. 3¾g fuel. Tyres, 3.00 × 21in(fr), 3.25 × 20in(r). 95mph. £93.

The ohc single-cylinder Internationals, rarely referred to by their catalogue titles of Models 40 (350) and 30 (500), came on to the postwar stage little changed from 1939. What differences there were concerned the front fork, tank, mudguards and gearbox end cover, with further minor variations in handlebar controls. The new fork was a telescopic Roadholder and the long, narrow tank held 3¾ gallons. The gearbox had its selector mechanism, previously exposed as a separate unit, decently hidden under a new, enveloping cover; the mudguards were larger; and the silencer was a big absorption type that managed to diminish power almost as effectively as it cut decibels.

Wins for Ivor Arber and Geoff Duke in IoM Clubman's TT events – when the silencer was abandoned in favour of a straightthrough pipe – were the most outstanding sporting successes of the postwar International. In ordinary roadgoing 500 form it was credited with a top speed varying from 89 to 97mph, and a standing-start quarter-mile time of around 16.4 seconds.

Other than a switch to light-alloy for cylinder and

vibration through the handlebar. It took me a while to realize the importance of the brass plugs, and longer to find them.

The pre-war Inter was the most handsome motorcycle of its day; and for long after. The long narrow fuel tank held 3¾ gallons and was artfully scalloped along the base joins, with a cutaway on the right, at the rear, for the TT10 Amal carburettor. The six-pint oil tank had a long neck, putting the filler cap clear of the small Dunlop rubber saddle. The Norton, once Sturmey Archer, gearbox carried its selector box on view at the top, and the change had a superb, if rather long-travel, action.

The 1938 Inter was the equivalent in performance terms of a "works" Norton five years older. There was difficulty in arriving at a top speed to do it justice when a proper silencer was fitted. The valve timing was phased to work best with an open pipe ; conventional baffles curtailed revs and bhp. With a Brooklands "can" attached, it made a very agreeable sound and would reach 95mph. This happened to agree pretty well with the maker's findings who – in those non-inflationary days – advertised the International as providing 1mph for every £1.

You could specify an International to racing specification, with refinements such as an aluminium cylinder head. All Inters, of whatever description, were labour-intensive to build and showed little profit for

Willie Wilshere on his 1950 490 Norton International.

Superb Featherbed-frame Manx Norton.

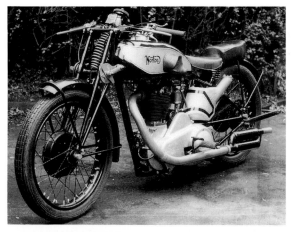

Norton overhead-camshaft CS1, 1929.

head, there were no changes to the long-stroke motors. They retained shaft-and-bevel drive for the single overhead camshaft, exposed hairpin valve springs and a modest compression ratio. Finally, in 1953, they were housed in the new race-bred Featherbed frame. In this form the "Inters" were equipped with an 8in single-side front brake, later incorporated into a full-width hub, and a neater "horizontal" gearbox, as well as a broader tank to sit on the wide-apart top rails of the McCandless frame.

By 1956 sales had fallen to an uneconomically low level, and Inters became available only by "special order", which was one of the industry's euphemisms for finished.

Specification, 30/40: Single-cylinder, ohv, 490cc (79 × 100mm). 29.5bhp/5,000rpm. 348cc (71 × 88mm). 24bhp/5,500rpm. Four-speed gearbox. Magneto/dynamo. 3¾g petrol, 6pt oil; from 1953, 3½g petrol. Telescopic/plunger; pf from 1953. Tyres, 3.00 × 21in(fr). 3.25 × 20in(r); 3.00 × 19in(fr), 3.25 × 19in(r) from 1953. 370-390lb. 97mph (500); 84mph (35).

Norton CS1

The CS1 Norton of the 30s was the poor man's International. That seems a reasonable judgment. However, it *can* be seen as a superior ES2, with the ohv engine replaced by a cammy unit. Either way, the CS1 was something of a mongrel, and not many were sold – probably fewer than the total over the years for the more expensive International.

The CS1 line falters in the 30s after a clear cut beginning in 1927 on Walter Moore's drawing board. It was designed as a replacement for the long-stroke pushrod engines that had obviously come to the end of their useful racing life in the previous year's IoM TT. Moore had no time to lay down a totally new design. Instead he altered the timing chest of the ohv motor to take the lower drive for a camshaft across the head. Through bolts, in place of separate studs and nuts, held the head and barrel, and there was new dry-sump lubrication, governed by plunger pump and fed from a tank under the saddle. Bore and stroke remained as before, at 79 × 100mm. The frame was new, a full

Norton CS1 of 1929 with triple-stays rear frame.

crade, with provision for pivoting adjustment of the gearbox, and was to remain much the same, apart from excision of the middle chain stays, for 20 years or more.

After a first-time-out win in the 1927 TT, the CS1 struck trouble in '28 and '29. In 1929 Moore went to Germany, to work at NSU. He took his CS1 design with him because, he said, he had drawn it in his own time, not Norton's. A young man named Arthur Carroll replaced him and was given the task of improving, perhaps obliterating, the work of Walter Moore, by then classified as something of a non-person. He made changes to the timing chest, introduced angular bevel boxes and a rightside magneto chaincase.

The CS1 was catalogued in 1930 in this form, with the exhaust pipe on the left side; a 350 version, the CJ, had the exhaust on the right. Two years later the International models made their appearance and stole much of CS1/CJ thunder. Thereafter the ohc models became increasingly alike, so far as the engines were concerned, although the Internationals remained by far the more handsome, with larger tanks and brakes and generally more attractive running gear.

A 1935 version of the CS1 (for example) was supplied in standard form with a small (2¾-gallon) tank that had nothing of the rakish good looks of the International's tank. The oil tank was smaller, too, being much the same as that fitted to the ohv range. The engine, at first glance very similar to the International's, had coil valve springs and a small-bore carburettor on a horizontal intake. The compression ratio was a lowly 6.5:1, and the top speed of 85mph fell short of an International's by 10mph or so. It was, however, an extremely oil-tight engine, one road-tester claimed.

There seemed no pressing reason in the 30s why anybody determined to buy an overhead-camshaft Norton should be persuaded by a saving of only £15 to forgo the snob appeal of an International in favour of the CS1.

Specification, CS1 (1935): Single-cylinder, ohc, 490cc (79 × 100mm). Four-speed gearbox. 2¾g fuel. Tyres, 3.25 × 19in. 86mph. £75.

Norton 16H

The 16H was Norton's equivalent of BSA's M20. In 1948, however, it acquired something of a sporting image, which even the most devoted M20 fan would not have claimed for the BSA. As late as 1947 the 16H, though garnished with teles, had looked much like its pre-war ancestor. The following year its old-fashioned

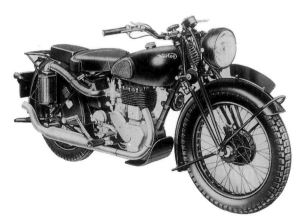

Early version of the Norton WD 16H side-valve, with special air-cleaner.

Norton 16H in 1954, with 8in front brake. This was the final year of the side-valve models.

cast-iron head was exchanged for a large-finned, light-alloy casting; and there were new flat-base tappets and other modifications to raise power to 15bhp and promote sorely needed high-speed stamina on long-distance runs – the sort of usage that would have given the earlier model the vapours.

Specification, 16H: Single-cylinder, sv, 490cc (79 × 100mm). Four-speed gearbox. 12bhp/4,000rpm. Magneto/dynamo. 2½, later 3¼g petrol, 4pt oil. Telescopic/rigid. Tyres, 3.25 × 19in. 370lb. 73mph.

Norton Big Four

From 1907 to 1954 the Big Four side-valve single featured regularly in Norton's new-season brochures, where it was invariably pictured with a vast sidecar lashed to its side, promising nothing more than long and faithful service.

Norton Big Four, 1951, following a major redesign of the engine, with capacity down to 596cc.

Its 82 × 113mm 596cc engine was changed in some essentials for 1948, sharing the move to light-alloy for the cylinder-head and modifications to the valve chest that were designed mainly to enhance the appeal of the 490cc 16H. But its role as workhorse was never altered.

Specifications, Big Four (1948): As 16H but 596cc (82 × 113mm).

Norton 19S

In the heyday of the British motorcycle, manufacturers were not shy of big pistons, long strokes, and vast (single-cylinder) cubic capacity. Throughout the 1940s and 1950s a selection of big singles around 600cc was on offer, intended mainly for sidecar hauling. Norton was unique in having both side-valve and ohv big bikes. The overhead-valve Model 19 dated back to the 1920s. By 1958, its last year, it had a light-alloy head, a neat four-speed gearbox, pivoted-fork rear springing and all the other mod. cons. distinguishing AMC manufactured Nortons. Yet dimensions had not changed from 1933, when the originally even longer stroke was reduced to 113mm and the bore opened up from 79 to 82mm.

An overgrown relation of the Model 18/ES2 (externally they were near identical), the 19S had

Norton 596cc 19S, 1956: mainly for sidecar work.

pulling power as its overwhelming characteristic. Though reluctant to rev, it was guaranteed to make light work of hauling the weight and bulk of a double-adult sidecar.

At a time when the twins were moving into the age of the ac generator, the 19 retained the old-fashioned Lucas Magdyno.

Norton 500T

Norton's postwar trials machine, the 500T, appeared in 1949. At first it was little more than a hasty rejig of the Model 18, with additional ground clearance achieved mainly through use of a 21in front wheel, and an upswept exhaust. The lightweight open frame was the one used in the wartime 16H. Within months the bike was modified to a more acceptable standard, with an all-aluminium engine, small tank, improved steering geometry, and weight reduced, the factory claimed, to 300lb. (Riders sweating to manoeuvre the bike in tight trials sections were not convinced.)

The gearbox retained a separate, exposed, selector mechanism, a throwback to pre-war years, throughout the 500T's six-year life. During this period it was

The 500T trials model Norton in 1949.

ridden solo by stars as diverse as Geoff Duke and Jeff Smith, and powered a sidecar outfit driven by the Humphries brothers, who numbered a win in the British Experts Trial among their more successful outings.

Specification, 500T: Single-cylinder, ohv, 490cc (79·× 100mm). 21bhp/5,000rpm. Four-speed gearbox. Magneto. 2g petrol, 3pt oil; dry sump. Telescopic/rigid. Tyres, 2.75 × 21in(fr), 4.00 × 19in(r). 300lb.

Norton Model 7 Dominator

Norton's 1948 twin, the Model 7 Dominator, was designed by Herbert Hopwood. The engine was all new but the rest was ES2, apart from the mudguards and tank, which were more handsome than those on the single. With a bigger stroke than bore measurement, the Hopwood engine had an iron barrel flange-bolted to a vertically split crankcase, and an iron head with integral rocker boxes, and widely splayed exhaust ports. Steeply angled valves, giving a shallow combustion chamber, were actuated from pushrods in a tunnel cast in the barrel and driven from a single, front-mounted camshaft. The crankshaft was of 360° type, with a chain-driven magneto at the rear of the engine and a Lucas dynamo at the front, driven from a fibre gear meshing with a camshaft-end pinion.

Power output, with a single Amal carburettor, was 29bhp – more than the Speed Twin, somewhat less than the Tiger 100. Not surprisingly, on-the-road performance of the Dominator was roughly mid-way between the levels set by those "standards" of the parallel-twin world.

Norton fans who had long foretold instant annihilation for Triumphs when "the winner of 21 TTs" got round to making a twin became a little subdued when the Dominator's road-test figures were released. They rallied by pointing out the Norton's superlative gearbox and transmission and – though this was not so certain – its superior roadholding.

Specification, Model 7: Twin-cylinder, ohv, 497cc (66 × 72.6mm). 29bhp/6,000rpm. Four-speed gearbox. Magneto/dynamo. 3¾g petrol, 6pt oil; dry sump. Telescopic/plunger. Tyres, 3.00 × 21(fr), 3.25 × 19in(r). 420lb. 88mph.

Norton Model 7 Dominator (1953)

One of the most pleasant if least-remembered Nortons was the 1953-56 Model 7 Dominator, which had its 497cc engine housed in a hybrid frame consisting of the existing single-front-downtube design as far back as the gearbox, at which point it was joined to a new pivot-fork layout, in place of the usual plungers. This frame was the one newly featured on the ES2 where, inexplicably, it made little difference to that robust single's manner of going. But with the twin it was a notable success.

Norton Model 7 Dominator, 1954, with single-tube main frame, pivot fork rear springing.

Norton Dominator 88

My first sight of a Dominator 88 occurred in an early month of 1953, when I watched V.H. Willoughby, a short man, attempting to clamber aboard one of these new Featherbed-frame twins. No ordinary 88, even in the matter of seat height, this pre-production model had been the editorial runabout of A.B. Bourne, editor of *The Motor Cycle*, who had bequeathed it to staff writer Willoughby on his (Bourne's) elevation to the Board of the publishers.

Blessed with extra-long legs and some conceit of himself as amateur mechanic, Mr Bourne had wasted little time in hoisting the Dominator's seat on to a lofty plinth knocked up from mild-steel strip and supported by disused valve springs and other bric-à-brac.

It took Willoughby a day to restore the Norton to original specification, and rather longer to regain a good opinion of his chief.

Despite those early traumas, the Bourne-Willoughby Dominator gave a good account of itself during several years; which is not surprising, for the 88 was an excellent machine.

Apart from a new light-alloy head, the engine was virtually unchanged from the 1948 original. But fitted into the Rex McCandless-designed Featherbed frame, it powered a bike that appeared able to outpace all rival roadgoing 500s.

The very first 88 had a valanced, fixed front mudguard but this was changed within weeks for a neat, unsprung type. Kidney-shaped silencers lent a distinctive look, and exhaust note. The tank was wide, because it sat on widely spaced top rails, and this militated against a really first-class riding postiion. In

1960 the rails were moved closer together and the tank was narrowed to a more acceptable 14in.

The 88 had a top speed in early years of around 90mph. What few modifications were made were not to the engine but to the frame, which acquired gusseting at the steering head and a welded-up union of main and rear sub-frame tubes, in place of a bolted-up layout.

It was not until 1956, following a good showing for specially prepared Dominators in the Daytona races, that some hotting-up, with new cams and pistons and a strengthened bottom end, was carried out to production-line 88 engines.

Specification, 88: As for 7 apart from Featherbed frame, tyres 3.25 × 19in(fr), 3.50 × 19in(r), light-alloy head.

Norton Dominator 88SS

Introduced in 1961, the 88SS had many of the go-faster components previously tested and incorporated in the 650 Nortons. Among these were lighter-than-standard pushrods, special valve springs, opened-out valves, twin 1¹⁄₁₆in-bore carburettors and a sporting camshaft. The result was a power increase to 36bhp/7,000rpm, boosting top speed to 110mph.

The brakes (7in rear, 8in front, both single-leading-shoe) were contained in full-width hubs, the rear one being designed to permit speedy withdrawal of the wheel. Early models had a siamesed exhaust system, which left the nearside of the Norton looking rather naked, and coil ignition; later changes included a downdraught-induction head and reversion to two pipes, two silencers.

Specification, 88SS: Twin-cylinder, ohv, 497cc (66 × 73mm). 32bhp/6,500rpm. Four-speed gearbox. Coil ign (later magneto)/alternator. 3½g petrol, 5pt oil; dry sump. Telescopic/pf. Tyres, 3.00 × 19in(fr), 3.50 × 19in(r). 410lb. 110mph.

Norton 497cc 88SS in 1963, with twin carburettors and downdraught manifold. Top speed was 105-110 mph.

Norton Model 99

Developed from the Hopwood-designed 497cc twin, the 597cc Model 99 Dominator appeared in 1956. It had a Featherbed frame, and up-dated features included a light-alloy cylinder head, "Daytona" camshaft, and full-width hubs carrying 7in-diameter

Norton Model 88 Dominator, 1954, with kidney-shape silencers.

Norton Dominator with full-width hubs, 1958.

Norton 750 in action at Cadwell park.

brakes. By 1958 the dynamo had been dispensed with in favour of an ac generator driven from the crankshaft, and coil ignition.

Road-testers in those days had an astonishing tolerance of vibration levels which, experienced now, would send any motorcycle reporter into a decline. *The Motor Cycle*'s man, writing about a 1958 Dominator 99, restricted his criticisms on this score to little more than. . . . "consideration which dictated the speed to be sustained . . . (was) a vibration period . . ." Seasoned analysts of road-test parlance will know how to assess that remark.

Fitted with an AMC-made gearbox, the 99, handsome in polychromatic grey and chrome, had a top speed of 100mph and average fuel consumption of 55mpg.

Specification, 99: Twin-cylinder, ohv, 597cc (68 × 82mm). 31bhp/5,750rpm. Four-speed gearbox. Magneto/dynamo;later coil ign/alternator. 3½g petrol, 5pt oil. Telescopic/pf. Tyres, 3.25 × 19in(fr), 3.50 × 19in(r). 410lb. 100mph.

Norton 650SS

Norton's Dominator 650SS was one of the outstanding derivations of Herbert Hopwoods's 1948 design. Usefully faster than the 597cc Model 99, yet sacrificing little of the sweet running of the smaller-engined bikes, the 650SS was a success from the moment it was released.

It had a top speed not far short of 120mph and would accelerate from zero to 60mph in six seconds. Yet vibration, that curse of the twin-cylinder classes, was mercifully low. In hindsight, it appears that 650cc probably was the sensible limit for enlargement of the 497cc twin. When the engine went to 750cc, as in the Atlas, vibration became intolerable and made sweeping changes inevitable (in the event, to the frame rather than the engine).

Specification, 650SS: As 99 except for: longer stroke (89mm) to give 646cc; 49bhp. Magneto/alternator, 115mph.

Norton Jubilee

In looks and character not unlike a Honda Super Dream, the Norton Jubilee 250 of the 1950s and 1960s had a general "oneness" of design that was in sharp contrast to the bitty appearance of more successful 250s such as the BSA C15 and Royal Enfield's Crusader.

Designed by Bert Hopwood, the twin-cylinder Jubilee appeared in 1958, at a time when the British four-stroke 250 was almost invariably a single. Of oversquare dimensions, the high-camshaft engine had separate cast-iron barrels, with four polished "mushrooms" for the rockers sprouting over the one-piece light-alloy head. A four-speed gearbox, arranged in unit, transmitted power through a fully enclosed chain to a rear wheel partly shrouded by streamlined bodywork scaled and styled to match the contours of the tank and the flowing, valanced front mudguard.

Norton Dominator 650SS on test in 1962.

Norton 250 Jubilee twin, 1962.

Brakes in full-widths hubs of Francis-Barnett/James pattern struck a rather cheap note in the otherwise all-new design but were well able to cope with Jubilee speeds, which rarely exceeded 70mph. The general impression was that the Jubilee, though adequately noisy and vibratory, was a shade underpowered – which it probably was. This, when a four-stroke 250 had to be pre-eminently a sporting device to survive, was the downfall of the Jubilee.

Specification, Jubilee: Twin-cylinder, ohv, 249cc (60 × 44mm). 16bhp. Four-speed gearbox. Coil ign/alternator. 3g petrol, 3½pt oil. Telescopic/pf. Tyres, 3.25 × 18in. 340lb. 70mph.

Norton Navigator

In 1960 the Jubilee had the first of its two reworkings when it was enlarged to 350cc and named the Navigator. No mere stroking or boring-out job, the Navigator's engine had totally revised measurements of 63 × 56mm to give a capacity of 349cc. The once-separate cylinders were cast as one unit; this apart, there was very little externally to show that the Navigator had a bigger engine than the 250. An immediate give-away, though, when the bike was viewed as a whole, was provided by the heavyweight Roadholder forks and bigger front brake.

Norton Navigator De Luxe, 1961.

Norton Electra ES400, 1964.

And after the Navigator – the Electra 400, with electric starting, which came along in early 1963. It was destined for the USA, where riders had been seduced by electric-start Hondas and were clamouring for a similar aid on British twins.

Specification, Navigator: Twin-cylinder, ohv, 349cc (63 × 56mm). 22bhp/7,000rpm.
Electra: As for Navigator apart from 66mm bore, to give 383cc, electric starting, 12-volt system.

Norton 750 Commando

British ingenuity at odds with limited financial resources, and finally triumphing, produced the Commando. In 1967 the main asset remaining to the motorcycle offshoot of the Manganese Bronze empire (comprising what was left of AMC – mainly Norton – allied to Wolverhampton Villiers) was the tried and proved, if somewhat outdated, 750 Atlas engine. BSA/Triumph were known to be developing a 750 triple.

Norton 750 Commando in 1968.

There were rumours of a Japanese 750 superbike. The Atlas was the power basis for assorted Norton and Matchless models of indifferent sales potential. What was to be done? Enter Dr Stefan Bauer, late of Rolls-Royce, accompanied by Bob Trigg and Bernard Hooper.

Trigg came up with the idea of directing the vibration of the big Atlas into the rubber mountings of a sub-frame to be suspended within a new main frame. This Isolastic arrangement, as it was called, worked extremely well. The engine, tilted forward, rocked the bike up to a fast tickover – but from then on no particular vibration was detectable up to the 5,500rpm peak.

Steering and road holding of a well-maintained Commando matched the standards set by the previous Featherbed layout, though a close watch had to be kept on the adjustment of the rubber mountings.

The tank of the early Commando was made of glass-fibre, as was the combined seat support and tail section. Altogether, the styling was of a very high standard.

Norton 750 Commando Interstate

The Commando did not, of course, remain for long as a nicely insulated 750 with agreeable, if not startling, performance. It got faster, and ran into trouble.

In 1968 the engine was a 20-year-old design. Originally it had produced 29bhp. Now, with no basic structural changes, it was expected to cope with not far short of double that figure. Main bearings began to give trouble at a low mileage; the pivot bushes tended to run dry, and wear; the general handling at high speed seemed to be dependent on critical adjustment of suspension, tyre pressures and steering-head bearings.

Troubles peaked in 1972 when the makers introduced a Combat edition of the engine with 10:1 compression ratio, high-lift camshaft and revised induction. The effect, with a newly stiffened crankcase, was to increase performance in the short term at the expense of total collapse at around 4,000 miles from new, following all-too-easy indulgence in high revs well beyond the safety limit of this long-stroke, ideally low-revving unit.

Remedial changes to the main bearings (with a new design called Superblend) and the auto-advance unit, and higher gearing, worked wonders. From 1973 the

Commando began to retrieve some of its reputation for quality and reliability.

Specification, 750 Commando: Twin-cylinder, ohv, 745cc (73 × 89mm). 65bhp/6,500rpm (Combat form). Four-speed gearbox. Coil ign/alternator. 5½g petrol, 5pt oil; dry sump. Telescopic/pf. Tyres, 4.10 × 19in. 415lb. 115mph.

Norton 850 Commando

In 1973 the situation was further improved on the introduction of an 850 Commando in Interstate, Roadster and Hi Rider forms, extra capacity being achieved by boring out the 750 to 77mm, to give 829cc. With an "easier" compression ratio and a lower state of tune, strengthening of the gearbox, clutch and rear fork, and modifictions to the Isolastic mounts to reduce the need for preventive maintenance, the 850 was more pleasant to ride than the 750 and rapidly acquired a better relibility record.

Last of the Commandos – an 850 of 1977 with electric starting.

The final edition, the Mk III, was equipped with an electric starter, which was supposed to answer the criticisms of owners of less than Mr Universe stature, who found it impossible to stir a long-stroke Commando on winter mornings. Unfortunately, the electric starter, too, usually found the job too much. With the starter went a change of gear-pedal position, to the left side, to conform to the practice of the leading Japanese makers and new US laws, and substitution of a disc brake for the rear-wheel drum unit.

Specification, 850 Commando: As for 750 apart from 77mm bore, to give 829cc. 55bhp.

Norton 750 Commando Dunstall Special, 1969.

Norton 750 Commando S, 1969.

OEC

For some, this firm is forever the Odd Eng. Co. The Osborns, who owned the company, were not afraid to try something new. Their best-known "oddity" was the duplex steering system, which was not true hub-centre steering, but a cheaper substitute which worked.

It was unfortunate that OEC, which gave motor-cycling its first practical monocar – the Whitwood, with full enclosure and jockey wheels – and held world's records, should have had to rely on indifferent engines and gearboxes. The way of the innovator is hard. Had commonsense prevailed, they would have stuck to the conventional. Motorcycling would have been poorer for it.

OEC 500 Duplex

Mr John Osborn, who with his father represented the O in front of Engineering Company in OEC, should not complain, wherever he is, if the motorcycles bearing his name are chiefly remembered for the so-called duplex steering which he designed and which was fitted, from 1927, to many of the machines turned out in a succession of small factories in the Portsmouth area.

In its affinity with its pedal-cycle forebears the motorcycle inherited one major design drawback above all: a weakly supported steering head, which had to exert pivot control over a fork and wheel from (comparatively) afar. Hub-centre steering early on found articulate supporters. But the difficulties faced in designing a system on these lines that would be both sufficiently neat and able to accommodate a useful brake in a front hub occupied, to the exclusion of almost all else, by the steering pivot, proved pretty well insoluble. John Osborn side-stepped the problem, but still got away from the traditional concept of the steering head with a duplex steering arrangement about which cleverer minds than the compiler's have had to admit defeat, when grappling with the task of describing it in an intelligible way. No faint-heart, C.E. Allen backed down when faced with the chore, and wrote: "Give me a working model – an old-fashioned three-leg clothes horse will do at a pinch – and I will demonstrate how the system works. Without such a prop I will not even try."

With its restricted steering lock – deserted three-lane highways or airfield runways are called for if an OEC owner is to execute feet-up turns – a duplex steerer is not all roses, by any means. Its apparently unshakeable stability takes some getting used to; during trial outings near-panic can be induced in the novice to OEC ways who attempts slow-speed cornering by handlebar leverage. Turning has to be done by leaning the machine, for the self-centring tendency is too strong to overcome; the steering geometry, designed to lift the front of the machine when the wheel is turned, is such that the bike's weight resists any move from the straight ahead.

OEC riders have always found enjoyment in demonstrating the unique stability of their machines. They are much given, at any suitable venue, to thundering along at indecent speeds while administering knocks and shoves to the handlebar, which usually refuses to budge – or, if it does move, straightway returns to its original setting with only a barely perceptible shake.

Duplex steering was allied to some undistinguished power units, such as the 350 side-valve JAP, in the 30s. It was put to better use, at the other end of the scale, when fitted to the 1,000cc big twin OECs used in several speed-record attempts.

OEC 500 Commander with Matchless Clubman engine, 1938.

A 500 "duplex" OEC, the Matchless-engined Commander of 1938, had a good turn of speed (82mph maximum) and was more than averagely comfortable because of its 2in-travel rear-wheel springing which had radius arms, with adjustable damping, giving something of the chain-tension control of Ariel's link-action system. *Motor Cycling* tested such a machine and, mindful of its reputation for thoughtful evaluation, declared that it had long debated why many OEC owners appeared to be committed to their machines. The magazine was "prepared to think that it was because of inherent steadiness of the model under all ordinary road conditions".

Specification, Commander (1938): Single-cylinder, ohv, 498cc (82.5 × 93mm). Four-speed gearbox. 3g fuel. Tyres, 3.25 × 19in. 82mph £80.

A 1935 OEC with duplex steering and rear springing.

OEC De Luxe ST2

Late in 1952, in time for a traditional unveiling at the Earls Court show, OEC produced two new models, powered by (of course) the tried and proved 197cc Villiers engine/gear unit. The de luxe ST2 touring version had a valanced front guard and rectified battery lighting; and, in common with the other model, featured a frame made in square-section tubing (is that a contradiction, in technical terms?), with pivot-type rear suspension, the fork being made in 16-gauge mild steel of rectangular section. At OEC, in those days, round was not beautiful.

The front fork was of telescopic pattern.

The other 200, known as ST3, a competition machine, had a rather ingenious three-chain crossover transmission system to guarantee constant chain centres – hence no variation in chain tension – for the rear drive. Alloy guards, competition tyres and trials handlebars came with this model.

OEC ST3, 1952, with 197cc Villiers.

OEC Apollo

In 1952-54 OEC dallied briefly with the Brockhouse-made side-valve 250 engine, as fitted in the small Indian of the day. Running on a 6.3:1 compression ratio, the alloy-head single was no more impressive under a tank bearing the OEC name than it was powering the Indian. In November 1954 the Apollo, as it was called, was dropped from the firm's promotional literature, and Brockhouse-Indian had the tiny market for 250 sv enthusiasts to itself again.

Specification, Apollo: Single-cylinder, sv, 248cc (64.5 × 76mm). 8bhp/4,750rpm. Three-speed

gearbox (four-speed optional extra). Flywheel magneto. 3g petrol, 2½pt oil. Telescopic/rigid; pf optional extra. Tyres, 3.00 × 19in.

OK-SUPREME

The name was merely OK until 1927, when Supreme was added by Ernie Humphries on buying-out his partner, Charles Dawes, from the family firm that had built motorcycles since the turn of the century. Dawes went his way into cycle manufacture and Humphries felt free, in a new factory, to realize his road-racing ambitions. There was a streak of megalomania in Humphries' personality. He could see no reason why OK-Supreme should not rival Velocette, another small firm that had made good on the race track, or even Norton. He tended to disregard OK's limited finances, which were better suited to the small-scale manufacture – or assembly – of proprietory-engined roadsters. His enthusiasms, no longer subject to check from Dawes, led to some interesting, costly and ultimately loss-making projects that enlivened 30s motorcycling.

An ohc 250 that became known as the "Lighthouse" kicked off the decade for OK-Supreme. Designed by G.H. Jones and Ray Mason, it had a glass inspection window in the sloping aluminium tower housing the camshaft – hence the nickname – with the cams at the top of the shaft operating the valves through an ingenious arrangement of sliding tappets and bell-crank rockers. The engine was made by an outside contractor. It required skilled – expensive – assembly. Even at the advertised price of £73 10s, which was big money for the times, there could have been little profit for Humphries in the Model TT/30. The "Lighthouse" was replaced by a more conventional ohc layout, again a Mason design, in 1934. From this date, OK-Supreme's grand-prix ambitions took a back seat; Humphries turned to the "bread-and-butter" side of the business. JAP-engined roadsters from 250 to 500cc were pushed into the limelight; the cammy 250 remained as a classy backup, available in sports or full racing trim. By the end of the decade Humphries had found a more effective outlet for his ambitions as a sporting manufacturer. OK-Supremes with modified roadster frames and powered by nothing more esoteric than

OEC Apollo, 1952. The engine is the Brockhouse sv 250.

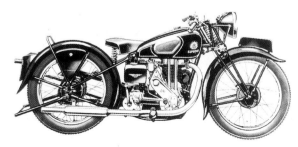

OK-Supreme overhead-valve 350 of 1937.

the overhead-valve speedway JAP were trouncing opposition on the short-circuit tracks of the Midlands. A smaller stage, admittedly, than the IoM TT course . . . but not so expensive.

OK-Supreme OHC 250

Freelance designer Ray Mason had no employment problems in the Depression years. Engaged in 1933 by Levis to lay out an ohc 250, he elected to have the camshaft driven by chain, in the AJS manner. A few months later he began work on a similar brief, for ebullient Ernie Humphries, boss of the OK-Supreme concern. This time, no slave to precedent and influenced by the forceful views of Mr Humphries, he favoured a vertical shaft, with bevels, to spin the cams.

With bore and stroke of 66 × 72.5mm, giving 249cc, the new engine was installed in a range of machines having the general name of Silver Cloud. The flywheel assembly was supported on ball bearings and the big-end on a double row of rollers; all conventional enough, and continuing to be so in the arrangement of the vertical shaft, with bevels top and bottom, and Oldham couplings. Where the design struck a new note was in the layout of the overhead gear, the rockers especially. Each rocker was made in two sections and secured on a taper with a Woodruff key, which neatly sidestepped the usual requirement for a slot in the cambox; each rocker shaft was able to protrude at the nearside, with an outer arm attached to it at that point. Oil leakage was discouraged by a special rubber washer. A further novelty was providing for the cylinder head to be removed without disturbing the timing, or the mesh of the bevels; all that had to be done was to unscrew the ring nut at the top of the tube enclosing the vertical shaft, the break being made at the Oldham coupling. Mr Mason assured investigative owners that reassembly entailed nothing more onerous than ensuring correct line-up of timing marks on the shaft.

A duplex Pilgrim pump fed oil through the drilled main shaft to the big-end bearing, with a by-pass sending a supply via an external pipe to the cambox, whence it drained by way of the vertical shaft to the crankcase.

In standard form the barrel and two-valve head were of all-iron construction, with a slightly domed piston giving a compression ratio of 6.5:1; in racing tune the

OK-Supreme ohc 250, 1935: top speed was 70mph.

head material was changed to bronze-alloy, the piston to a high-compression type, and the cams were treated to a sizeable hump. Mr Humphries seemed to find it all very impressive and 18 months after its debut at Olympia, in 1934, entered one for the 1936 Lightweight TT in the Isle of Man. Entered it; but did not see it start, because it failed to qualify.

Known to *Motor Cycling*'s test expert in 1936 as Pilot models, while everybody else who was interested kept to the original name of Silver Cloud, these ohc 250s in sports (ie, non-racing) form were attractive, reasonably fast (70mph at 5,600rpm), quiet and almost, but not quite, oil-tight; those special rubbers in the cambox were not, it appeared, 100 per cent efficient after all.

Specification, CG OHC (1936): Single-cylinder, ohc, 249cc (66 × 72mm). Four-speed gearbox. Tyres, 3.00 × 19in(fr), 3.25 × 19in(r). 70mph. £54 10s.

OK-Supreme Dauntless

Sales of their racy ohc 250 gave OK-Supreme plenty of publicity but not much money in the bank. It was an expensive bike to make, yet had to be sold at a reasonable price. Hence the 250 JAP-powered Dauntless of 1935. It had a three-speed, hand-controlled gearbox, pressed-steel forks, all-black finish – and the selling price was £34, which meant a useful profit for the makers.

The management persuaded a magazine to test it over sporting-trial terrain. The new model was to be shown living up to the image suggested by its name. The thinking seemed to be that photographs of the Dauntless leaping over hillocks and ploughing through glutinous mud would convince potential buyers that, by contrast, urban commuting on this latest OK would be a doddle.

OK-Supreme 250 Dauntless, 1935, selling at £34 13s.

Much was made of the rust-proofing incorporated in the paintwork though *Motor Cycling* was unable to offer a conclusive judgement on its worth. What is certain is that enamel in all those places – tank, handlebars and wheel rims – where chromium was the rule with other makes helped to keep the selling price low. Coil ignition, with a rubber-mounted Lucas battery, gave reliable starting. Customers with an extra £2 17s 6d to burn, and ill-founded faith in more traditional motorcycle electrics, specified a separate dynamo and magneto.

Specification, Dauntless (1935): Single-cylinder, ohv, 249cc (62.5 × 80mm). Three-speed gearbox. 3g fuel. Tyres, 3.00 × 19in. 58mph. £34 13s.

OK-Supreme SV/39

In the 1939 "utility" market, dominated by the Red Panther at £29 17s, nobody's thoughts turned unaided to OK-Supreme. You'd have needed to be a long-time fan of this Birmingham firm – perhaps have been an earlier owner of one of the cammy models – to favour the cheaper end of their range when money got tight. The SV/39 was a 250 side-valve and sold at £38 17s, which was not very cheap.

The JAP engine was of 64.5 × 76mm bore and stroke, was all iron, of course, and had a separate cylinder head. Total-loss lubrication was metered via an adjustable Pilgrim pump mounted on the offside timing chest. The big-end ran on rollers, the crankshaft on rollers on one side and a plain bush on the other. It was a very ordinary engine, and in the context of this particular OK none the worse for that. Top power was around 10bhp and top speed on the highest (6:1) of the three gears, 55mph. The petrol tank was handsome, though, and unexpectedly large at three gallons, serving to attract a critic's eyes up and away from the engine. The wheels were enamelled, but lined – which must had added a shilling or two to the price – and the brakes were tiny, and commensurately ineffective. But this was of little concern in view of the bike's moderate performance.

Specification, SV/39 (1939): Single-cylinder, sv, 249cc (64.5 × 76mm). Three-speed gearbox. 2¾g fuel. Tyres, 3.00 × 20in. 59mph. £38 17s.

PANTHER

The "sloper" Panther was probably the longest-running British motorcycle design. The 600cc "Big Pussy" gave great economy and sidecar-pulling torque, but scared off soloists. It was, apparently, unburstable. Smaller Panthers in conventional frames having a down tube from the steering head to the crankcase were equally long-lasting, and economical, in 250 and 350 capacities. These were slow sellers until the London dealers, Pride and Clarke, pulled off a bulk-buy deal with the makers, Phelon and Moore, which allowed them to sell the 250, advertised as the Red Panther, for as little as £29 15s.

350 Red Panther

Most people with an interest in motorcycle history know of the under-£30 250 Red Panthers sold by Pride and Clarke in the 30s. But shrewd Mr Pride (or was it Mr Clarke?) did not make a deal with P and M for 250s alone. There were 350 Red Panthers on offer, too, from

those famous premises in Stockwell. Somehow, though, a 350 for £35 15s lacked the advertising appeal of a £29 15s 250. The price differential of £6 or so was crucial at a time when the average weekly wage was no more than £4.

Outwardly, the 350 Red Panther was a double of the 250 and, like the smaller machine, went uncommonly well – rather better, in fact, than a number of more highly regarded and expensive competitors. For a start, the ohv Panther engine, with 77mm bore and 88mm stroke, was a natural "revver". Some engines are, with no particular merit in their design to suggest why they should be; others, though painstakingly designed and evolved to produce the goods, never take kindly to being hurried. The Red Panther would rev to well over 6,000rpm and had a top speed of 75mph. It was fairly quiet, though this aspect was not deemed to be of major importance, and it did not leak oil. It was reliable, and reasonably comfortable.

Panther 350 Model 80, 1934, a de luxe, twin-port version of the Red Panther.

Where it showed humble origins was in the gearbox, which was not merely a three-speed but was controlled by hand – enough to damn this excellent motorcycle in the eyes of any red-blooded rider raised on the exploits of TT heroes. (The BSA sports 350 of the day cost £20 more . . . a lot of money for an extra gear and foot control.)

Specification, Model 30 (1937): Single-cylinder, ohv, 348cc (77 × 88mm). Three-speed gearbox. 2g fuel. Tyres, 3.25 × 19in. 74mph. £35.

Panther Model 100

After the war, indeed after either world war, one bike above all others had "sidecar" written all over it: the Model 100 Panther. It was not usually referred to in this way. More often it was the "sloper" or "600" or plain "big" Panther.

Phelon and Moore did not go in for change lightly. Not for this manufacturer the annual frenzy over new engines, frames, colour schemes. When they made a good thing, they stuck with it – for half-a-century, if sales kept up.

This exaggerates the "sloper" story, of course, but only a little. As far back as 1901 P and M introduced a bike with a tall, sloping engine as most of the "chassis". The same layout was still the most notable thing about

P and M Panther 500cc Model 100, 1938.

Panther model 100S De Luxe, 1962.

Panther 100 with Oleomatic forks, 1948.

Panther 650cc model 120, 1963, with Canterbury sidecar.

the last big Panther as the factory closed for good in 1966.

The immediate (by Cleckheaton standards) forebear of the 600 was the overhead-valve 500 of 1924, enlarged to 598cc in 1927, from which date it continued largely unaltered, apart from trifling improvements such as valve enclosure, to 1959 and a final capacity increase to 650cc.

The twin-port all-iron engine was tall: perhaps not so much tall as long, for its considerable forward tilt meant that most of a big Panther's geography from steering head to rear wheel consisted of lanky cylinder running to massive crankcase. There was every justification for the engine appearing tall/long, for the stroke was 100mm. The crankcase held a flywheel reputed to weigh 14lb.

Starting a 600 did not call for a great effort to overcome compression. (At a nominal 6.5:1, the cr was on the low side.) It was the long stroke, and the inertia of the vast flywheel, that gave the problem. Even the burliest Panther owner could find that the thrust of 14st or thereabouts at the kick-starter had been dissipated long before it generated useful reciprocating motion. It was like stamping on an old-fashioned tyre inflator with a leak; but more tiring. The Panther had a half-compression facility, controlled by a lever on the timing chest, which raised the exhaust valve off its seat. With this in operation, a little more speed could be introduced into the start-up

procedure; and when the engine fired it would continue to run, with an odd, chuffing note, until the lever was released.

Big Panthers had exactly the right sort of power for hauling a double-adult, or larger, sidecar: their engines, 600 or 650cc, were all slog, all torque. And because the carburettor was of small bore, fuel consumption was always better than might have been expected.

Specification, 100: Single-cylinder, ohv, 598cc (87 × 100mm) 23bhp/5,000rpm; 645cc (88 × 106mm) version introduced 1968. Four-speed gearbox. Magneto/dynamo. 3g petrol, 4pt oil. Telescopic/rigid; pf available from 1954. Tyres, 3.25 × 19in(fr), 3.50 × 19in(r). 390lb.

Panther Model 45/50

A particularly good-looking Panther, in the two-stroke idiom, was the Model 45, circa 1958, with 324cc (57 × 63.5mm) twin-cylinder engine. Earles-type forks and a harmony in the treatment of the rear-end styling, plus practical improvements such as 7in-diameter brakes in place of 6in, made the 45 stand out in the Panther range.

In 1959 the 3T Villiers engine of the 45 was subjected to a little tuning, gaining higher-compression pistons

A 1959 Panther model 50 Sports, with Villiers two-stroke engine.

and a bigger-bore carburettor, and the Earles fork was swapped for a heavy-duty telescopic. Brakes went up to 8in, there was further enclosure at the rear, and siamesing of the exhaust system. In this format it gained the name of 50 Grand Sports.

Red Panther

One of the last Panthers to be sold, in 1967, was a 250cc two-stroke twin for which, fittingly, the title Red Panther was resurrected. Fittingly because the name echoed the one given 30 years earlier to the ohv 250 which P and M, desperate for cash, had disposed of by the lorry load to Pride and Clarke, for selling at a bargain price.

In 1967 it was the turn of the latter-day Red Panther to be discounted, this time by George Grose of New Bridge Street, London EC4. But though the price was no more than £149 10s, there were few takers.

The bike had all the then usual equipment, such as telescopics and pivot-fork rear springing, and the engine was one of Villiers' better efforts. But perhaps the motorcycling public, in the Wilson era, was not so desperate to save a bob or two as it had been during the Depression days of the 1930s.

Red Panther 35ES Twin 250 two-stroke, 1967.

PHOENIX

Though this book is mainly concerned with motorcycles, there has to be some reference to the scooters that became, in the 1950s, a notable part of the scene, and contributed to the demise of the British motorcycle. At least one native design was the work of an ex-racing man who had served his time on the best of Britain's racing bikes and might, therefore, have been expected to turn out something that would steer and handle rather better than the all-conquering Lambrettas and Vespas.

Phoenix T250 twin-cylinder scooter, 1961.

Ernie Barrett's Phoenix, circa 1956-62, available in several sizes from 150 to 324cc, was produced by a work force limited to Mr Barrett and, at most, a half-dozen like-minded associates (paid? unpaid? who knows) working in a few sheds in a yard in darkest Tottenham. The Villiers power unit was set roughly amidships on a flat baseboard, with simple framework helping to carry the steering head, rear wheel and body panels, the latter having the minimum of expensive curvature. The body was secured by overcentre clips which happened to be cheaply available but were promoted in Phoenix sales literature as a thoughtful design aid to dismantling.
Specification, Phoenix: Single-cylinder, two-stroke, 147cc (55 × 62mm), changed to 31C (57 × 58mm) engine in 1958; 173cc (59 × 63.5mm); 197cc (59 × 72mm). Twin-cylinder, two-stroke, 249cc (50 × 63.5mm); 324cc (57 × 63.5mm). Three-later four-speed gearbox. Flywheel magneto/generator. 2½g petroil. Leading link/swing arm. Tyres, 3.50 × 8/10in. 250-300lb.

QUASAR

Late in the postwar era another variation on the old theme of a "protected" two-wheeler appeared. The

Phil Read in a Quasar at Buckingham Palace, 1980.

work of one Malcolm Newell at Bristol, prototypes of the Quasar were built in the early 1970s, and limited production began in 1977.

The Quasar had a long-wheelbase space frame of small-diameter 531 tubing incorporating a roll bar and a front section designed for progressive collapse, in automotive style, in a head-on crash. Glass-fibre bodywork going up and over the frame, with a long, shallow-sloping Perspex windscreen, gave protection from rain and made for a fine aerodynamic form that was not only effective in minimizing drag against head winds but also reduced the effect of side-wind buffeting.

The engine was an all-alloy, water-cooled 848cc Reliant four with overhead valves producing some 40bhp, with final drive by gears. Twin discs at the front, and one at the rear, in cast-aluminium wheels shod with tubeless Avons provided braking.

Custom-made to suit the requirements of individual customers, the Quasar repaid a considered approach on the part of a new owner, who was well advised to forget ordinary riding techniques and to concentrate instead on not keeling over from the unfamiliar, low seating position.

Never thick on the ground, the Quasar in its bid for acceptance had to contend not only with its unorthodox looks and manner of going but also with cost increases which raised the retail price, in 1981-82, to more than £6,000.

RALEIGH

A household name in pedal cycling, Raleigh never made a comparable impact with their motorcycles. Under the Sturmey-Archer name, they made excellent gearboxes for use by such famous firms as Norton and Brough Superior. Their motorcycles of the early 30s were entirely conventional, well-made, and unremarkable. It was no surprise when they were abandoned, around 1934, to make way for the (even less successful) Safety Seven three-wheeler.

Rather more surprising has been the longevity of the heir to the Safety Seven, the Reliant.

Raleigh 500

Nineteen-thirty marked the final year for Raleigh's vertical-engine 500; within months it followed BSA's lead into the "sloper" era, though it was never to enjoy a comparable following. In 1930 form the 496cc Raleigh was well engineered and handsome. It owed something of its performance to the pioneering work carried out on the firm's TT racers by the Brooklands wizard of tune, D.R. O'Donovan.

A well-finned barrel and head, with exposed valve springs and wide-spaced parallel pushrods in plated covers, looked impressive above a large crankcase with forward-projecting casting for the Magdyno drive. The frame was a diamond pattern, and the girder forks were of Raleigh manufacture, as was the excellent three-speed gearbox; this was known by the Sturmey Archer label that Raleigh used at will on many of the items turned out in their Nottingham factory (including the engine itself, when it was sold for use by other manufacturers).

Raleigh 500 two-port, 1930.

A top speed of 70mph was well up to the standard of the class and a low "dry" weight of around 330lb contributed to brisk acceleration. The compiler has memories of riding a Raleigh on open stretches of beach. It had very little in the way of silencing and the gearbox had been converted, none too skilfully, to foot control. No doubt the din, soaring to gull-frightening heights during missed gear changes, added nothing to performance. Its effect on the imagination, however, was potent beyond words. The Raleigh seemed a very fine motorcycle.

Specification, MA30 (1930): Single-cylinder, ohv, 496cc (79 × 101mm). Three-speed gearbox. 2½g fuel. Tyres, 3.25 × 19in. 75mph. £46.

REYNOLDS

Albert E. Reynolds was to say that his earliest glimpse of a Scott, during pre-World War I schooldays in Liverpool, fired his enthusiasm for the marque. He owned his first Scott in 1920; was repairing them, in a small way, at home the following year; and by 1924 had formed a business to sell Scotts that rapidly prospered into a full-blown agency in the centre of Liverpool. In the period 1927-30, golden years for the Scott concern, with 3,901 machines made and sold, Reynolds advanced through the dealership ranks until he could boast that he held the largest stock of Scotts to be found under one roof. His success was such that, in 1930, as Scott Motorcycles Ltd. ran into financial trouble with the onset of the industrial slump, he was able to step forward with an offer to buy out the Shipley works. It was refused. The result was that Reynolds, on the rebound, a little annoyed at being turned down, put his money into expanding his business, acquiring the chief outlet for Scotts in Manchester. His next move was to tell Scotts, struggling along under a new title and desperate for sales, that he wanted an extra-special model made exclusively for him, to be sold only from the showrooms of A.E. Reynolds Ltd. Scotts needed money; they could hardly do other than agree. Reynolds wanted the very best ... a TT Replica-type engine (in both 498 and 596cc sizes) assembled to the highest standards, Brampton bottom-link forks, a foot-change mechanism (modelled on the trend-setting Velocette pattern), and twin Lucas headlamps.

Handlebars were free of control wires (they went inside the bars). The exhaust pipes blended into fishtailed Howarth silencers. Other de-luxe fittings included a Binks twin-float carburettor, Jaeger 100mph speedometer and a Boyce thermometer on the chromium-plated radiator. The tank had snap-on filler caps and a particularly eye-catching colour finish, with purple side panels predominating. Leather toolbags ... beautifully tooled, of course ... went each side of the rear wheel. All the alloy castings were polished. On the tank were discreetly styled motifs, in gold, for "Aero Special".

A student of human nature, Mr Reynolds had acquired further insights into the thinking of potential, and existing, Scott owners during his retail years; thus he had no hesitation in setting the price of the Aero

AER 350 twin, made by A.E. Reynolds: price was £65.

Special high, at £105. This was £30 more than Shipley charged for their 1931 Flying Squirrel de Luxe, with a basically similar specification. For their money, buyers of the Aero Special were assured that they were getting "a Scott for connoisseurs ... built for enthusiasts prepared to pay for that little extra which means so much."

In 1932 the name Aero Special was dropped; in its place went a new emblem, The Reynolds Special, which decorated the tanks of two new models priced, in standard form, at 100 guineas and, when fitted with an ingenious form of rear springing designed by Gordon Barnett of Wembley, at 110 guineas.

The separate exhaust pipes and silencers of 1931 were replaced by a two-into-one system.

Reynolds Specials were sold up to the autumn of 1933, when they were fitted with the detachable head newly introduced by Scotts, and throttle-controlled oil pumps. It is thought that 100 or so were registered.

ROYAL ENFIELD

Royal Enfield was one of the longest-established firms in the industry, turning out a host of worthy, undistinguished motorcycles.

Some of the features that were to be found on the very last of the Royal Enfields, in 1967, originated a half-century earlier. The "floating" big-end design, for instance, introduced in 1935; cush-drive at the rear-wheel hub, 1912; and the oil reservoir in the crankcase, 1903. Like many firms in the British industry, Royal Enfield did not lightly indulge in change.

The Enfield Cycle Company was formed three years before the end of the 19th century, with a factory at Redditch in Worcestershire. Founded on a pedal-cycle business, it came to powered two-wheelers by way of De Dion single-cylinder engines (for trikes) and Minervas mounted on the front downtube of solo bikes. Then JAP supplied a vee-twin for a 6hp sidecar model of 1912. The most attractive pre-1914 Enfield, however, was the 350cc vee-twin solo, beautifully made, if conventional in every way apart from the smallness of the engine. A team of 350s was entered in the 1914 Junior TT, and the best finished third. After the war Major Frank Smith, son of one of the founders, came back to Redditch as assistant managing director, taking over the top job on the death of his father in 1933. Long after another war, in 1939-45, Major Smith was still in control of Enfield affairs.

In 1927 the first of the big singles appeared, a 488cc (85.5 × 85mm) side-valve, supplemented a couple of years later by an ohv version.

Technical innovation in the 1930s was represented by a four-valve 500, the model JF, later depleted to three valves (two inlet, one exhaust). Apart from displaying their advanced engineering brains, with all those valves, the Enfield design team broke away from the practice of having (potentially) leaking external

A Royal Enfield ridden by Peter Head leads in a section of the 1938 International Six Days Trial in Wales.

A two-valve 499cc Royal Enfield Model J of 1936.

tubes for the pushrods, which instead were installed in integrally cast tunnels in the barrel and head.

By the mid-1930s a Bullet range of ohv sports bikes, at 250, 350 and 500cc, was on sale, together with a neat 150 which had all-enclosed valve gear that made the Bullets appear, by contrast, noisy and old-fashioned.

The long-serving big-twin, especially in 1,140cc form, was well thought of by sidecar-outfit owners.

During the war a staple military two-wheeler was Enfield's 350cc side-valve, girder-forked and with an oil reservoir in the crankcase. For a couple of years after 1945, renovated examples of the side-valve were on sale from enterprising London dealers who had no other hope of satisfying the demand for personal transport.

The side-valve was not a part of Enfield's official programme for the postwar era, which comprised the 350 Model G (with single down-tube frame, a telescopic front fork and valanced front mudguard), a 125cc two-stroke and, a little later, the 500 single-cylinder Model J. In 1948 the Bullet line was resurrected, with a pivot-fork 350, and augmented within a year by the 496cc twin. Through the 1950s and 1960s Royal Enfields proliferated. The 250s, starting off with the basically pre-war-style, long-stroke S series, were facelifted into a 70 × 64.5mm range which ended with the five-speed, 90mph Continental GT.

In the last years of the 1960s, when the Redditch plant had been sold, a series of 736cc Interceptor models was turned out in an underground cavern at Bradford-on-Avon; then in 1967/68 this remnant of a once-prosperous company was closed.

Royal Enfield Model X

Though very few makers, even in the depressed 30s, managed to produce motorcycles to sell at under £20, there were plenty of bikes on offer in the £20-£30 bracket. In 1933 Royal Enfield, for instance, brought out the Model X, with 148cc two-stroke power unit, at £23 17s 6d. At this price it had direct lighting. For another £1 it could be equipped with a separate 6-volt dynamo, tucked away between the rear engine plates and driven by chain from the crankshaft.

Twin exhaust pipes, a dash of chrome on the 1¾-gallon tank, a valanced front mudguard, adjustable footrests and handlebars and a spring-up rear stand were part of the specification of the Model X, which allowed Royal Enfield to claim they catered for all sections of the market.

Specification, Model X (1933): Single-cylinder, two-stroke. 148cc (56 × 60mm). Three-speed gearbox. 1¾g fuel. Tyres, 3.00 × 19in. 45mph. £23 17s 6d.

Royal Enfield Cycar

In 1931 tax concessions for two-wheelers, previously based on weight limits, began to take account of engine capacity. This was the year when the Chancellor of the Exchequer authorized an annual tax of 15s for motorcycles with engines of up to 150cc, to come into operation in 1932. It was intended as a fillip for the hard-pressed motorcycle industry; and of course made vote-catchingly plain that the government was concerned for a less well-off section of the motoring population. Royal Enfield's spirited response was the 146cc two-stroke Cycar with all-covering, pressed-steel bodywork and large leg shields. The panelling ran back, under and parallel to the fuel tank, to the rear-wheel spindle, with slots at appropriate places through which projected necessary cranks and knobs for kick-starting and gear-changing (by hand, of course). It was not lovely; but aesthetics had been low among Royal Enfield's priorities, which tended instead to favour price-cutting. It appeared, however, that even the humblest motorcyclist wanted something more attractive than the Cycar on which to lavish his 15s road tax. Even a selling price of under £24 did not tempt him. Next season Royal Enfield undertook cosmetic work, with a profusion of gold lining. Sales picked up, marginally. A year or so later the price was down to 19 guineas, and then, in 1937, the Cycar was no longer available.

Specification, Cycar Z2 (1932): Single-cylinder, two-stroke. 146cc (56 × 60mm). Three-speed gearbox. 2g fuel. Tyres, 2.75 × 19in. 45mph. £23 17s 6d.

Royal Enfield Model K

Motorcycling recollection puts "11.50" firmly in Brough Superior country. But there were in the 30s more than a few big sv vee-twins with other names on the tank; and at least one, the Royal Enfield K, had an engine that equated almost precisely to 11.50, at 1,140cc. (The Brough Superior's big JAP was 1,100cc, the "50" a power rating.)

The model K was made available to the British motorcyclist in 1937. Prior to this date it had been reserved for the remoter areas of the Colonies where, harnessed to enormous sidecars and receiving the minimum of attention from mahouts more familiar with bullock-power than the ic engine, it performed prodigies of uncomplaining service. For sale in the UK it was smartened up a little, with a plated tank, but continued to be equipped, in standard form, with a foot-operated clutch, for the makers concluded that few buyers would hazard solo trips on this 8ft-long heavyweight; for those who insisted on hand-control, a substitute fitting was available.

Royal Enfield Model K side-valve twin of 1140cc, 1938.

Total valve-gear enclosure, dry-sump lubrication (the oil being carried in a compartment in the crankcase, in customary RE style), magneto ignition, a four-speed, hand-controlled Albion gearbox, and a large duplex cradle frame were other features of this effortless performer, which sold to any worshipper of side-valve power who might be approximately £100 short of the £170 that Mr Brough charged for *his* 11.50. **Specification, Model KX (1939):** Twin-cylinder, sv, 1,140cc (88.5 × 99.25mm). Four-speed gearbox. 3½g fuel. Tyres, 4.00 × 19in. 58mph. £102 (with sidecar), £77 (solo).

Royal Enfield Bullet JFL31 (1930)

Motorcyclists with sporting interests and a long memory recall Royal Enfield mainly on the strength of the Bullet models. It was a good title for a bike with a little extra performance; in view of the company's puzzling motto, Made like a Gun, the only surprise is that the early 30s had arrived before it was used.

The most interesting Bullet of the early series was the 500 (there were 250 and 350 versions) which was

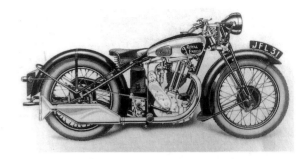

Royal Enfield Bullet JFL31, a four-valve 500, 1930.

based on the single introduced at the London Show of 1930. Known as JFL31, this model was sized at 488cc (as were previous REs in the same category) but departed radically from earlier practice in having a four-valve cylinder head. Parallel sets of valves were operated by totally enclosed rockers running on roller bearings. The compression ratio was no more than 5.5:1, with the bike in showroom trim, but an under-barrel plate could be removed by owners in search of higher compression and more invigorating performance. The factory talked of a 3hp increment for the four-valver, even in low-compression tune, over the two-valve model in the range: top speed was supposed to be 80mph. The engine was canted forward in the frame which, for reasons best known to the management, had only a single front down tube (to the top of the crankcase) at a time when much was being made of a new duplex-tube full cradle featured in the specification of, among others, the F31 346cc side-valve.

The Bullet name first appeared in 1933 catalogues, when the 500 headed the line. Retaining a four-valve engine while the other Bullets inherited two-valve units, the 500 ran on a high compresion and was said to be good for more than 85mph. Indeed, with a modicum of additional preparation, and taller gearing, the bike would see "the ton", RE claimed; and at this point decided that the time had come to substantiate such brave talk. The outcome was an early-morning session in which the firm's Jack Brooker, more usually seen on mud-plugging Enfields, took a Bullet through an independently timed flying quarter-mile to record a mean 99mph, which readers of the motorcycle press generously accepted as proving Royal Enfield's claims.

In 1933 the Bullet had a cradle frame, a four-speed foot-change gearbox and the almost mandatory high-level exhaust system. It sold for £59. **Specification, JFL (1930):** Single-cylinder, ohv, 488cc (85 × 85mm). Four-speed gearbox. 2½g fuel. Tyres, 3.25 × 19in. 80mph. £50.

Royal Enfield Bullet LO (1935)

Two years on, the 500 Bullet was still priced at £59 – testimony to the financial rigours of the Depression years which required any commercial undertaking that was to remain in business to pare retail prices to the bone. Not that the 1935 Bullet was the same bike at the same price; it had been extensively redesigned and developed, for another lesson of the 30s for survivors in the hard-hit motorcycle industry was that, somehow or other, specifications had to be upgraded, year by year, while prices must remain constant. It was a difficult, if not impossible, proposition. In 1935 the Bullet's engine lost one of its valves. The new arrangement featured a single large exhaust valve and two smaller valves for the inlet. All were set vertically and, with springs and rockers, were totally enclosed within an extension of the cylinder-head casting. For 1935 the pushrod tunnels were incorporated in barrel and head, giving a cleaner, if less glittery, aspect on loss of the usual chrome-plated tubes. Clearance adjustment was provided at the base of the pushrods, behind a removable cover, instead of on the rocker arms. The inlet valves were operated through a bridge piece pivoting between the valves and taking its motion from a single rocker. The downdraught mixing chamber of the Amal carburettor was mounted horizontally (for the engine remained inclined and space beneath the frame top tube was limited). With its integral pushrod tunnels and well-ribbed crankcase holding oil in the forward section, this engine took on much of the familiar appearance of all four-stroke Royal Enfields during the remainder of the company's life, to well beyond World War II.

Running gear remained much as before, with the exception of the 6½in diameter brakes, which in 1935 acquired ribbed, cast-iron drums in place of the flimsier pressings of earlier years.

It would be pleasing to record that the painstaking design work involved in the three-port head, and all the other changes, had resulted in a radically better motorcycle; unfortunately this was not the case. The model LO, as they called it, was an indifferent performer. Many Bullet enthusiasts thought it represented a climb-down from the '34 version. This was a period when four valves were seen as a good thing (not that Rudge, the main exponent, could boast of spectacular sales). Three valves were considered more odd than appealing. It took Honda, 40 years on, to make three valves acceptable.

Specification, Model LO (1935): Single-cylinder, ohv, 488cc (85 × 85mm). Four-speed gearbox. 3¼g fuel. Tyres, 3.25 × 19in. 80mph. £59 7s 6d.

Royal Enfield Bullet sloper LO500, 1935.

Royal Enfield Bullet J2 (1938)

By 1936, the three-valve Bullet had reverted to four valves and was known as the JF. It was not, however, merely the model of 1934 brought up to date; the JF had a new engine patterned on the one raced by Cecil Barrow in the 1935 Senior TT, where he finished a creditable eighth at 73.94mph. Capacity was a more familiar 499cc, obtained with a 90mm stroke and 84mm bore, and there were two well splayed exhaust ports and low-level pipes with flattened silencers. The four-speed gearbox had a positive-stop foot control and the primary chain ran in a pressed-steel oilbath case. Because the engine was now upright in the frame, there was adequate room under the tank for a vertical carburettor on a longish (horizontal) inlet tract; in the space between rear finning and mixing chamber was a Lucas Magdyno.

Royal Enfield Bullet J2 500, 1938.

In its progress to the outbreak of World War II the 500 Bullet underwent further surgery, with the loss of one exhaust valve and one for the inlet. As some compensation, the factory indulged in much brochure talk of the "special two-port head" while pointing out the extra depth of finning implanted on head and barrel. On the road, though, the Bullet was shown to have lost its edge, with a top speed of no more than 76mph, and a 0-60mph time of 16 seconds that was hardly memorable.

Smooth and tractable, with benefits from the customary RE cush drive in the rear hub, the Bullet by 1938 had slipped out of the fast road-rider's reckoning. It never climbed back to favour.

Specification, J2 Bullet (1938): Single-cylinder, ohv, 499cc (84 × 90mm). Four-speed gearbox. 2¾g fuel. Tyres, 3.25 × 19in(fr), 3.50 × 19in(r). 76mph. £64.

Royal Enfield 125

In November 1945 Royal Enfield's 125cc two-stroke returned to the market as the "Flying Flea". It had flown, and it was very small. The name was bestowed in recognition of service during the war, when the 125 was used on parachute drops and advertised by its makers as the only vehicle capable of "winning through".

After the war, despite its battle record, the Flea sold in only modest numbers. It might have disappeared

Royal Enfield 125 Flying Flea, 1952: weight was under 150lb.

Royal Enfield 350 Bullet, 1952.

Royal Enfield Bullet Scrambler, 1956.

altogether but for the loyal writings of "Torrens", famed columnist of the big-circulation weekly *The Motor Cycle*, who interspersed reports on his number-one bike, the 100mph Ariel Square Four, with occasional tales of fishing expeditions undertaken on the tiny Enfield.

In 1946 some trifling improvements were carried out to the big-end bearing. For the rest the bike was as before, with flat-top piston, light-alloy cylinder head, unit construction for the three-speed gearbox (with hand control), and a built-in Miller flywheel magneto. The front fork was made in pressed steel and springing was by rubber bands. It had folding footrests and a 26½in-high saddle, and at a pinch could be stowed in the boot of Torrens' 2½-litre Riley.

Royal Enfield 350 Bullet

Five years into the postwar era, a 1950 346 Bullet, ranked as a sports machine, had a top speed of no more than 73mph. But high speed was never – the late-model 700s excepted – a dominant characteristic of a Royal Enfield; comfort was, and flexibility; and a generally pleasant performance.

Based on the Model G; the Bullet was first seen in 1948 when, in competition trim, it was entered for one of the early-season national trials. It had an alloy head in place of the Model G's cast-iron head and a taller crankcase, to accommodate the cylinder spigot to an unusual depth. But the engine, with its bolted-up gearbox, was almost the least of the Bullet's new features. What really marked it out from its roadster predecessors, and most other makes, was the pivot-

Royal Enfield Model G 350 in 1945 with fixed front mudguard.

fork frame. In March 1948 Royal Enfield was the first manufacturer thus to equip a postwar machine.

The Bullet was made available in trials, scrambles and roadgoing forms. The 1950 roadster version retained a light-alloy head, a plain big-end bearing, ball and plain main bearings and a compression ratio of 6.5:1. Power output was 18bhp at 5,750rpm.

Little faster than the all-iron Model G, the Bullet was considerably noisier mechanically but had undeniable virtues in improved handling and greater comfort.
Specification, 350 Bullet: Single-cylinder, ohv, 346cc (70 × 90mm). 18.5bhp. Four-speed gearbox. Magneto/dynamo. 3¾g petrol, 4pt oil; dry sump. Telescopic/pf. Tyres, 3.25 × 19in (road version). 350lb. 73mph.

Royal Enfield 496 Twin

The 496 Twin was designed by Tony Wilson Jones and appeared in late 1948, for delivery the following year.

Twins newly produced in 1945 by other manufacturers were advertised as high performers. Only the self-deceived among the Enfield clan would have claimed that this 25bhp newcomer was anything more than a mild-mannered tourer.

With separate cast-iron barrels, each with its own head in light-alloy, the Twin had a 250 Enfield's bore and stroke measurements (64 × 77mm). In many other ways too it followed customary Enfield design. For instance, it had an oil reservoir within the crankcase and a double-end plunger pump for oil

Royal Enfield 496 Twin, 1954.

circulation. The crankshaft, an alloy-iron casting, was carried on one ball bearing and one roller bearing. The twin camshafts, exhaust at the front of the engine, inlet at the rear, were driven by a jockey-tensioned chain and actuated short pushrods. Coil ignition with behind-the-engine distributor distinguished the Enfield among the other new twins of 1948, which were faithful to the magneto.

Though the engine was distinctly unsporting in looks and performance, it was housed in probably the best-contrived frame on the maket. A double of the 350 Bullet's, it was fitted with pivoted-fork springing and gave hydraulically damped movement noticeably in excess of that provided by the primitive plungers of most contemporary designs.

By way of modest specification changes – mainly from coil ignition to Magdyno to alternator – the 496 Twin (its catalogue title) carried on through an unremarkable career till 1958, when it gave way to the 70 × 64.5mm Meteor Minor.

Specification, 496 Twin: Twin-cylinder, ohv, 496cc (64 × 77mm). 24bhp. Four-speed gearbox. Coil ign/ dynamo or alternator. 3¼g petrol, 4pt oil. Telescopic/ pf. Tyres, 3.25 × 19in(fr), 3.50 × 19in(r). 400lb. 78mph.

Royal Enfield Clipper

Once overlooked in the attention given to Bullets, Meteors, Constellations and the like, the 250 grew from humble beginnings to dominate Royal Enfield production in the 1960s. By then it was the outstanding 250 on the home market. It had become the archetypical low-capacity (but high-performing) sports bike for the learner rider, following the 250s-only law of 1961.

The first postwar Enfield 250, the Model S, was as per 1939 – plus a telescopic fork. Thus it had a 64 × 77mm cast-iron engine with four-speed gearbox and a rigid frame. It was not very exciting and, as far as the compiler recalls, was seldom seen outside a 20-mile radius of the Redditch factory, where its popularity might have been explained by workforce loyalty, sustained by special buying terms granted by the management.

In its later Clipper form (from 1954), the 250 Enfield achieved more sales mainly because of new pivot-fork rear suspension and practical, cosmetically pleasing changes to the fuel tank (up in capacity to 3¼ gallons) and the fork-top headlamp area, shrouded by what the publicists termed a casquette. The Clipper was discontinued in February 1958.

Specification, Clipper: Single-cylinder, ohv, 246cc (64 × 77mm). 13bhp/5,750rpm (earlier 11bhp/ 5,500rpm). Four-speed gearbox. Magneto/dynamo. 3¼g petrol, 3pt oil. Telescopic/pf. Tyres, 3.00 × 19in. 280lb.

Royal Enfield Crusader

The Enfield 250 was reborn as the Crusader at the Earls Court show of 1956. Layout of the oversquare (70 × 64.5mm) engine broke new ground for Enfield, and for the remainder of the British industry, in having the bottom half as a smoothly contoured *bloc* housing, in separate compartments, gearbox, Lucas ac generator, oil-bathed primary drive, and of course the big one-piece crankshaft/flywheel assembly. The big-end bearing was split-shell, white-metal. Pushrods were concealed in integral tunnels and the rocker-box cover was a neat light-alloy casting. It was all so smooth, so bland that it might have been taken for a two-stroke.

The wheels were reduced to 17in diameter, under valanced guards, and the brakes, still of 6in, were concealed in full-width hubs. The tank held three gallons and was deep and shapely; finish could be in green, maroon or black. Top speed, despite those promising looks, was no more than a busy 70.

Royal Enfield Clipper 250.

Royal Enfield Crusader 250, 1957.

Royal Enfield Continental GT

The five-speed Continental GT, first shown in 1962, was the culmination of progressive development of the Crusader which had taken in such stages as Crusader Airflow – 1958 (with glass fibre fairing), Sports – late 1958 (high compression, high-lift cams, bigger inlet valve, light-alloy head), and Super Five – 1962 (five-speed gearbox, leading-link fork).

The Continental GT, with fairing and rear-set footrests, had a top speed genuinely in the mid-80s, the product of about 25bhp at the crankshaft. It remained in production almost to the end of 1966, chief of the roadgoing 250s in an Enfield programme comprising no fewer than nine 250s and overshadowed by only a pair of bigger bikes.

Royal Enfield Continental GT, 1962, with leading-link fork.

Continental GT in 1966: note big-bore carburettor.

Specification, Continental GT: Single-cylinder, ohv, 248cc (70 × 64.5mm). 25bhp/7,500rpm. Five-speed gearbox. Coil ign/alternator. 3½g petrol, 3pt oil. Telescopic/pf. Tyres, 3.25 × 17in. 300lb. 82mph.

Royal Enfield Constellation

The Constellation of 1958 might be reckoned as the first of the superbikes. At 692cc it was big – the biggest vertical twin on the market – and had plenty of performance. Descendant of Super Meteor, and Meteor 700, the Constellation followed usual Enfield practice in having the oil compartment incorporated in the crankcase, which meant that the latter was adequately big and, by design, strong enough to be used as part of the frame.

Another very "Enfield" characteristic was reliance on chains to drive the twin camshafts, the magneto and the gearbox. Adding to the general whirr and rustle produced by the chains were further noises-off from the cams, specially formed (the makers claimed) in the

Royal Enfield 692cc Constellation, 1959.

interests of "racing efficiency" ... another way of saying that they had no quietening ramps. Compression ratio was 8.8:1. The crankshaft was of one-piece design, in graphite-cast-iron, supported by a ball bearing on the drive side and rollers on the timing side. From the beginning, the Constellation's crankshaft was dynamically balanced. An alternator driven from the left end of the crankshaft provided lighting power, a rear-mounted magneto the sparks.
Specification, Constellation: Twin-cylinder, ohv, 692cc (70 × 90mm). 40bhp. Four-speed gearbox. Magneto/alternator. 4½g petrol, 4pt oil; dry sump. Telescopic/pf. Tyres, 3.25 × 19in(fr), 3.50 × 19in(r). 410lb. 100mph.

Royal Enfield Meteor Minor

By the spring of 1958 Royal Enfield had thought of a new name for the "496 Twin". However, the Meteor Minor De Luxe was more a combination of ideas and components from the smaller Crusader and the 692cc Constellation than an upgrading of the original 500.

The all-welded lightweight frame, rear-chain enclosure and smallish wheels were copied from the 250. The engine continued in the familiar Royal Enfield mould, with light-alloy heads and iron barrels, one-piece crankshaft, bolted-up Albion gearbox and oil reservoir in the sump. But it was more eyeable, and a shade more efficient, with extra finning extending up around the integral rocker boxes and new,

Royal Enfield Meteor Minor 500 twin in 1962.

Meteor Minor 500 Airflow with Royal Enfield's Belgian distributor aboard, in 1958.

"oversquare" dimensions to permit interchangeability among 70mm-bore models.

The small headlamp was shrouded by something known to Enfields and the motorcycling press as a casquette. A siamesed exhaust system, with the pipe from the left (nearside) head sweeping round to join the other in front of the timing chest, saved a few pounds but did nothing for the quality of the exhaust note.

As before, this was a sound, reliable, inoffensive motorcycle that nobody ever thought enough of to cannibalize in any way (the ultimate mark of respect in the two-wheeler world).

Specification, Meteor Minor: Twin-cylinder, ohv, 496cc (70 × 64.5mm). 30bhp/6,250rpm. Four-speed gearbox. Coil ign/ac generator. 3¾g petrol, 4pt oil. Telescopic/pf. Tyres, 3.25 × 17in. 410lb. 90mph.

Royal Enfield Rickman-Metisse

In 1972 Rickman Bros, frame builders and suppliers of performance equipment, had an order to produce the rolling chassis and cycle parts . . . everything except the engine/gearbox . . . for a batch of sporting 750s to be sold in the USA. The engine would be the Royal Enfield series 2 Interceptor 736cc parallel twin.

Rickman duly fulfilled the order. But by some means Elite Motors of London were able to snap up 50 Enfield-engined Rickmans for the home market. Over the ensuing months they were surprised and disappointed to find that these fine bikes were slow sellers.

The frame was beautifully made in Reynolds 531, hand-welded, and finished in dull chrome. The front fork was of racing type, having large-diameter, flex-free stanchions. The disc brakes, in alloy-rim wheels, were the very best Lockheed pattern, to racing standard. Everything was of first quality, and assembled by craftsmen. The Enfield engine had never been in such high-class company. It proved, surprisingly, a very suitable choice.

Rickman with Royal Enfield engine/gearbox.

An indication of the innovative approach of the Rickmans was the way in which the footrests were attached not to the frame but – as it happened, more conveniently – to the exhaust pipes.

The price of these handbuilt twins with racer-like handling was £550.

Specification, Rickman-Metisse: Twin-cylinder, ohv, 736cc (71 × 93mm). 56bhp/6,750rpm. Four-speed gearbox. Coil ign/alternator. 3g petrol, 4¾pt oil; wet sump. Telescopic/pf. Tyres, 4.10 × 18in. 375lb. 115mph.

RUDGE

If there was a different way of engineering a component, *that* was Rudge's way. They used fine splines where other firms were content with taper and key, needle rollers in circumstances when most settled for plain bushes or nothing at all. There were huge, interconnected brakes on Rudges at a time when rival makers had narrow linings in 6in-diameter drums. Yet Rudges *looked* conventional; possibly the only feature that singled them out, at a glance, was the unusual lever on the left side . . . a hernia-saving method of operating the centre stand. The immortal radial four-valve 250 came straight off the drawing board to score 1, 2, 4 in the 1931 Lightweight TT, and later showed it was far from finished with a 1, 2, 3 record in 1934. Two of the TT "greats", Jimmy Simpson and Graham Walker, had never managed an IoM win until they rode 250 Rudges.

A 1929 500 Rudge raced by Willie Wilshere.

1934 Four-valve TT-style 250 Rudge.

Close-up of the 1934 two-fifty.

Rudge 500 Special

Along with much else in motorcycling, the nomenclature favoured by the manufacturers of the 30s had a Mad Hatter quality that defies rational explanation. Thus the *standard* 500cc Rudge was known as the Special.

A Rudge Special of the late 30s was a handsome motorcycle having nicely valanced mudguards, discreet gold lining on (usually) black enamel, huge brakes, and a well-balanced disposition of curves, with the minimum of angularity. The engine, too, with its single cover for the pushrods and a polished-aluminium valve-gear box, was pleasingly rounded, with generous finning.

Rudge 500 Special, 1935, with four-valve engine.

It was the Ulster model, of course, named after Graham Walker's 1928 Ulster GP-winning machine, that stole the thunder in Rudge circles. Justly, perhaps; the Special tended to live up to its handsome, florid looks, if not its name, by being a tame performer on the road. In at least one respect, however, the Special had a decided advantage. Like the Ulster, it had a four-valve head, but the valves were arranged in parallel pairs and operated by double rockers; on the Ulster, the radial layout of the exhaust valves with their interacting transverse rockers called for frequent maintenance. Almost unnecessary to add that tales of this drawback never succeeded in denting the Ulster's reputation . . .

The brakes were interconnected, both coming on, via a spring compensator, on pressure of the rear-brake pedal. At 8in diameter, the front brake of the Special followed Rudge practice in being unusually large. This was more obvious in the early 30s, when the brakes on other makes were, in comparison, much smaller than they were to become by 1937 or thereabouts. Fearing steering imbalance in heavy use of this powerful brake, Rudge altered the dish of the hub in the front wheel to place the brake nearer the middle. It probably was unnecessary but remains as another feature setting Rudge apart from other manufacturers. As does the left-side footchange control for the gearbox (which lasted till 1937); and the hand lever to haul the bike on to the centre stand; and the infamously complex gearbox with its mass of needle-roller bearings; and, of course, the devotion to four valves for a single cylinder, which produced little extra power (in the case of the Special, at any rate) but undoubtedly added to the price.

Specification, 500 Special (1938): Single-cylinder, ohv, 499cc (84.5 × 88mm). Four-speed gearbox. 3½g fuel. Tyres, 3.25 × 19in. 75mph. £69.

Rudge Ulster

In 1928 Graham Walker was sales manager of Rudge Whitworth. Towards the end of the year he won the Ulster Grand Prix at 80.078mph on a 500 Rudge. It was the first time more than 80mph had been recorded in a major road race. Speedy Walker was also no slouch in the public relations field. He baptized the following year's sporting 500 the Ulster. The name and the bike remained prominent for 10 years. In the 30s it was probably the fastest 500 – bar the more expensive International Norton – on sale to the public. See what you got for your money in 1930. A four-valve head giving a bigger port area, and an easier life for the valve springs, than any rival two-valve design. A stiff, deeply ribbed crankcase. Ball and roller-bearing main bearings. Race-developed crank assembly and con-rod. A four-speed gearbox on needle rollers. Enormous, interconnected brakes. Quickly detachable and interchangeable wheels (this latter facility was of dubious benefit because the front wheel was an inch larger, at 21in, than the rear). Above all, there was individuality. All for £70 (plus £5 if you insisted on dynamo lighting).

Rudge Ulster photographed at Brooklands. Lever operates stand.

Top speed of an Ulster Rudge was around 90mph and acceleration was more than adequate, because the bike weighed under 300lb. Getting maximum pick-up required no special skills. The Ulster rider could happily ignore the on-the-cam techniques beloved of Norton and Velocette men, for there was no cam-effect with the four-valver. All he had to do was turn the twistgrip and pay some necessary attention to avoiding hedges, pedestrians and other obstructions.

Later in the decade, with new owners for the company, the valve gear was totally enclosed, which was not an unmixed blessing, for seize-ups ensued before further modifications eased the problem. The price rose a little, by about £10, but options to compensate were race camshafts, a bigger-bore carburettor and polished ports, which kept the bike competitive despite increasing bulk and weight.

Specification, Ulster (1938): Single-cylinder, ohv, 499cc (84.5 × 88mm). Four-speed gearbox. 3½g fuel. Tyres, 3.00 × 21in(fr), 3.25 × 20in(r). 92mph. £82.

SCOTT

The Scott engine was a twin-cylinder two-stroke from the beginning. Alfred Angas Scott, inventor and engine designer, was 23 when he made his first motor, of 2hp, and installed it at the steering head of a modified Premier bicycle, driving the front wheel via a friction roller. It was almost certainly the first vertical twin engine of any consequence.

The first complete Scott motorcycle appeared in 1908, with a capacity of 333cc (58 × 63.5mm). The barrels were air-cooled but water circulated by thermo-syphon effect through jackets fitted to the integral cylinder heads. The crankcases were separate but part of a one-piece casting, recessed to take a flywheel between them, with a sprocket fixed to either side of the centre flywheel. This arrangement accommodated the two-speed gear that was a feature of Scotts for many years.

Within five years the design had changed to watercooling throughout. Thereafter, from his works at Saltaire in Yorkshire, Scott produced some of the most distinctive and esteemed motorcycles of the age, in capacities ranging from 498cc through 532cc to 596cc. Scotts won the Senior TTs of 1912 and 1913 but missed the hat trick in 1914, the year war broke out. During the war the company made machine-gun carriers (modified sidecar outfits) and gun cars for the military, while A.A. Scott busied himself with an odd-looking three-wheeler, like a mechanized crab. When described in the weekly press in 1916, the Sociable, as it was called, aroused a great deal of interest that was to be rekindled when an example was shown post-war at Olympia, in 1920.

Scott was the most original of all motorcycle designers. The principles he laid down before World War I sustained his successors (he severed con-

Scott circa 1929.

Scott Flyer of 1930.

Rear-sprung Scott Clubman Special.

nections with the Scott company in 1918, died in 1923) through the vintage period. By the 30s, however, the Scott, so long in the forefront, was falling behind. There was little sign of the design activity that had been evident in earlier years – though a 750, later 980cc, three-cylinder engine, designed by William Cull, should be mentioned. It was exhibited in 1934 but never went into production.

Fashions were changing. The watercooled two-stroke twin, though in detail much developed from the founder's time, appeared to be rooted in vintage, even veteran, ideology. In a practical way, too, the passing years were exposing shortcomings in the design, for the engine was nearing the limit of its power. Every styling change brought in, year by year, to match evolving fashion meant extra weight and a loss in performance. The final chapter to the story was written round the 1939 Clubman Special. The engine of this sleekly styled but grossly overweight roadster was tuned to unreliability in Scott's efforts to achieve parity with other (four-stroke) manufacturers.

After the war the Scott was unchanged from 1939 apart from a regressive move to a solid rear end and substitution of an air fork for the old-style girders. The retail price was very high. Sales were minimal. The public, it seemed, had no enthusiasm for rorty two-strokes, yowling or otherwise.

At Christmas 1950 manufacturing rights were taken over by the Aerco Jig and Tool Company of Birmingham. Becoming the owner of a new Scott was even more difficult than before. Sales were conducted on a protracted, bespoke principle that gave customers individual attention not experienced since the days of Mr Brough and his superior vee-twins.

Scott Flying Squirrel

"Fascinating," said *The Motor Cycle*'s tester. "Possibly even more fascinating than its predecessors, because it is more docile, more flexible, and faster."

What promoted these paeans of praise? Nothing less than a 1935 498cc Scott Flying Squirrel, sole representative (with a 596cc stablemate) that year of the famous Shipley concern. After a bout of price cutting in '34, the decision had been made to prune the range. For the first time in many years Scott enthusiasts, with or without a useful bank balance, were unable to indulge their fancy among Super Squirrels, Flying Squirrels, Sports Squirrels, Flyers and Replicas, Aeros and Tourers. In place of all these permutations there were the Flying Squirrel, as the 500, and when enlarged to 596cc, the Flying Squirrel De Luxe.

The new cylinder head, with compression plate, was introduced with the aim – realized, according to *The Motor Cycle* – of increasing efficiency, to give higher speeds and cooler running. It was secured to the block by no fewer than 14 studs and two bolts. In most respects this head was based on the one fitted to the sports engine known as the Power Plus, which had been available to special order in 1933 and featured hemispherical combustion chambers and central plugs. It was said to produce around 27bhp in 500 form, and 31-32bhp as a 596. Lubrication was, as usual, dependent on a twin Pilgrim pump mounted on the rightside crankcase door. The nuisance of petrol dripping on to the magneto chain, long familiar to Squirrel owners, was ended by moving the carburettor float chamber to the nearside. A neat, peculiarly "Scott" fitting in this area was a small, lidded cup containing oil to lubricate the magneto chain via a wick feed.

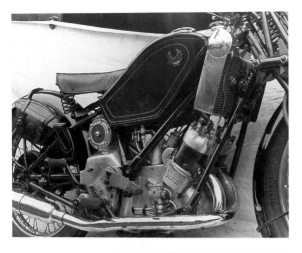

Scott 596cc Flying Squirrel de Luxe.

The revitalized engine, with three-speed gearbox (foot change was available as a £3 10s extra), was fitted in what was claimed to be the old TT frame brought up to date. It had a shorter wheelbase than earlier production frames and was noticeably lower, in the interest of "reduced pitching at high speeds". With a lower frame, the saddle, not unnaturally, was lower too. This proved to be a mixed blessing for at least one tester who commented, a little petulantly, that he had been unable to prevent the saddle nose from pointing upward. The factory claimed that it was possible to alter the position of the saddle "in a horizontal plane", which rather side-stepped the problem. Despite this criticism ... it was unclear whether it was based on aesthetics or a consideration of personal anatomy ... the tester found much to admire in the new Scott.

596 Scott Flying Squirrel of 1955.

"The handling of the machine at speed was admirable on both dry and wet roads. Even at the maximum speed of 77mph in top gear, the steering damper was unnecessary while the fork action was ideally suited to the machine. The maximum speed reached in second gear was 65mph, while 43mph was the best figure in bottom gear. On a long run 60mph could be maintained indefinitely."

But all was not exclusively sweetness and light. Scott buffs familiar with test-report jargon would have known how to interpret ... "As a precautionary measure a generous oil setting was given for high speeds, and this noticeably affected the two-stroking qualities of the engine on light throttle at low speeds." Ah.

With a Lucas Magdyno fitted, the 498cc model sold for £75. When the 596cc engine was installed, the price rose by £3.

Specification, Flying Squirrel (1936): Twin-cylinder, two-stroke. 498cc (66.6 × 71.4mm). Three-speed gearbox. 2¾g fuel. Tyres, 3.25 × 19. 79mph. £75.

Scott Three

To the motorcycle world at large the Scott sensation of 1934/35 was the William Cull-designed three-cylinder. It was not so welcome to diehard members of the Scott clan, who saw little merit in anything that interrupted a pure bloodline stretching back to the founding father.

But Cull, if not a designer of genius, as Scott undoubtedly was, had engineering skills aplenty. His three was a car engine in miniature ... not so miniature, in fact, for in prototype form it began life at 747cc, and ended only a few cc short of one litre. Originally, the crankcase was cast in one piece, in Elektron, and separated into three chambers by alloy discs or drums forming housings for the main bearings of the 120° built-up crankshaft, which was inserted

Scott 986cc water-cooled three of 1934.

Scott Three under the bonnet.

from one end of the case. The connecting rods were of light-alloy, with split big-ends to allow installation via the mouths of the crank chambers. On later versions, as shown in a last-minute appearance at the 1934 Olympia exhibition, the crankcase was horizontally split, with the chambers rendered (theoretically) gas-tight by flooding the main bearings with oil at a higher pressure than that of crankcase compression. On it was set a monobloc casting for the cylinders, with water cores to mate with those in a detachable, light-alloy head fitted with a recessed induction manifold fed by a car-type RGA carburettor. The deflector-head pistons were of split-skirt type.

In later form the engine retained an ingenious Cull-designed system of lubrication controlled by a throttle-linked swash-plate pump; extra pump capacity was introduced by two gears, for primary and scavenge, driven off the front end of the crankshaft.

Behind the block was a flywheel-speed clutch, with a spiral-bevel joint to switch the drive into chain from a four-speed gearbox. All this helped to make the 5cwt superbike more than averagely long . . . wheelbase was 60in, which was in the Brough Superior class . . . and something of a handful. It was, said the factory, good for 95mph. Off-the-record comments by the forthright Allan Jefferies, however, who was acting as official tester, indicated that it was anything but good at 90. The frame was weak and the steering head flexible. Even Jefferies, a fearless performer whose credentials included setting fastest time in the infamous Scott Trial, appeared a little shaken. Among the changes made in an attempt to improve handling was substitution of Webbs for the original Brampton forks. Not that doing so made much practical difference, as far as the public was concerned, for the Three never went into production. Cull and his men at Shipley became progressively discouraged by setbacks with cooling . . . the radiator, prettily styled to flow into the bodywork, was prone to boiling . . . and carburation, which managed to be simultaneiously uneven and rich, and gave horrendous mpg.

It is no simple matter to elucidate the reasoning behind the splash with this 750, later 1000cc, three-cylinder during a pre-war period of financial trauma.

Receivership was looming when the company embarked on the costly business of setting up a new motorcycle of such complexity that only one member of the workforce was able to assemble it!

Specification, Three (1939): Three-cylinder, two-stroke. 747/986cc. Four-speed gearbox. 3½g fuel. Tyres, 3.00 × 20in(fr), 4.00 × 19in(r). 90mph. £115.

Scott Swift

The Scott's famous exhaust "yowl" was heard but rarely after the war and then, in the main, it came from pre-war silencers. Though Scotts exhibited at some Earls Court shows after the war, and there was stirring news from time to time of changes to frame and engine, very few people actually took delivery of these famous two-strokes.

For some years in the early 1950s would-be Scott buyers in the Birmingham area had the frustrating experience of catching sight, or being told, of new Scotts being tested on the road. Always a prototype, never a production bike, it seemed.

Then in 1956 "production" was announced, and details of one or two changes to the specification were given in the press. Still a 596cc model at this stage, the Scott was advertised at £275 but nobody, as far as the compiler knows, ever managed to become the owner of a new Scott in 1956 or 1957.

In 1958 one of the more important revisions in the A.A. Scott canon took place. A new model, successor to the Squirrel and to be known as the Swift, was fitted with flat-top pistons in place of the old deflector type, necessitating extensive changes to the crankcase layout to provide new transfer porting. Of smaller capacity, at 500cc, than the traditional 596, the Swift had a top speed of about 90mph, which made it almost as fast as a pre-war Scott.

Eight-inch-diameter brakes (the front a double unit) in full-width hubs produced by the Scott company, Aerco Jigs, gave braking that was unprecedentedly efficient for a Scott. The lubricating process continued in the charge of the age-old Pilgrim pump working on the "total-loss" system.

But the Swift, too, never went into production. Finally Matt Holder reverted to the old 596 engine in a big duplex frame.

Scott 592cc Swift, 1958: seldom seen.

SEELEY CONDOR

The Seeley Condor was a graceful motorcycle found (but not very often) among the treasures salted away by collectors in the early 1970s.

Why so rare? Because Mr Seeley made so few – fewer than 10, apparently.

Colin Seeley gave up a career as sidecar racer in 1966 to devote himself full-time to making frames for racing solos. Displaying much attention to the honoured principle of straight-line triangulation, and impeccably finished (usually in nickel plating), Seeley frames housed AJS 7R and Matchless G50 singles. His business being successful, Seeley did not hesitate when the chance came to buy the stock of A M C's redundant race shop at Woolwich, together with manufacturing rights to the ohc engines. This is how the Condor was born. When Seeley decided in 1970 to make a sporting roadster for the discerning (and wealthy) few, he had the right ingredients to hand. It was a simple matter to "detune" the 498cc G50 and insert it into the race frame.

Seeley Condor: a G50 engine in a special frame.

With a front-of-engine generator for lighting power, Norton-pattern primary-chain case, large silencer with terminal reverse cone, and many bits and pieces in aluminium, the Condor was an eye-catching package. And by all accounts it went pretty well, too.

But then again, a high-compression single with lurid valve timing handicapped by exhaust muffling might not be as impressive in action as its looks would suggest.

SILK

The Silk Special was dreamed up and built by George Silk, an engineer trained by Tom Ward of Nottingham, who traced *his* mechanical know-how back to days with the great A.A. Scott himself.

The 700S Silk with twin-disc front brake.

Silk showed his bike publicly for the first time at the London Sports Machine Show of 1971. The engine, based on the 596 Flying Squirrel but increased to 653cc, was fitted into a 250-size frame constructed by Spondon Engineering of Derby, who had an enviable reputation for their work in the racing field. Spondon also made the front fork and the brakes, which reversed the practice established by the Japanese by being a drum at the front and a disc at the rear; later Silks had a rear-drum or all-disc set-up.

Available in various states of tune to suit the requirements of individual customers, the engine was fitted with a 12-volt alternator and car-type contact-breaker, and was said to produce at least 30bhp, more than enough to propel this light-weight (300lb), superb-handling motorcycle at over 100mph – 10mph better than any previous production Scott had ever managed.

In a production span of 10 years more than 100 Silks were sold at prices ranging from the original £600 to around £2,500 in 1980.

Specification, Silk: Twin-cylinder, two-stroke, 653cc (76 × 72mm). 48bhp/6,500rpm. Four-speed gearbox. Transisitorized ign/alternator. 3g petrol, 3½pt oil. Telescopic/pf. Tyres, 3.60 × 18in(fr), 4.10 × 18in(r). 300lb. 95-100mph.

SOS

Originally produced by Len Vale-Onslow, the SOS was without doubt the most exclusive and best developed Villiers-engined light-weight of the 1930s. They were first made by Vale-Onslow in his home village of Hallow, near Worcester, when it was the frame, rather than the engine, that attracted interest. As Hallow was (in the late 20s) beyond the reach of Worcester's gas supply, Vale-Onslow was unable to braze-up his frames, in the usual way. Instead he settled for electric welding, and the SOS became the first British motorcycle to have an all-welded frame. Later he

SOS 250 of 1936: a watercooled model, with all-welded frame.

A 1934 250 SOS.

established a small factory for the Super Onslow Special in Birmingham, and it was in the 30s that his adaptation of Villiers two-strokes to watercooling became well-known. So successful was he that Villiers themselves investigated watercooling, finally entering the market with watercooled units in 1933, when their customers included Excelsior and Vincent-HR, as well as SOS.

In the mid-30s the marque was taken over by another great two-stroke exponent, T.G. Meeten, of Kingston-on-Thames (when the rubric became So Obviously Superior), who continued to produce them until World War II. He had a better head for publicity than Vale-Onslow, making much of the 250 SOS as a sidecar-hauler. Even so it is doubtful if production ever exceeded 15-20 bikes a week.

STEVENS

In many ways the Stevens of the 1930s was more of a traditional AJS than were the machines bearing those once-revered initials which were made at the Colliers' factory in London. The Stevens brothers were left with many AJS engine components when they sold out in 1931. The money-shortage which precipitated the crisis, and the sell-out, proved to be temporary. Creditors were paid off, and the brothers, sitting in

their vacant factory in Retreat Street, Wolverhampton, were soon tempted back into the motorcycle business. They couldn't use the AJS name – that had been bought, with much else, by the Colliers – but there was nothing to prevent their turning out virtual replicas of the AJS line, as last produced at Wolverhampton, under a "Stevens" emblem. These were good, straightforward motorcycles and in at least one respect notched up something of a lead in being, probably, the first production roadsters to have a megaphone-type silencer.

350 LL4

When they picked up the threads of their old motorcycle business, the Stevens brothers produced a few machines to order powered by engines which, though bedecked with "Stevens" logos, bore a striking resemblance to the AJS units turned out by the brothers in happy, pre-crash days. Road-test reports appearing in the weeklies were intriguingly coy about the engines. Not for a Stevens write-up the customary detailed rundown on the internals ... merely (in the case of the 350) a terse line: "74 × 81mm (347cc) single-port ohv Stevens." Bob Currie, most knowledgeable of motorcycle historians, remarked on the resemblance and concluded, "... the only possible answer was that Harry and George [Stevens] had bought back, from Matchless, a number of surplus-to-requirement AJS jigs and tools."

Stevens 350 LL4, 1936, with megaphone silencer.

Whatever the parentage of the Stevens engines, they were at the heart of some thoroughly good if underrated motorcycles. A 1935 LL4 350, for example, had a sturdy cradle frame with twin front down tubes, a separate oil tank mounted in front of the crankcase, BSA style, a four-speed foot-change gearbox, and an oil-bath case for the primary chain that, like the engine, bore much resemblance to the equivalent item on Plumstead products.

The relationship was underlined by both makes leaking oil in the same way in this area.

Weighing some 300lb, the LL4 had a top speed of 70mph and could manage nearly 80mpg at a constant 35mph. Ahead of their time, the Stevens brothers had arranged for a stop-light to be connected to the rear brake. Similarly, a year or two later they pioneered the use of a megaphone-style silencer, with detachable

baffles, on a roadster motorcycle. The old skills were a long time dying at Retreat Street, Wolverhampton.
Specification, LL4 (1935): Single-cylinder, ohv, 349cc (74 × 81mm). Four-speed gearbox, 3g fuel. Tyres, 3.25 × 19in. 67mph. £52.

SUN

The Sun was among the Villiers-powered lookalikes that thronged the pages of the motorcycling press, if not the dealers' showrooms, after the war.

The company's postwar programme was based at first on the 98cc two-speed Villiers. The "Motor Cycle" (it was given no other name) of 1947 had a rigid frame, tubular, link-action fork, 4in-diameter brakes, 1½ gallon tank and a very modest top speed.

By 1955 the Sun-with-no-name was called Hornet and had been joined by a scooter, the Geni, for which the old "98" had been advanced to 4F specification, with comfort and control provided by a leading-link front fork and pivoted-fork rear suspension. Parallel with these developments was the continuing evolution of a plunger-framed 125 (Villiers 10D) that became 150 Challenger and then 200 Challenger, using, successively, Villiers 6E, 8E and 9E engines.

By the mid-1950s telescopics, or Armstrong leading-link forks, and full rear springing were commonplace through the range. The decade ended with another scooter, this time in the Lambretta idiom and known as the Sunwasp, which was fitted with Villiers' newly introduced scooters-only 173cc (59 × 68.5mm) fan-cooled power unit, Earles-type fork and swing-arm rear suspension. Having nicely styled bodywork, it was a pleasant, useful runabout but, unfortunately for Sun, no Lambretta as far as sales were concerned.

The biggest Sun was the Overlander, announced in October 1956, powered by a 2T 249cc inclined twin two-stroke with four-speed gearbox. The frame had (of course) pivoted-fork rear suspension, and a leading-link front fork.

Sun Challenger MkV, 197cc, 1956.

Sun Overlander 250 twin, 1956.

Sun Wasp 173 scooter, 1959.

Sun 98cc Geni, 1956.

SUNBEAM

It is not widely known that Sunbeam, a pillar of the motorcycle establishment, passed from private ownership into the maw of Imperial Chemical Industries as early as 1928. Not that there was any noticeable drop in the quality of the product . . . at least, not for a while. The standards of decades of John Marston craftmanship were too well implanted in the workforce to be lost in months, or even in a year or so. As Sunbeam historian R. Cordon Champ has noted: ". . . the popular idea of Sunbeams going into a swift decline because of the activities of some faceless 'group' is far from the truth. They did decline, but only gradually."

Sunbeam 350, 1929/30, soon after the ICI takeover.

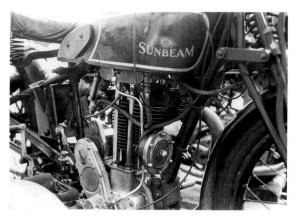

Model 95 Sunbeam with hairpin valve springs, 1931.

Model 90 Sunbeam with hand change in 1928.

It was not until the middle 30s that any change in Sunbeam manufacturing and design "integrity" occurred. The accountants made plain that the company was not pulling its weight; ICI standards of profitability were not being met. Sunbeam, whose machines, like Rolls-Royces, had long been more notable for their fine finish than for any startling originality, was given a flick of the whip. An attempt was made to spread the sales net with an underdeveloped high-camshaft 250, which ended disastrously, and a scarcely more promising light 350 with under-engine sump. The traditional Sunbeams, residue of Marston days, were clearly outdated. A half-hearted attempt to introduce some modernity into the Lion models, with plated tanks, turned out no better than the wholly new designs.

The path was clearly downhill. Entries in the IoM TT achieved little. Something positive had to happen; the alternative was a steady rundown to extinction. The "something" was a surprise sell out to Matchless (later Associated Motor Cycles) in 1936. To AMC's credit, it may be said that they achieved a definite "Sunbeam" character with the high-camshaft design that appeared shortly before the outbreak of war. Some, at least, of the cycle parts of these ill-starred machines displayed much of the old Marston quality of finish.

Sunbeam Model 90

The 1930s was not the happiest decade in Sunbeam history. As one of the innumerable companies comprising mighty ICI (but, as contributor to the collective purse, rather low in the pecking order), the old-established works at Wolverhampton entered the period trailing fast-fading clouds of glory from successive TT wins in 1928 and 1929.

Replicas of Charlie Dodson's Senior-winning bike, catalogued as the Model 90, were available to the public in the early 30s at around £90. This was £15 up on the price asked for the Model 9, the basic touring version with crossover gearbox and distinctive, lengthy offside rear chain, usually enclosed in the famous Sunbeam oilbath case. The TT Model 90, to give the full title, though closely allied through identical bore and stroke (80 × 98mm) to the Model 9, was much racier in appearance, having an impressively – vertically – finned two-port head with hairpin valve springs, a foot-change gearbox and a selection of other features which could be varied to suit a buyer's preferences. Thus a typical Model 90 of 1930-32 might carry a larger-than-standard oil tank with nearside filler, a breather on the fuel tank and quick-filler cap, a racing mudguard pad, and rear-set footrests; internally, the valves could be larger (1¾in for the inlet, 1¹¹⁄₁₆in for the exhaust), with highly polished ports and connecting rod; and there might be a raised compression ratio.

The Motor Cycle wrote in 1930 that the Model 90 was, more than ever, the speedman's ideal, and managed to discover such further improvements as detachable and interchangeable wheels, a four-speed gearbox and a system of direct lubrication of the valve guides. At £90, this 90mph single challenged the best that Nortons could provide with their Carroll-designed camshaft models; unfortunately, there was much to remind the public that the Sunbeam was, however worthy, a 20s design. Sales slumped and in 1934 the Model 90 was discontinued, and when this happened any lingering pretensions to a sporting connection for the Sunbeam firm vanished also.

Specification: Model 90 (1931): Single-cylinder, ohv, 493cc (80 × 98mm). Four-speed gearbox. 3½g fuel. Tyres, 3.25 × 19in. 91mph. £90.

Sunbeam Model 16 250

A salutary comment on the value of reports published, after too brief experience of models on test, in journals having intimate ties with industry is provided by *Motor Cycling*'s enthusiastic 1935 write-up on a machine which remained in production for a mere 12 months and later earned notoriety among Sunbeam enthusiasts as being "perhaps the worst motorcycle ever produced by the factory".

This was the high-camshaft Model 16 250 designed by Sunbeam's one-time chief mechanic, George Stephenson, and shown for the first time at the November 1934 Olympia show. Rather handsome, having something of an ohc racer look, with a tall timing chest containing a high-mounted camshaft, hairpin valve springs and a downdraught, big-bore carburettor, the Model 16 captivated *Motor Cycling*'s tester. He enthused over its appearance and practicality, summing it up as being "a distinct credit to the firm . . . carrying on the well-known reputation for gentlemanly high performance."

A sourer, but sounder, verdict based on extended acquaintance might have dwelt on such features as the weakly sited engine studs and valve gear which turned out to be unequal to the loads imposed by race-strength hairpin springs. As the valve guides wore, so the rockers and shafts cracked up, with other troubles arising from the shaky timing-case, held insecurely by a multitude of tiny Whitworth-thread screws.

Handsome it may have been, and something of a trendsetter too as the first Sunbeam to be sold with a proprietory (Burman) gearbox, but the Model 16 turned out to be a disaster.

Specification, Model 16 (1935): Single-cylinder, ohv, 248cc (64 × 77mm). Four-speed gearbox. 2½g fuel. Tyres, 3.25 × 19in. 65mph. £49 10s.

Sunbeam "AMC" B24

My personal experience (the compiler writes) of a "Matchless" Sunbeam concerns a 1939 350 owned by a schoolmaster who in middle age was more interested in the chronicles of imperial Rome than in motorcycling. His riding style owed much to observation of veteran motorcyclists threading through 1920s traffic on belt-drive single-speeders. He was happy to let me borrow the Sunbeam, when I offered to carry out sorely needed maintenance on it; less pleased later when the engine seized, during one of his leisurely outings, from oil starvation caused by a length of small-

A 1939 AMC-made Sunbeam 350.

bore "Petroflex" with which I had replaced a suspect pipe in the lubrication system.

I thought it was a pleasant 350, though a little noisy and possibly not as good a performer as a less expensive Matchless of similar age.

The 350 Sunbeam was announced in October 1938. It was one of several capacity variations, from 246 to 598cc, on a common design which had as its most obvious feature an enormous timing chest inscribed with the word Sunbeam in appropriately large, flowery script. Inside the case ran a lengthy, Weller-tensioned chain driving both the high camshaft and the rear-mounted Lucas Magdyno. Short steel pushrods were concealed in a single plated tube for the height of the barrel before entering an internal passage in the well-finned cylinder head/rocker box casting. Hairpin springs, completely enclosed of course, returned valves with chromium plated stems to their seats in the iron head.

Thought to be the work of Bert Collier, the new engine emerged from the Plumstead Road works to a blurb more notable for hype than fact. "It is the dream of all designers," it ran, "but the good fortune of few, to be given the opportunity of producing the best design that knowledge and experience can suggest, without limitations imposed by cost, past design or even by plant deficiencies. One limitation only was imposed, that no unproven feature be used, and for this reason the design is not revolutionary."

Well finished, though heavy (at more than 400lb), the new breed of Sunbeam had little time to make a name for itself, good or bad, before September 1939, when the Colliers cut production in favour of the cheaper, G3-style AMC single for wartime contracts.

Specification, B24 (1939): Single-cylinder, ohv, 347cc (69 × 93mm). Four-speed gearbox. 3¼g fuel. Tyres, 3.25 × 19in. 71mph.

Sunbeam S7

Introduced for the 1948 season and made by BSA at their Redditch factory, the Sunbeam S7 designed by Erling Poppe represented a big stride towards an ideal frequently advocated but, when realized or even

Sunbeam 487cc Model S7, 1952.

Sunbeam S8, 1951: lighter, faster than the S7.

approached, seldom bought by motorcyclists, who were, and remain, extremely conservative in their two-wheeler tastes.

The S7 was quiet and sedate – attributes amounting to a guarantee of modest sales. The crankshaft of the ohc twin was in line with the frame and the exterior of the unit was smoothly contoured, to an extent unique among British models of the day. The most striking feature was the balloon tyres, seemingly as big as those on the average family car of the 1940s. The wheels were quickly detachable and interchangeable; the spring frame had a reputed 3½in of movement; there was shaft final drive from the unit-construction gearbox.

On test the S7 had a top speed of 78mph, average fuel consumption of 60mpg, and was found to be remarkably quiet, mechanically and on the exhaust. Outstanding too was the degree of rider comfort, which owed more to the large, telescopic-sprung saddle than to the fairly basic plunger rear suspension. Other features of merit were enclosure of battery and electrical gear, an overall "oneness" of design, and a dignified black finish.

Sunbeam S8

Motorcyclists who liked the new Sunbeam S7 but complained that it fell short in the all-important matter of performance would point out that *Motor Cycling*'s editor, Graham Walker, had tested a sports version of the in-line twin in 1946, when he had intimated that it might go into production. It never did; but Sunbeam took the hint, and in 1949 managed the next best thing by installing the S7's engine in a lighter frame equipped with a BSA front fork and ordinary-size wheels and tyres.

With less wind resistance, and hauling fewer pounds, the S8, as it was called, had improved acceleration (four seconds saved over the ss quarter-mile, at 18.2 seconds) and a top speed of 83mph, compared with the S7's 78mph.

The S8 usurped whatever sales potential existed for

these smooth, quiet Sunbeams in the years to 1958, when both were pensioned off.

Specification, S8: Twin-cylinder, ohc, 487cc (70 × 63.5mm). 25bhp/5,800rpm. Four-speed gearbox. 3¼g petrol, 4pt oil. Coil ign/dynamo. Telescopic/plunger. Tyres, 3.25 × 19in(fr), 4.00 × 18in(r). 420lb. 83mph.

SWALLOW

Britain had its very own scooter a year or two before Vespas invaded. Not that the Gadabout seemed to have much in common with any pert Italian. It was about twice Vespa size, heavier, and a good deal slower; and when it met the foreign competition it slunk away and sensibly died.

Swallow Gadabout scooter of 1948: no match for the Italians.

The engine was a 125cc Villiers under large, squarish rear panelling, with a three-speed gearbox. A simple leading-link fork allowed some vertical movement for the front wheel on loading of bonded rubber in torsion. The Swallow Gadabout was on sale from 1947 to 1951.

Specification, Gadabout: Single-cylinder, two-stroke, 122cc (50 × 62mm). 4.9bhp/4,400rpm. Fywheel magneto/rectifier. 2½g petroil. Rubber-sprung front fork/rigid. Tyres, 4.00 × 8in. 200lb.

TANDON

Mr Devdutt Tandon, born in India and casting about for a remunerative occupation in postwar Britain, raised money to launch a motorcycle manufacturing business. In July 1948, the first model bearing the 'TM' (Tandon Motors) symbol appeared, being powered by the pre-war-designed 9D Villiers of 122cc.

In 17 years of making motorcycles, mainly powered by Villiers, but occasionally by British Anzani twins of 242 and 322cc, the Tandon concern turned out markedly ordinary models at a factory on the Watford bypass in Hertfordshire while being guided through financial crises by Mr Tandon, whose talent for commerical brinkmanship was at all times superior to his professional skills as a motorcycle manufacturer.

Tandon 242cc Supreme on test in 1954.

Life for the workforce had something of a dream quality. Supaglids and Milemasters (sic) were assembled to a communal chant of 'Wonderful, wonderful Devdutt Tandon' (the tune being 'Wonderful, wonderful Copenhagen'). Long after the factory's closure in 1955, uncertainty remains as to whether there was an ironic edge to the lyric.

Tandon Special MKT

In June 1948 Tandon brought out the Special MKT and declared that it had been in development for 2½ years. As this 160lb – but man-size – device represented absolutely basic motorcycling, a natural reaction to news of the prolonged gestation was: *Why?* The Lycett saddle was on a pillar, pedal-cycle style, which contributed nothing to good looks but had some practical point; the tank was slab-sided; the brakes, at no more than 4in, seemed almost extravagantly efficient when measured against the 45mph maximum speed and 0-30mph in 12.2 seconds performance of the 125cc two-stroke.

Tandon machines were fitted with telescopic forks in 1949 and, in de-luxe versions, with a form of rear springing through rubber bands arranged horizontally. By 1954 there was a pivoted front fork, with taper-roller head bearings.

Tandon Special MKT, 1948; note bicycle-type saddle.

Tandon Supaglid

The most fervent admirers of Mr Tandon would not have claimed he had much of a way with words. A memorable example is Supaglid. Mr Tandon came up

Tandon Superglid, 1951: more power and style.

with that one for his 1952 122cc lightweight, and then expanded it to Supaglid Supreme, denoting a 197-powered version. Both had a twin-loop frame (the loop comprising that part of the frame running from saddle to engine plates, rather than the front section, which was a single tube) and pivoted-fork rear springing in which the suspension medium was a 14in-long synthetic-rubber cartridge set horizontally under the engine. Inspiration deserted the design team when it came to the front fork, which had to soldier on as a normal telescopic.

"Milemaster" was another Tandon flight of fancy, adopted for a rigid-frame, telescopic-fork model wherein mastery was exercised by a 122cc Villiers engine fitted with hand-change three-speed gearbox.

TRITON

The Triton was offered in more than a few shapes, and at any engine size from 500cc up, in the 1960s. Memorably simple, though for some more evocative of marine mythology than a fast motorbike, "Triton", as a name had no difficulty in beating "Norumph", advanced by another faction at the outset of the vogue for mating Triumph and Norton. The first almost invariably provided the engine, and the latter the frame.

Best known of the hybrids was the Dresda Triton turned out by ex-racer Dave Degens in south-west London. It had a badge on the tank saying as much when similar Specials had no proper name at all.

Degens made his Tritons for around five years, to 1965-66, most of them with 650cc T110/Bonneville power units. Probably little faster than the contemporary all-Norton 650SS, a 650 Dresda Triton was considerably lighter, at no more than 320lb, and therefore handled rather better. And motorcyclists had always preferred Mr Turner's engine to any other vertical twin.

Dresda Triton, 1965, powered by 650 Triumph.

TRIUMPH

Triumphs always had connections with Coventry. It was in a small factory in the city's Much Park Street that the first all-Triumph machines were made in 1904. The engine of this epoch-maker was a 300cc side-valve designed by one Charles Hathaway at the behest of the German-born owners of the company, Siegfried Bettman and Mauritz Schulte.

In 1906 the Triumph Cycle Company, as it had become, was turning out annually 500 of these machines, by then much improved over the original, and the search was on for bigger premises to accommodate greater production. Finally a move was made to a disused factory in Priory Street, where Triumphs were to be made for a further 30 years, into the Second World War.

Plans for replacement of the first model were put in hand. The 3½hp side-valve single took over for 1907 and then in its turn was superseded when a development of the 1907 TT model made an appearance. This sv 495 could be obtained fitted with a three-speed Sturmey Archer gear in the rear hub and was regarded as one of the jewels of the young British motorcycle industry.

When the First World War began Triumphs were producing annually 4,000 of the 499cc singles (upped to 550, in some versions) and had experimented with a Franch-made sv vertical twin layout. Known as the Model H, the big single acquired a tremendous reputation for reliability during its service in all theatres of war. It has been estimated that 30,000 Triumphs, most of them the Model H, were turned out by the end of hostilities in 1918. Not that the Armistice signalled the end of the Model H: it carried on, bulwark of Triumph's peacetime range, well into the 1920s.

A link with a Triumph subsidiary in Germany, which had resumed production at much the same time as Coventry, was broken when the Nuremburg TWN plant elected to go fully independent.

In the early 1920s the first of the ohv Triumphs, with four-valve cylinder head designed by Harry (later Sir Harry) Ricardo, were raced in the 1921 Senior TT but failed to impress; it took another year's development before Riccy Triumphs got the measure of the IoM circuit and one climbed to second place.

The most famous Triumph to appear in that postwar decade was the 494cc side-valve Model P, which took the motorcycle world by storm in 1925, mainly on account of its absurdly low selling price of £42. Within months, the Model P was coming off the Priory Street benches at the rate of 1,000 a week – a production figure the company was to match only very occasionally thereafter, and then with vastly improved plant and in bigger premises. Triumph's Model P was the Model T of the motorcycling world. Unlike much of the motorcycle industry, which tended to go downhill during the depressed years of the 30s, Triumph made a remarkable recovery from early setbacks. It came in

The 550 side-valve Triumph of 1929. It was used by the AA sidecar patrols.

two parts. First, their old-fashioned late-vintage range was junked in favour of new models laid down by the brilliant Valentine Page, who had joined the company on the closure (temporary, as it proved) of Ariel, his previous employers. He turned out sleek fair-sellers, from a 150cc runabout to an advanced 650cc vertical twin. Even bigger sales were needed, however. This was a period when the firm was concentrating on car manufacture. The prime requirement was capital. The solution was to hive off the motorcycle side in 1936, for a very considerable sum, to the Ariel mogul, J.Y. Sangster, who had reconstituted his old company in '32 and fought back to a leading position in the industry. With Mr Sangster to Triumph at Coventry came 35-year-old Edward Turner, as chief designer and general manager. The changes wrought by this wiry new broom were considerable, bringing an upturn in Triumph fortunes that was both immediate and long-lasting. Page's machines, previously rather sedate in a sombre shade of plum, were given the benefit of Mr Turner's ideas on finish . . . tasteful, but striking, combinations of silver-sheen and chromium plate . . . and a new family name of Tiger. The Page-designed 250 became the Tiger 70, the 350 the Tiger 80

Tiger 100 engine in 1952.

and the 500 Mark V the Tiger 90. Not that the changes were all so superficial: there was a definite move towards higher performance, with polishing of flywheels and cylinder-head ports, stronger valve springs and an improved cylinder-barrel finish. Later there were new single-tube frames and upswept exhaust systems. Motorcyclists could not get enough of the Tigers; they were a sellout for the firm, a morale-booster for the assembly-line workers (who had taken a drop in pay on Mr Sangster's takeover), and further confirmation, were it needed, for Turner that his was the magic touch. He cheapened motorcycles, lightened them . . . above all, gave them *style*. The Speed Twin of 1938 set the seal on Triumph's – and Turner's – success.

The Speed Twin ranks as the first truly modern powered two-wheeler. It changed the face of motor-cycling in Britain, and ultimately throughout the world. Yet, like many other "revolutionary" ideas, it was basically simple, no more than the refinement of a long-established standard. In this case the standard was the industry-old single, liked and trusted by generations of riders the world over. Turner took the single and thrust it into the middle of the 20th century. He split it, introducing two pistons where there was one, doubling the firing strokes, bringing in a different rhythm, a different sound. Of course, Page had done much the same five years before, with his well-engineered 650. But it was Turner's particular talent, genius perhaps, that made him turn *his* twin into a double, in looks, of a single. It was as light, almost as familiar, as one of Page's singles (and was, as a matter of fact, very little faster, though a good deal more accelerative).

Finally, it was cheap to make, hence profitable to sell, because Turner had not allowed any grand-design philosophy to blind him to the advantages of production economies. He made sure that the new twin, from its basic dimensions of 63 × 80mm through a range of components and fittings, had common ground with existing singles.

It was a great success. Even the destruction of the Coventry plant during bombing raids in the early 1940s, leading to a mid-war transfer to a new factory at Meriden, was not enough to dampen the enthusiasm of the workforce. In five years of war Triumphs turned out more than 50,000 motorcycles, most of them 3HW 350 singles. Light and wieldy, this model was pencilled in by Turner as part of the postwar range. But when details of the 1945 models were released, it was an all-twin range. With the Speed Twin and the sports Tiger 100 was a 350 twin, the 3T, making its first public appearance since a planned but war-aborted 1940 debut.

All were telescopic-forked; in everything else they were virtually identical with their late-1930s predecessors. The main difference was a drop in top speed and acceleration, occasioned by use of a lower compression ratio to suit the poor-quality Pool petrol of the time.

Another wartime Triumph product was a 500 twin engine, with aluminium head and barrel, which had been used to power stationary generator sets for the RAF. Tuned by development engineer Fred Clarke, and mounted on a modified Tiger 100 crankcase, this was the engine that powered the 120mph Triumph ridden to victory by Irishman Ernie Lyons in the first postwar event to be held in the Isle of Man, the Manx Grand Prix of 1946. Edward Turner's device for springing the rear wheel was seen in action for the first time on the MGP bike. Highly ingenious, but providing only a restricted movement, the Spring Hub came ready laced in the wheel, which could be fitted straight into an existing rigid frame. It was soon on sale at £20. Lyons' bike, with its Spring Hub, was the prototype of the Grand Prix racer which from 1948 provided an interesting and sometimes competitive over-the-counter alternative to the Model 30M Norton.

In 1949, in answer to the demands of the company's distributors in North America, Triumph brought out a 650. Little more than an enlarged Speed Twin, the Thunderbird was well received and was developed, after a season or two, into the sporting Tiger 110 and, later, the Tiger 120/Bonneville.

Triumph was acquired by BSA in 1951, and there was a certain coming together of the two firms; but not to any marked degree. When Triumph decided to market a small-capacity single, it appeared that existing BSA designs were sacrosanct. Turner designed the 150cc Terrier from scratch. The appearance – more than that, the reality – of intense competition between the firms was maintained throughout the 1950s and into the 1960s.

Triumph Trident in 1975 was fast and handled well.

Finally, however, as Turner's influence faded after his retirement in 1961, a more rational programme, covering the products of both concerns, was introduced, to be demonstrated most clearly in the common design for the 1968 750-3s.

In the 1970s, following the rundown of the BSA group and its eventual merger with Dennis Poore's government-backed Norton Villiers Triumph con-

sortium, the long "sit in" took place at Meriden. It was staged to prevent closure and sale of the factory, planned as part of NVT's strategy to concentrate motorcycle production at BSA, Small Heath. With the coming of a Labour government in early 1974, the picket-line workers declared their intention of forming an independent co-operative to operate the Meriden works. Government approval, and £5 million of public money, launched the co-operative in 1975; production was resumed of the 750 twins developed from the 650s in the last year of the old regime. Two years later, with help from a sympathetic Lord Weinstock, who made £1 million of GEC money available, Meriden bought its freedom from NVT, until then empowered to handle sales for the co-operative.

The last years saw changes in the co-operative's "management" philosophy and personnel, and further reductions in an already thinned-out workforce. Production rates veered between 100 and 400 machines a week. The 750s were developed to a stage where they became top of the best-seller lists, for their category, in the UK.

Finally, the co-operative failed. Meriden was sold. Production continued for a few years at an independent factory in the west country.

Triumph 3H

Mr Turner (though devoting much time in the mid-30s to the sporting Tiger range) had a shrewd appreciation of the needs of ride-to-work riders. For these people, he eschewed eye-catching model names – and inflated selling prices – and concentrated instead on slicking-up Val Page's earlier designs just enough to give them showroom appeal at rock-bottom cost. Hence the 3H at £55. Taken to the limit, cosmetically, it became the Tiger 80, at £60+. The 3H was transformed from Page's day by a curvier tank, more chromium plate, and highly buffed alloy around the engine.

There was very little that needed to be altered in the design, for the 70 × 89mm, 6:1 cr engine was a naturally good performer, giving an easy 70-75mph. Power output was quoted as 20bhp at 5,700rpm. A mildly inclined Amal fed a two-valve head topped by a light-alloy rocker box supplied with oil from external pipes. The oil reservoir was contained in Triumph's usual shapely tank under the saddle.

Triumph 3H, 343cc, 1938. Slightly modified, it was supplied to the army in the 39-45 war.

During World War II the 3H was pressed into service and became the 3HW, losing its alloy rocker box in favour of an iron chest formed integrally with the head. In 1945 there was talk of relaunching it in the civilian world, but soon the twins took all attention and the idea was dropped. What few 350 singles carried on to postwar times were either remnants of the late-30s or drabber military versions, the latter often installed in modified frames carrying Matchless Teledraulic forks. The result could be a very effective trials machine, for the engine was lighter, and livelier, than many that were provided by the major trials-bike makers. It was a fitting end, more in a sea of mud than a blaze of glory, to the career of many of these Page-Turner 343cc singles.

Specification, 3H de Luxe (1939): Single-cylinder, ohv, 343cc (70 × 89mm). Four-speed gearbox. 3g fuel. Tyres, 3.25 × 19in. 72mph. £55.

Triumph 650 6/1

When the 40-year-old Val Page went to Triumph as chief designer in the early 30s he found the firm in the doldrums. Sales were low because the models on offer were old-fashioned. Page was given the job of designing a new range. As a flagship – something to fire the enthusiasm of the editors of the weeklies and bring the Triumph name into prominence – he designed a 650cc vertical twin. Why side-by-side cylinders, at a time when twins meant vees? Page later said: "All the vee-twins I had worked on had suffered from distribution problems due to the unequal firing intervals. It seemed to me that a parallel twin with its equal firing intervals would be a better proposition." Cool, understated ... the words of a professional designer; Page had nothing of the showbiz style of Edward Turner, the man who was to succeed him at Triumph.

The 6/1, as it was catalogued, came out in 1933 and deserves to be remembered as forerunner of the vertical twins that were to flood the market. With plain big-ends and a single inclined pushrod tunnel at the rear, the 6/1 had a large flywheel outside the crankcase and in the primary-drive section, where it was helically geared to the gearbox, which was bolted to the rear of the crankcase. The crankcase was the oil reservoir. The engine was offset to the right, to facilitate sidecar fitting – the 6/1 was designed mainly as a sidecar hauler – and despite a generous gap between the cylinders, trouble could be experienced with overheating of the left cylinder, partly masked from air flow by the front mudguard.

Bore and stroke were 70 × 84mm and power developed was 25bhp at 4,500rpm, enough to propel the bike, plus a handsome Triumph sidecar newly designed for the job, at an easy 65mph. It was, however, a disappointing seller. In hindsight, reasons are not difficult to find. It was rather expensive, more than £70 at a time when money was short, and it was very different from any other motorcycle; this alone

was sufficient reason for conservative-minded motorcyclists buying only 100 twins in the three years of production, 1933-36. It was also extremely noisy.

However it was reliable, as was demonstrated by a successful foray into Maudes Trophy competition, with a run in the International Six Days Trial followed by 500 miles in 500 minutes at Brooklands. Standard fittings included coupled brakes, ratchet parking brakes and a folding kickstarter. In 1935 the hand-change was dropped in favour of foot control.

Specification, 6/1 (1932): Twin-cylinder, ohv, 649cc (70 × 84mm). Four-speed gearbox. 2¾g fuel. Tyres, 3.25 × 21in(fr), 3.50 × 20in(r). 76mph. £74.

Triumph Speed Twin (1938)

The most important motorcycle of the decade was Edward Turner's Triumph Speed Twin, introduced in 1937. Its impact was immediate. Its influence on design and development among the motorcycle industries of the world was enormous and continues to the present.

Edward Turner, lately arrived at Triumph at the behest of Jack Sangster, the firm's new owner, had no doubt that his moment had arrived. Playing himself in with successful "face-lifting" exercises on the existing singles (as described elsewhere), he turned to a fresh sheet of paper for his masterwork. Perhaps not an

Mick Broom on the Geeson brothers' 1938 Triumph twin.

C.E. Allen's 1938 Speed Twin: light, low and flexible.

entirely fresh sheet: the idea of a vertical twin – in effect, two singles mounted side by side – had of course occurred to Val Page, Triumph's chief designer, in 1932.

It has been claimed that Turner took inspiration from Page. Perhaps he did; and certainly there is truth in the suggestion that Turner was motivated by a desire to outshine Page. Whatever the emotions that shaped the new venture, the facts at least are conclusive. Page's 650 never caught on, while Turner's Speed Twin was an instant and continuing success. Turner did not have Page's originality but, in a commercial world, his talents were more happily balanced to take him to the top. He was a competent designer; above all, he had an instinct for what motorcyclists wanted. Indeed, he knew, with a touch of genius, what motorcyclists wanted before they knew themselves. Had he not chosen the motorcycling world for his operations, he would have risen to eminence in some other field. The idea of Turner as a Hollywood movie mogul is not too fanciful.

Page's 650 could be identified at first glance as more than a single – mainly because it was noticeably larger than a single. Turner realized that the motorcyclist of the day was ultra-conservative and would stomach nothing that departed too radically from his idea of the single. The Speed Twin, no larger, no heavier than the average 500 single, and in profile astonishingly like one, got off to a very good start by offending nobody. Its good looks (on any count), intriguing exhaust note and fine performance did nothing to inhibit its appeal. Its price in 1937 was £77 15s. Bert Hopwood, a one-time Turner assistant, sometimes given the task of improving the great man's less than polished draughtsmanship, has confirmed that Turner's Speed Twin marked a turning point in Triumph's fortunes. According to Hopwood, from the launch date of the twin at the '37 Show at Earls Court, the company was never short of orders.

The principal design features of the Speed Twin were hemispherical combustion chambers, short rockers and separate, fore-and-aft pushrods, all owing something to the layout of the Riley car engine (Turner drove a Riley Nine). Something of a rattler, which was natural, because of the train of gears in the timing case, the Speed Twin developed 27bhp. Bore and stroke measurements, at 63mm and 80mm, were those of the existing 250 single, and there were many other parts of the twin that were close, and sometimes identical, to components used in the existing range. Thus Turner cut costs from the start. As to the looks of the new machine, Turner, no victim of false modesty, got it right when he said, "The general proportions of this engine were most eyeable, and in performance it was even more remarkable..."

Remarkable; but not simply as a high performer. The manner in which the all-iron engine developed its power was endearingly smooth. It was a naturally flexible engine, able to sustain a high gear at low rpm and providing unfussy, but distinctly rapid,

acceleration at a turn of the grip. Perhaps there was, literally, extra flexibility in the crank assembly of the early jobs compared with the apparently identical engines turned out after World War II, for a '38-'39 Speed Twin is noticeably "softer", with a wider top-gear range, than a postwar version.

Specification, Speed Twin (1938): Twin-cylinder, ohv, 498cc (63 × 80mm). Four-speed gearbox. 3g fuel. Tyres, 3.25 × 19in. 82mph. £78.

Triumph Tiger 100

When the Speed Twin proved a runaway success, designer Edward Turner might have found himself in a quandary. It was, however, a situation he had prudently anticipated, and resolved, before it materialized. The manufacturer of a best-seller can be the victim of his own success. How is he to encourage sales beyond those achieved by his chart-topper? Turner was sure that the Speed Twin was going to succeed. When it did, he was ready to launch the second part of his masterplan, the Tiger 100. There was, of course, little to surprise in this development. It followed the usual pattern of the motorcycle industry

Tiger 350 80 Triumph, 1937: one of Edward Turner's good-lookers.

Tiger 80 controls. An oil-pressure gauge was a popular fitting pre-war.

of those days, when a bread-and-butter model – hardly a fair description of Turner's Speed Twin, perhaps – would be paired with a sports version intended to cream off sales at the wealthier end of the market. There was a parallel already in Triumph's own range, with Tigers 70, 80 and 90 as de-luxe versions of comparatively anonymous, and cheaper, singles. It wasn't all plain sailing behind the scenes, however, for experiments to raise the Speed Twin's 27bhp to 33bhp, for the Tiger 100, brought a rash of broken cranks – and displays of temperament from Turner.

These difficulties were ironed out, and the Tiger 100 was announced for the 1938 season. It was popularly thought to be capable of 100mph, and with a skilled – and nose-on-the-tank – rider, this undoubtedly was the case. The finish was in the usual silver sheen of Triumph Tigers.

A restored 1938 Tiger 100.

Turner, with unerring instinct, had specified a larger fuel tank than was fitted to the Speed Twin. It held four gallons and was recessed to take the knee rubbers, slimming it in a vital area. The Tiger 100 was harsher, of course, than the Speed Twin, and thirstier, with a bigger-bore carburettor. But these were minor drawbacks ... in fact, not drawbacks at all, for they underlined the bike's sporting character to any proud owner, who could even specify a go-faster, bronze cylinder head as an extra.

The new Tiger 100s were expected to sweep the production-machine race at Donington. They did not. The story is that the tank-top instrument panels were shattered by racing-speed vibes. What is certain is that the extra performance of the Tiger 100 highlighted shortcomings in Triumph handling. Bert Hopwood has told of Freddie Clarke, Triumph's development engineer, and a fine rider, experiencing lock-to-lock steering wobbles while testing a Tiger 100. Clarke instituted a number of far-reaching modifications to the steering geometry with, apparently, beneficial results. He was prevented from carrying them through to the production stage by Turner who, with autocratic certitude, pronounced Triumph handling to be entirely adequate.

Over the years this opinion has not been endorsed by owners who have fallen victim at one time or another to the Triumph wobble. And if not the wobble, then it has been the weave, a secondary affliction that can prove equally unmanning.

Specification, Tiger 100 (1939): Twin-cylinder, ohv, 498cc (63 × 80mm). Four-speed gearbox. 4g fuel. Tyres, 3.00 × 19in(fr), 3.50 × 19in(r). 98mph. £82.

Triumph Speed Twin (1946)

The 5T Speed Twin circa 1946 was probably the best known motorcycle of the day. Its fame arose not only from its own considerable quality but because it was the chosen mount of London's police "mobiles". Like the Tiger 100, it was strikingly good looking but had an even more attractive finish in what Triumph advertisements were pleased to call amaranth red – a term promptly modified, according to one-time Meriden executive Ivor Davies, by customers living not a million miles from Bow Bells to "'ammer and thread".

Detuned a little to suit the low-octane Pool petrol of the 1940s, the Speed Twin's engine turned out approximately 25bhp at 5,500rpm, which was enough to power the bike at up to 85mph, 5mph down on 1937 test figures.

Specification, 5T: As for T100 except for 25bhp engine tune.

A 1952 Speed Twin. Rider is unknown, pump attendant is one Letty Albiston.

Triumph Tiger 100 (1946)

High-performance brother to the Speed Twin, the Tiger 100 returned to Triumph catalogues in 1946. As before the war, it had eight-stud fixing for the cylinder block, and polished flywheels and connecting rods. Changes had been made to the electrics, the dynamo being repositioned at the front of the block, leaving the magneto on its own at the rear. External oil piping was reduced compared with 1939 arrangements.

Tiger 100 in 1955, with pivoted-fork rear springing.

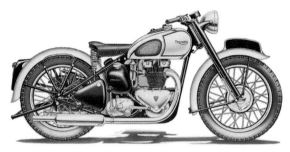

Postwar (1947) Tiger 100: 95mph on low-octane "pool" petrol.

Tiger 100 with rear spring hub.

Top speed was well in excess of 90mph. Save for the Vincent Rapide, at double the capacity, the T100 was the fastest standard tourer available, and is considered, along with the Speed Twin, the handsomest Triumph of all. It had uncluttered lines, a wide but recessed-for-the-knees tank with lined paintwork on chrome, centre-ridged mudguards, and a sweptback handlebar free of the usual levers for choke and ignition control. The 6pt oil tank was the "right" size and shape to blend with the toolbox. The front number plate, usually an afterthought, with cheese-cutter edge exposed, was framed in chrome beading. Even the tank-top instrument panel, with ammeter and lighting switch, though possibly a safety hazard in its invitation to the rider to drop his gaze from the road, was in keeping with overall styling.

In the first year or two of postwar production, with demand for all Triumphs running high, there were few changes to the T100. The most notable was the

provision of rear springing, as a £20 extra from late 1946, by means of the Spring Hub. This was a rehash of the Edward Turner design, conceived in the 1930s, in which a large-diameter hub was sprung around the wheel spindle, allowing about an inch of vertical movement, with no variation in chain tension. The extra weight was no more than 12lb, and a spring-hub wheel would go into the normal rear end of an unsprung Triumph. Press reports were very favourable, making much of the ingenuity of the design. On the road the spring hub was less impressive, its meagre travel being attended by some reduction in steering precision. Hard riders reckoned the result was more loss than gain.

In 1949 the tank-top panel was removed. Instead, a sheet-metal nacelle around the top of the forks and the headlamp carried the dials (less the oil-meter, finally abandoned) and the lighting switch. Where the tank panel had been were four threaded holes, there to support a chrome-plated luggage grid, should an owner wish. In those far-off days, before officialdom began to adjudicate on the danger posed by a ½in-high filler cap, motorcyclists were happy to trade safety for convenience (though they did not, of course, weigh the odds in those cold-blooded terms).

Specification, T100 (1946): Twin-cylinder, ohv, 498cc (63 × 80mm). 30bhp. Four-speed gearbox. Magneto/dynamo. 4g petrol, 6pt oil; dry sump. Telescopic/rigid/spring hub. Tyres, 3.25 × 19in(fr), 3.50 × 19in(r). 365lb. 93mph.

Triumph 3T De Luxe

A good-looking bike in black and chrome, the 1946 3T De Luxe was Triumph's attempt to repeat the success of the Speed Twin at a smaller capacity. But this 350cc vertical twin, though pleasant, was too short of performance to rise very high in the sales charts. It was at least 5mph down on contemporary BSAs and AMCs, at about 68mph flat out, and its acceleration was leisurely, with a standing-start quarter-mile time of 25 seconds.

Almost over-silenced on the exhaust, so that the not particularly noisy engine seemed, by contrast, obtrusively "clickety", the 3T was relaxing to ride and had flexible top gear performance down to a snatch-free 10mph. It was dropped in 1951.

The 1946 349cc 3T De Luxe: too well-mannered, and slow, to succeed.

Specification, 3T: Twin-cylinder, ohv, 349cc (55 × 73.4mm). 20bhp/6,000rpm. Four-speed gearbox. Magneto/dynamo. 3g petrol, 6pt oil; dry sump. Telescopic/rigid. Tyres, 3.25 × 19in. 340lb. 68-70mph.

Triumph Trophy

The Trophy, first listed in 1949 after ISDT successes, was Triumph's on- or off-road bike of the day. A mixture of Tiger 100 and Grand Prix detuned to one carburettor, and running on a compression ratio of around 6:1, the engine was housed in a specially shortened, high-clearance frame, with a siamesed exhaust system tucked above the primary case and ending in a lightweight silencer at rear-wheel-spindle height.

A 1954 Triumph 650 Trophy, as used in the ISDT.

Triumph Trophy TR6 650, 1959, with full-width front hubs.

Light and manoeuvrable, the Trophy was equipped with a full (but quickly detachable) lighting set, and thus was a practical all-rounder for workaday use and weekend sport. In 1955 the compression ratio was increased, which helped to boost power to 33bhp/6,500rpm, and then the 500 was joined by a 650 variant, listed as TR6, with new light-alloy cylinder.

Specification, Trophy: Twin-cylinder, ohv, 498cc (63 × 80mm). 25bhp. Four-speed gearbox. Magneto/dynamo. 2½g petrol, 6pt oil; dry sump. Telescopic/rigid. Tyres, 3.00 × 19in(fr), 4.00 × 19in(r). 304lb.

Triumph TRW

A side-valve twin was a departure for performance-orientated Triumph in 1949. The 498cc TRW was designed for Ministry of Supply use, in which flexibility and ease of maintenance took precedence over performance. With a built-up crankshaft running on plain and ball bearings, the light-alloy motor operated on a 6.3:1 compression ratio and produced 16bhp at 6,000rpm, to give a comfortable 60mph cruising speed. The carburettor was a Solex, and a 6-volt

TRW services model with 498cc side-valve engine, rigid frame.

generator was situated in the primary case, with the rotor on the end of the engine mainshaft.

Specification, TRW: Twin-cylinder, sv, 498cc (63 × 80mm). 16bhp/6,000rpm. Four-speed gearbox. Coil ign/alternator. 3½g petrol, 6pt oil. Telescopic/rigid; spring hub available. Tyres, 3.25 × 19in. 366lb. 72mph.

Triumph Tiger 100C

One of the most interesting of Tiger 100 variants was the C model, listed from 1951 to 1954, having a die-cast light-alloy cylinder block and head with close-pitch finning. The C stood for "convertible", which in Triumph's motorcycling interpretation of the term meant that it could be bought equipped with any combination of a wide range of extras, to turn it, ultimately, into something approaching a full-blooded racer.

Vic Willoughby, racer-turned-race writer, took a C Triumph down the A11 from London to Snetterton circuit where, after removing silencers and attending to one or two chores, he finished respectably high in several events before rounding off the day with a sedate 70mph cruise back to London.

The owner could specify for his new bike, or buy at a later date: two mixing chambers and remote float for the twin carburettors, close-ratio gearbox pinions, a race camshaft, high-compression pistons, stronger valve springs, rev-counter, and more than a few other aids to the fast life. Yet however much he spent in this way, he would end with a Triumph £100 cheaper than the discontinued Grand Prix racer.

A 1969 Tiger 100S.

Tiger 100SS with semi "bathtub" treatment – not a happy styling idea.

Triumph T100A

In 1959 the Tiger 100 was subjected to further change – in the opinion of some, not so much change as a complete redesign. A pivot-fork frame had been standardized back in 1954 when most of the C (for convertible) variations on offer had been dropped in favour of an integrated specification. Then in 1957 a new light-alloy head with wide-splayed ports – an echo of Hopwood's 1948 Dominator design – was fitted, together with a single-side 8in front brake.

Now the Tiger, in company with the trend-setting 350 Twenty One, was given a gearbox in unit with the engine, new oversquare engine dimensions, a single carburettor, smaller front brake (7in. in full-width hub), valanced front mudguard and "bath tub" – inverted bath tub – rear treatment. Top speed was no more than 85mph. The T100A's main distinction, compared with other Triumphs, was its Lucas alternator with energy transfer. Power output was given as 32bhp at 7,000rpm.

Specification, T100A: Twin-cylinder, ohv, 490cc (69 × 65.5mm). 32bhp/7,000rpm. Four-speed gearbox. Energy-transfer ignition/alternator. 3½g petrol, 5pt oil; dry sump. Tyres, 3.25 × 17in(fr), 3.50 × 17in(r). 375lb. 85mph.

Triumph Thunderbird

In 1946 Edward Turner took heed of the pleas of his important American customers and enlarged the Speed Twin by 150cc. Bore and stroke were increased from 63 × 80mm to something nearer "square" at 71 × 82mm, which worked out to 649cc and gave the bike, at 34bhp/6,300rpm, an 8bhp boost over the 500 and a noticeable surge of mid-range torque.

Under a polychromatic-blue tank, the engine was outwardly identical with that of the Speed Twin. But road performance was ahead even of the Tiger 100's. George Wilson of *The Motor Cycle* referred to its "racer-variety" speed as being "phenomenal".

Managing director Edward Turner with Thunderbirds and riders at Montlhery, France.

A 1958 Thunderbird; all-iron engine is very like that of original Speed Twin.

Triumph Tiger 110 in 1955, with 8in single-side front brake.

1960 Thunderbird, with duplex-tube frame.

Tiger 110, 1955, still with magneto ignition.

Introduced by a demonstration run averaging 90mph over 500 miles at Montlhéry in France, the new model, code-named 6T but already known as the Thunderbird (a Turner inspiration, from his visits to the USA), rapidly became a best seller. In addition to satisfying the urgent need for a high-performance model, the 6T made very good business sense. The company was able to demand a usefully higher price for what was no more than (in the advertising manager's later, disarmingly frank admission) a bike with "bigger holes in the barrel and pistons to match . . ."

Triumph Tiger 110

The Tiger 110 circa 1960 looked much like the earlier Thunderbird and the later Bonneville. However, it had virtues all its own. It first saw public light of of day during the 1953 International Six Days Trial, when it was ridden by British Trophy team member Jimmy Alves. Export marketing began later that year. Americans, especially, liked this hopped-up Thunderbird with its higher compression ratio and pivoted-fork rear end. Bigger inlet valves and a

stronger crankshaft helped too. For a few years it retained that nearly forgotten relic of the Golden Age, the advance-retard lever.

Early Tigers were at home on the track, finishing one-two-three in the 1955 Thruxton Nine Hour 750 class. Cylinder heads had a nasty habit of cracking at full revs, until Meriden put the matter right in 1958 with extra metal and smaller valves. In that year, too, the Tiger nearly became a Bonnie, with an optional twin-carburettor head. The 1959 Bonneville, while not fully eclipsing its stablemate, certainly cast a long shadow over it. The Tiger – no mention of 110 – with a 750 powerplant, and one carburettor again, remained in production to the 1980s, being especially popular in the USA, possibly because emissions restrictions officially vetoed its sale there.

Triumph Terrier

The Terrier was one of those seminal designs whose descendants go on to greater glory. It sired the Tiger Cub and, ultimately, a stable of BSA singles from 250cc up. The 149cc four-speed unit-construction single first appeared at the 1952 Earls Court show. It was an Edward Turner design. After devoting himself to 500s and above, Turner laid down his plan for a midget

Triumph 149cc Terrier in 1953, the first year of production.

Triumph 199cc Tiger Cub, 1956: fashioned on the Terrier.

because ". . . world economic conditions are such that the present high cost of producing expensive motorcycles cannot be maintained. A modern 150 will provide ample power for two, at 45-50mph, with 60 as top speed. That's enough for the majority of motorcyclists". Why four-stroke? "Because this is the way to get the maximum power output for a given capacity".

A star-studded Land's End to John O'Groats reliability run followed the London showing, featuring the designer, works director Bob Fearon and Alec Masters, the service manager. The trio of Terriers and their masters completed the "Gaffers' Gallop" successfully, from both technical and publicity points of view.

The Terrier's greatest attribute was its innovative bottom end, wherein crankcase and gearbox were arranged in a single casing, the crankshaft being inserted through the drive side and secured by the inner primary chaincase.

The Terrier barked for several years alongside its 199cc offspring, but after 1956 the Tiger Cub was on its own.

Specification, T15: Single-cylinder, ohv, 149cc (57 × 58.5mm). 8bhp/6,000rpm. Four-speed gearbox. Flywheel magneto/alternator. 2⅝g petrol, 2½pt oil. Telescopic/plunger. Tyres, 2.75 × 19in. 200lb. 60mph.

Triumph Tiger Cub

Born of Terrier, the Tiger Cub came into the world in 1954. More than a sports version of the 150, this 199cc Triumph obtained most of its extra speed from its extra capacity. An inclined ohv single, like the Terrier, with unit-construction for a four-speed gearbox driven by non-adjustable chain, the Cub had an oval timing-side casing and a generally neat appearance. It was equipped at first with plunger rear springing, later with a pivot-fork type. The Cub was an excellent performer, with a top speed of 65mph and plenty of acceleration to put it ahead of contemporary two-strokes of comparable size. But it vibrated and was noisy, both mechanically and on the exhaust. (*The Motor Cycle's* tester was moved to say, in what must rank as searing criticism by that journal's standards ". . . wide throttle opening evoked a hard, flat exhaust note of considerable volume").

It was as a trials bike that the Cub achieved distinction. When it became clear that 300lb 500s were too big and too powerful for trials riders facing the lightweights from Greeves and, soon, from foreign factories, it was the Cub that delayed for a while the inevitable changeover to the two-strokes. Other versions included a scrambler and the T20 SH Sports Cub, which had a 9:1 compression ratio and other modifications to turn it into a very effective production-machine racer in those relatively Yamaha-free days.

Specification, T20: Single-cylinder, ohv, 199cc (63 × 64mm). 10bhp/6,000rpm. Four-speed gearbox. Coil ign/alternator. 3g petrol, 2¾pt oil. Telescopic/plunger/pf. Tyres, 3.00 × 19in; later 3.25 × 17in; later 3.25 × 19in, 3.50 × 18in. 240lb. 65-72mph.

Tiger Cub competition model at work in 1959. The rider is Ray Peplow.

Triumph Twenty One

The Twenty One of 1957 represented Triumph's bid to make motorcycles, at least *their* motorcycles, more socially acceptable. The way to do this, they decided, was to cover up the conglomeration of tubes and engine plates and bits and pieces that made up the appearance of the average motorcycle. Undoubtedly, too, an envious eye had been cast at the popularity of the foreign scooter, with its all-enveloping bodywork.

So the Twenty-One arrived with what unkind critics described as an inverted bath tub around the rear frame, smoothly valanced mudguards and – proving that the revamping was not purely cosmetic – a kind of unit construction for crankcase and gearbox. It was the first 350 to carry the Triumph name since the 3T of 1946.

Triumph Twenty-One 350.

Army model 3TA, as shown at Amsterdam.

The engine was straightforward "Turner", with two gear-driven camshafts, split big-ends, cast-iron block and light-alloy cylinder head with separate rocker boxes. The four-speed gearbox was contoured to mate with the right-hand half of the crankcase. An alternator on the other side, on the crankshaft, was concealed by the aluminium case for the duplex-chain primary drive.

Finished in an all-over silver grey, the 21 (there seemed to be no firm authority on the correct way to give the name) was a bland-looking motorcycle. It came over as a diminished version of the traditional Triumph, while falling short in presenting the integrated styling of a scooter.

Specification, 21 3TA: Twin-cylinder, ohv, 349cc (58.25 × 65.5mm). 20bhp/6,500rpm. Four-speed gearbox. Coil ign/alternator. 3½g petrol, 5pt oil; dry sump. Telescopic/pf. Tyres, 3.25 × 17in. 340lb. 80mph.

Triumph T120 Bonneville

The Bonneville was Edward Turner's last triumph. A 1959-introduced 650 vertical twin developed from the Tiger 110 (which was developed from the Thunderbird, and before that the Speed Twin), it was aimed at the USA market. "Bonneville" commemorated near-150mph dashes across the Salt Lake Flats of Utah in the Autumn of 1958. Its performance was a response to the demands of the American riders no longer satisfied by the just-over-the-ton top speed of the Tiger 110. The Bonneville, of course, had a Tiger's heart. Essentially, it was the 110 with a splayed-port head in light-alloy, a pair of Amal Monoblocs, sans filters, and an increased compression ratio, all combining to boost power to around 46bhp at 6,500rpm.

The controversial "slickshift" semi-automatic clutch featured on many of the Triumph models was absent from the Bonneville's specification. The first year's

The T120 650 Bonneville in 1962, with unit construction of engine and gearbox.

Bonneville 750, 1976.

version sported the then-usual headlamp nacelle but, again, American tastes prevailed, and a more acceptable bare-bones look returned in 1960.

By late 1962 engine and gearbox were manufactured as a single unit, marking the end of the last direct-line descendant of the Turner Speed Twin of 1937.

It can be argued that Triumph never built a better bike than the early Bonnie, despite subsequent development over the years during which it gained a duplex frame, Amal Concentrics, high bars (for the USA), a five-speed gearbox, 10in front discs and, in 1972, an enlarged (750cc) power plant.

Critics chided Triumph for stubbornly keeping to an ancient design in high-tech days. Triumph in effect responded: *Why argue with success?*

Triumph Bonneville T120R

Claimed by the weekly *Motor Cycling* to be the fastest production roadster of 1961, the 650 T120R was credited with a mean maximum speed of 117mph. This was achieved with a Bonneville modified to the extent of having twin Monobloc carburettors, without air filters and supplied by a single float chamber. Though this seemed a very modest deviation from standard, Triumph said that it would enable the engine to attain 7,500rpm in all gears – 700 revs up on the usual figure – and this was precisely what the tester found during his performance runs.

Triumph Tina

In 1962 motorcycle sales were declining and the UK scooter boom was over. BSA/Triumph had failed to score with their big scooters. But the idea of tapping the market for cheap, simple transport that supposedly existed among all those men (and women) in the street still tantalized. The Tina, management said, was to be The Big One.

Meriden made room, and the Tina was launched. 'No gears, no clutch, goes at a touch', was the slogan. The Tina was tiny, with a 99cc two-stroke engine, and automatic transmission by belt over expanding and contracting pulleys. There was nothing original in this, of course, but what was new was the scale of the Tina operation.

To a degree unique in the British industry, the Tina was tooled for mass production. There were large plastic injection mouldings, elaborate die castings and pressings. The advertising campaign was the biggest ever undertaken by the company.

Despite Triumph's unprecedented expenditure on tooling, and the setting up of an assembly line in special premises, the Tina had not been thoroughly road-tested. The transmission seized on occasion, and if the road surface was wet when this happened the passenger was thrown off. This was not popular with housewives, who represented an important segment of projected sales. Nor was the temperamental starting.

Tina automatic transmission scooter with extra Wipac equipment.

Ken Craven undertook a Continental appraisal of the machine, riding it over three major Alpine passes and covering more than 1,000 miles during a long weekend. He wrote:

"It was a very comfortable little bike. Quite undemanding. All you had to do was open up to three-quarter throttle, sit back and admire the (slowly) changing scene. If you adopted a resigned attitude, you covered a lot of miles simply by keeping going. I did 440 miles the first day, from the Channel port into Switzerland, with very little fatigue. It also handled very well, with excellent roadholding over snow and mud, and in this respect was probably superior to other scooters. It had a lot of character and certainly did not deserve to join the ranks of the world's dismal motorcycles; perhaps it was a good idea which was not quite right for the time".

Triumph Daytona

Buddy Elmore took a race-kitted Tiger 100C around the Florida Daytona course for 200 miles in 1966, winning America's toughest road-race at a record 96.6mph.

In celebration, the 1967 twin-carburettor super-sport 500 was called the Daytona. This race-developed T100 had shallow combustion chambers, a 9:1 compression ratio, and a new frame with braced fork pivots, increased steering rake and lowered seat. The Bonneville's 8in front brake was borrowed as well. By 1969, brake diameter had shrunk to 7in but twin leading shoes were fitted. The official designation was T100R. A companion T100C single-carburettor "street

Triumph Daytona 500 in 1968, based on a race-winning model.

scrambler", with twin upswept exhaust pipes, was offered in that year, too. Both models survived until 1972.

Triumph Trailblazer

Final development of the C15-turned-C25 was the Gold Star 250SS of 1971. The Triumph version was the TR25W Trailblazer. Compared with the C15 engine, it had a new, stiffer connecting rod in duralumin and a larger bearing for the big-end. Power output, with a compression ratio of 10:1, was given as 22.5bhp at 8,250rpm, and the carburettor was an Amal Concentric R928. Electrical components consisted of an ac generator in the primary chaincase, driven off the crankshaft, with a capacitor to boost power at low rpm.

The engine was carried in a frame designed at Umberslade Hall, with an oil reservoir in the main tube and cam adjustment for the chain at the rear-fork pivot.

Trailblazer 250, 1971: the final version of BSA C25.

The brakes were at one side of conical hubs; the matt-black exhaust system pursued a winding, mainly uphill path inside frame tubes to the offside rear, where an overheated silencer was shielded from a rear-seat passenger's legs by a strip of plated, perforated tin.

Light and punchy, and forgiving on not-too-arduous going, the Trailblazer was well made and very likeable. In the 1980s it would have been a match for a 10 years-younger Honda single.

Specification, TR25W: Single-cylinder, ohv, 247cc (67 × 70mm). 22.5bhp, later 25bhp. Four-speed gearbox. Coil ign/alternator. 3¾g petrol, 6pt oil; dry sump. Telescopic/pf. Tyres, 3.25 × 19in(fr), 4.00 × 18in(r). 320lb. 80mph.

Triumph Tiger 750

The Tiger TR7RV, the 750cc single-carburettor Triumph of the late 1970s, weighed 100lb less than some of the Japanese 750-4s. This was too slight an advantage to boost its acceleration or top speed into the class of the fours, but paid dividends in handling.

Other aspects of the big twin which were equally British, but not so endearing, were its starting arrangements, vibration levels and reliability record. In an age of electric starting for all except the most humble Japanese runabouts, it was unusual to have to engage in a ritual familiar to any stormcoated enthusiast of a decade or two earlier. This sort of thing . . . Ignition on, fuel on, half choke, flood carburettor with tickler, get pistons just over compression: *kick!* One outspoken tester wrote, half admiringly, "There was no need to red line it. If you do stay near the upper rev range you will be rewarded with the choke vibrating on, the lights falling from the sockets inside the instruments and a tingling numbness in your body

Triumph Tiger 750, 1976: popular in the USA.

VELOCETTE

This was the archetypal family firm among British motorcycle makers. Veloce made good motorcycles because the directors, the Goodman family, were themselves motorcyclists and, consequently, their own sternest critics. Considered as a money-making concern, the firm for many years suffered the handicap of an addiction to racing, which tended to cream off profits. In company with Norton's not dissimilar bikes, Velocettes won for Britain a commanding position in international racing that was not seriously threatened until, late in the 1930s, foreign factories were sneaky ... state-subsidized ... enough to wheel out supercharged multis having a 20mph speed advantage over their British rivals.

But in the beginning . . . Anybody keen to demonstrate school linguistics would give "Velocette", and the firm's official title, Veloce Ltd., a French connection. But it is not so simple. Veloce, in the beginning, was more German than French. In fact, there was nothing French about it at all. German-born Johannes Gutgemann turned up in England in the 1860s, married, and settled down to making pills for the sick, in which enterprise he decided that his name was something of a handicap. He changed it to John Taylor.

Quite why or how Mr Taylor diversified from pills into motorcycle manufacture is unclear. The facts are that he teamed up with one William Gue, and in 1904 the pair took over a motorcycle business which promptly died. But by then "Veloce Ltd." had been registered. Recovering from his financial fright, Taylor began to make bicycles – pedal variety – in premises in Spring Hill, Birmingham.

Later his sons, Percy and Eugene, joined the company and John embarked again on motorcycle production. By 1910 two models were on offer, an ioe single of 272cc with two-speed gear, and a direct(belt)-drive 500. In 1911 it was name-changing time again, when the family applied by deed poll for "Goodman". Shortly after, the first Velocette two-stroke appeared.

Post-World War One Velocettes were two-strokes of 220cc, then 250cc, fitted with a reciprocating oil pump and capable of over 50mph. There was no hint of a poppet valve in the Goodman's deliberations until 1925, when Percy designed a sporting 350 which had not only overhead valves but an overhead camshaft.

In its second TT race, the 1926 Junior, the ohc Velocette scored an outstanding success, winning by about 10 minutes from a Big Port AJS. Further wins in the Junior brought big sales of the new model and helped to finance a move to the factory at Hall Green, Birmingham at which all future Velocettes were made until the company was wound up in the early 1970s.

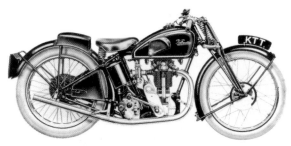

Mark 4 KTT Velocette, 1934.

Percy Jago on a 1939 ohc Velocette (number 109) and Walter Goodman on an ohv 1934 model.

Of classic design, with drive to the camshaft by vertical shaft and bevels, the ohc Velocette from the beginning displayed strongly individual touches that made it more of a "love it or hate it" proposition than the broadly similar Norton designed by Walter Moore in 1927. It was much quieter mechanically than the Norton . . . but there was the peculiar Velocette clutch, which operated on a kind of servo principle; and the inboard primary chain, which made changes in gearbox sprocket easy but everything else more difficult; and the narrow crankcase; and the new-fangled positive-stop foot change (though that came later, in 1928).

Racing (KTT) and sports roadster (KSS) 350s were on sale in 1928/29. The KTT series, running through the 1930s, was the ultimate racer for the privateer. Factory-prepared Nortons won more races, but the KTT enabled the clubman to take on the stars, and sometimes beat them.

Alongside the ohc bikes Velocettes sold revitalized two-strokes, first the U series and later the smooth, quiet GTP which, with well-finned engine, positive lubrication and coil ignition, set an unrivalled standard up to the Second World War. In the 1950s a 20-year-old GTP had a performance superior to that of many brand-new 250s.

Works 1933 350 "dog kennel" Velocette prepared for the TT.

Next, Veloce designed an ohv with pushrods. This was the 1933 high-camshaft, hence short pushrod, MOV that was followed within a couple of years by the 349cc MAC and the 495cc MSS.

It was these "bread and butter" bikes, created by production director Eugene Goodman to offset losses on the racers, that kept the firm in business. The success of the humble pushrod ohv series funded experiments with a twin-cylinder supercharged racer, the Roarer, tried out in practice for the 1939 IoM TT and then killed of by the war, and the roadgoing Model 0 parallel twin that was, perhaps, the most forward-looking design to emerge from a British factory in the 1930s.

Development of the ohc models continued. The roadster KSS was fitted with an aluminium head and complete enclosure of the valves and rockers, which further distanced it from noisier, oilier ohc Nortons. The racing KTT acquired more finning, more speed, and won several TTs.

During the war Veloce Ltd. installed new plant to fulfil government contracts and so went in to the postwar period well equipped. In 1946 girder-forked ohv MAC, MOV and MSS models, and the 350 KSS, appeared. By 1948 all (apart from the MAC) had been withdrawn in favour of a newcomer. The LE, first in 149cc form, later as a 192, was an outstanding design deserving better fate than remembrance as the "Noddy Bike" of countless police forces. Veloce had been confident that Mr Average was ready, at last, for a civilized motorcycle .. a watercooled, side-valve, horizontally opposed twin having shaft drive, hand starting, hand gear change, full enclosure, rider protection, making practically no noise, mechanically or exhaust-wise, and selling at a low price. But this confidence was misplaced. It took the firm a long time to recover the costs of tooling up for the bonanza that never arrived.

Some years were to pass, with solid selling of conventional, regularly up-rated MAC and MSS models and their high-performing derivatives (Viper, Venom and the like), before any further adventures were undertaken. Then they took the form of a sporting, air-cooled version of the LE with overhead valves, called the Valiant, and later in 1956 another variant, mechanically identical to the sv LE, which was partway to being a scooter. This was the Vogue, and it was no more successful than the Valiant.

Twice bitten, Velocette returned to the ohv "M's", and faster bikes. The Vipers and Venoms became Clubmen, and finally the Thruxton arrived as the ultimate sporting 500.

As the 1960s dawned, sales began to tail off. The Viceroy scooter, introduced in 1960, was no help. Large, rather too expensive to the public, cripplingly so to the makers, it accelerated the downfall of Veloce. In 1971 Hall Green closed. Founded by a German and bearing a quasi-French name, it had been a company displaying for half a century all those virtues which patriots like to think of as peculiarly English.

Velocette GTP

There was a fascinating ambivalence – some might say schizophrenia – in the Goodman family's attitude to motorcycling. Controlling Veloce, Eugene and Percy Goodman achieved world fame for their tiny firm with a line of GP-winning ohc racers. Yet they never gave up the idea of an "everyman" motorcycle that would put the world on two wheels. The LE – the "noddy" bike born in the 1940s – is the best example of this fixation.

Pre-war the Velocette contender for the "everyman" title might, with some stretching of definition, be taken as the GTP two-stroke.

It appeared every year from 1930 to the outbreak of World War II, and a few were produced after the war, for export. The GTP had bob-weights, a large external flywheel on the left, and started life with an iron barrel and head. The aluminium deflector piston and other internals were lubricated from an adjustable pump on the right side of the crankshaft. Coil ignition was a surprising feature in a magneto-dominated era.

GTP 250 two-stroke in a 1931 publicity stunt in Scotland.

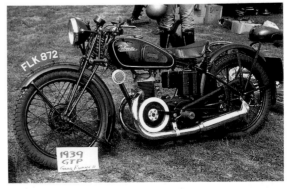

A 1939 GTP for sale at Brands Hatch auction.

Twin exhaust pipes with fishtail outlets, a traditional Velocette finish in black with gold lining (and a reminder in gold lettering on the tank of the firm's TT successes), and a general air of quality distinguished the GTP among the mass of 30s two-strokes. It was always a good performer, too, which further raised its standing. The fishtails gave a mellow exhaust note and, for a two-stroke, it would tick over uncommonly slowly – a tribute to the efficiency of the ignition system. Top speed was 60-plus.

By 1935 the hand-change three-speed gearbox had become a four-speed foot-change, the tank was bigger, and the primary chaincase had an oil bath. Later on, the tank was deepened again and some chromium plate incorporated here and there. It was one of the first motorcycles to have the oil supply linked to the throttle.

The compiler was happy to borrow a 1932 GTP for some hundreds of miles, and passed his Test on it. The owner used it as a (usually) mobile test-bed, experimenting with an ingenious form of water injection which was intended to reproduce the cool running of evening. At this time of day, especially after a long run in hot sun, he had detected an improvement in the GTP's performance. Power and speed had risen and there had been less of the dreaded two-stroke rattle, presaging seizure. He metered water via some kind of Schrader valve into the GTP's interior. The flow varied from mere dampness to gusher proportions.

Specification, GTP (1936): Single-cylinder, two-stroke. 249cc (63 × 80mm). Four-speed gearbox. 2g fuel. Tyres, 3.00 × 19in. 57mph. £38.

Velocette KSS/KTS (Mark I)

A half-decade on from Percy Goodman's original design for an overhead-camshaft single, the K-series Velocettes of the early 30s enjoyed the renown of TT success and the practical asset of a tried, and modified, and finally proven engine that claimed a near-fanatical following. It was a remarkable achievement for an engine that began life with some worrying disabilities arising from Mr Goodman's light-hearted approach to lubrication. He arranged for "total-loss" oil to be helped on its way to the oh cams and rockers by the action of a plunger pump; after doing its work in the camshaft area, oil was to drain via the vertical shaft to the crank assembly. This failed to occur, and overheating and seizure were not uncommon. As a consequence, the lubrication system was totally revised, to a dry-sump layout, with flow up the vertical shaft and into the bevel housing governed at up to 12lb psi by a double-gear unit driven from the mainshaft and installed in the rightside half of the crankcase. Henceforth oiling problems were few ... and those mainly concerned with *reducing* the oil supply, particularly from the rockers to the exterior of the engine.

The designation KSS was chosen at an early stage, some years before the end of the 20s, and represented

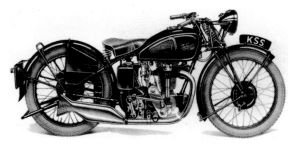

The 348cc KSS in 1935, final year of the Mk 1 series.

the initials for "super sports" tacked on to the engine identification.

With improvements to the cam box (to keep more oil inside), to the steering head, gearbox and clutch (still uniquely Velocette in its wafer-thin construction and servo-action, but stronger, less pernickety than the original, lifted from a low-powered two-stroke), to the petrol tank, and exhaust silencing, the KSS went into the 1930s with an enviable reputation, and a price of £62 10s. At this figure a new owner was unable to verify that part of the Velocette's enviable reputation which rested on out-and-out speed, for having a speedometer entailed extra cash outlay. And if he wished to indulge in speeding after sunset, and see both speedometer *and* road, there was little choice other than to find still more money – £5 6s, to be precise – for a dynamo lighting set.

Experts admit that the early 1930s KSS, for all its racing pedigree, was not an invariable 80+ performer. A 6.75:1 compression-ratio piston, running to advantage on a 50/50 mixture of No 1 petrol and pure benzol, helped towards fair if not startling acceleration. General handling was unapproachable, with narrow section 21in tyres giving a steering precision that had become a by-word.

Titch Allen, a cammy Velocette enthusiast for years, has written of the pleasures of riding a K series. "The overall impressions are the effortless steering, the solid cammy feel, and the incredible smoothness of engine and transmission, smoothness which must be inherent in the engine design for the only cush device in the transmission line is a simple engine-shaft cam-type shock absorber."

By 1932 the standard hand-change control for the four-speed gearbox could be dumped, in consideration of a £1 15s charge, in favour of the famed positive-stop footchange originated by Harold Wills and lately further developed by that talented engineer. In 1934 the positive-stop foot control was standardized, together with a new and shapely four-gallon tank; developments which underlined Velocettes' reputation for combining a unique blend of style and speed with solidly based engineering.

And then, around 1935, the KSS and its touring partner, the KTS, seemed to hang fire, disappearing from the sales catalogues. Speculation, shortly followed by gloom, became intense among clannish cammy chaps. Had there been a sellout at the works in

favour of pushrods? It was a dark year for the K men.
Specification, KSS (1935): Single-cylinder, ohc, .
348cc (74 × 81mm). Four-speed gearbox. 2½g fuel.
Tyres, 3.00 × 21in(fr), 3.25 × 20in(r). 80mph.
£62 10s.

Velocette KSS/KTS (Mark II)

The clouds lifted at show time, in November 1935, when the factory announced the return of the cammy 350s, which were to be available by Spring of the following year. The suspicions expressed by the ohc loyalists turned out to be well founded, however. The Goodmans had been so pleased with sales of the newly introduced ohv models that there had been talk of dropping the oh camshaft 350s, which by comparison were expensive to produce (less profitable to sell) and, because of their tendency to leak oil, a continuing source of irritation to the service department. Finally sentiment prevailed; that, and a feeling that in a reasonable world it should be possible to copy at least one aspect of the new ohv engine's specification in any redesign of the cammy unit. The M series bikes, as well as being cheaper to build, were oil tight; all the valve gear, not merely the rockers, was enclosed. The contrast between a dry-finned MOV or MAC and even a newish KSS, with oil-dewed cambox and clacking, open rockers, was striking. Number-one priority for the Mark II K models had been full enclosure of the valve gear.

Velocette KSS Mark II, 1938, with alloy cylinder head.

Contemporary reports on the oiling system devised for the new models (there was, as before, to be a touring KTS as well as the KSS) show that Percy Goodman had been extremely thorough in his redesign. A separate 4pt tank was mounted on the seat tube, with a duplex gear pump operating to fill the lower bevel case, the vertical shaft housing and the bevel box. An adjustable ball valve in the base of the bevel housing bypassed lubricant pressurized in excess of 10lb psi back to the suction side of the pump. The big-end was served by a supply taken through the centre of the crankshaft and controlled by a lightly loaded ball valve.

A small-bore external pipe from the bevel housing to the top of the cambox (discontinued from 1938) fed a generous wash of lubricant to the cams, with drainage into two pockets formed in the head to hold

the valve springs, and thence to the crankcase through external piping, in classic Y formation, on the left side of the engine. In the crankcase the "top-half" lubricant, together with surplus oil from other areas, was scavenged by the larger side of the duplex pump and returned to the tank.

As for valve enclosure, that was very well done; indeed the entire engine was more impressive than the Mark I, and remained unaltered, apart from trifling modifications, throughout a production life which lasted until a year or two after World War II. Formed as an aluminium-alloy casting with the cylinder head, the cambox was clear of the centre of the head, giving plenty of air-flow. With twin inspection covers in position, it formed a complete enclosure for camshaft, rockers, valves and springs. Tappet adjustment was provided at the rockers, which were on spindles having an eccentric mounting.

The cylinder head-plus-cambox was larger than any similar casting turned out by Velocette in early years and was set on a new, deeply finned cast-iron barrel; the overall effect was distinctly pleasing to all the fans who had fears about cammy status in the wake of the M models' sales successes.

Jeff Clew and Bob Burgess, the latter a Veloce employee for more than 30 years, documented the development story of the Mark II in detail. In their book, *Always in the Picture*, they have related how production suffered a setback when early examples were found to be low-achievers; they were, it appeared, no match for the oil-slinging Mark I, and the trouble was not unconnected with the new lubrication system. A full-skirt piston with a chamfered oil-control ring had been specified, in place of the slipper type that had given faultless service in earlier years. The result (as prophesied by a humble employee, who was roundly told off by the management for speaking out of turn) was a general "oiliness" – internal, of course – that depressed power. The slipper piston, with slotted oil-control ring, went back; this and changes to the silencing system and valve timing restored sparkle to the Mark II's performance.

Many of the cycle parts of the new machines were taken from the latest of the ohv variants, the 500 MSS, introduced in 1935. The forks, for example, and frame, and gearbox; and the wheels, tyres and mudguards, in the case of the KTS. The KSS continued to rely on a difference in wheel size, at 21in front, 20in rear, to give it a sporting edge over the KTS, with its 19in rims.
Specification, KTS (1938): Single-cylinder, ohc, 348cc (74 × 81mm). Four-speed gearbox. 3½g fuel. Tyres, 3.25 × 19in(fr), 3.50 × 19in(r). 78mph. £75.

Velocette KSS (postwar)

Shortlived in the postwar era, but perhaps the most attractive Velocette to get to the interesting side of 80mph, the 350 KSS was the only "cammy" Velo marketed after 1945. It returned to the roads in late 1946 largely unchanged from seven-year-old MkII

KSS Velocette in 1948, shortly before it was withdrawn from production.

Velocette 248cc MOV in 1937. It proved a big seller.

specification. This 348cc sohc alloy-head single, camshaft driven by vertical shaft and bevel gears, rockers positively lubricated in integral chambers, churned out civilized power with the very minimum of mechanical noise.

Narrow mudguards, bigger-than-usual wheels, a 3-gallon tank finished in black and gold, and elegant, efficient Webb girder forks contributed to the good looks of the KSS. But, as ever, the centrepiece of this old-fashioned model was the engine. Powerful, economical, undeniably a classic, its only – but decisive – drawback was that it was expensive to make . . . at least, in relation to any realistic price that could be charged for the bike.

The KSS was dropped in 1948, a few months after being kitted out with new Oleomatic forks.

Velocette 250 MOV

In the opening years of the 30s the health of the Veloce concern's bank balance depended on sales of the ohc K series three-fifties and the 249cc GTP two-stroke. The company's forays into the "black" were spasmodic, and never deep. While sales were reasonably satisfactory by volume, the profit margin on the camshaft machines – priced at £60 – was small. They did not lend themselves to economical manufacture. A skilled workforce was called for to master the niceties of assembly. Meshing the bevel gears in the ohc drive was a finicky operation. The GTP, too, though apparently a simple two-stroke, was in reality much more sophisticated than a Villiers engine. Eugene Goodman was in no doubt that the firm had to have another selling line. His first attempt involved a 350 side-valve single set in a GTP frame and driving through a GTP's three-speed gearbox. It was not a success in test sessions, being a mediocre performer, and noisy. The next step was to design an overhead-valve 250. This must have seemed no more than a logical progression from the disappointing 350. The simple valve gear had

gear-driven cams mounted high in a large timing chest, driving very short pushrods. The gear train included an intermediate pinion on a spindle, allowing for some adjustment, which enabled precise – hence quiet – meshing to be obtained without recourse to expensive machining. (Later the straight-cut gears were dispensed with in favour of helical-teeth gears.)

Lubrication of the upper parts was first entrusted to oil mist floating up, via the tubular pushrod cover, from the timing chest. The deficiencies of this arrangement becoming apparent, steps were taken to ensure a more positive supply through an external pipe running to the rockers from the top of the timing cover.

The engine was installed in a frame originally intended to accommodate the stillborn side-valve 350. The new frame was the first of full cradle type made by Veloce. The forks were Webbs, to Velocette specification, made in Birmingham, the brakes of GTP origin.

It was a very pleasant 250, so obviously "right" that a 350 version was commissioned within a few weeks of the 250's maiden outing. The 250 was given the identification MOV, M being the type letter (as in K, in KSS . . . but what happened to L?) and OV standing for overhead valve.

The MOV was to sell extremely well, in company with the 349cc MAC (no adequate interpretation of those initials is available). They contributed much to the financial stability of Veloce Ltd. By 1938, after five years of continuous MOV production, top speed had crept up from a shade over 60 to 72mph, which compared favourably with the performance available from more sporting 250s, such as the Excelsior Manxman. Fuel consumption averaged 80mpg. The price of an MOV in 1938 was £58, with such items as a speedometer, pillion seat and footrests being included in the standard equipment.

Specification, MOV (1938): Single-cylinder, ohv, 248cc (68 × 68.25mm), Four-speed gearbox. 2½g fuel. Tyres, 3.25 × 19in. 72mph.

Velocette 350 MAC

The 349cc MAC was probably the most successful model turned out by Veloce. It was derived from the MOV by the simple, inexpensive expedient of increasing the piston stroke from 68.25mm to 96mm.

A 1938 MAC Velocette.

Pre-war belt-driver, ohv models had front-mounted Miller dynamo and rear magneto.

In this way, piston, valves and cylinder head were interchangeable between the two models, and manufacturing costs maintained on the same level.

With its 250-designed fittings and running gear conferring a favourable power-to-weight ratio, the MAC was able almost to match the heavier, complicated KSS in performance.

Specification, MAC (1934): Single-cylinder, ohv, 349cc (68 × 96mm). Four-speed gearbox. 3g fuel. Tyres, 3.25 × 19in. 74mph.

Nearer camera – a 1936 MAC, ridden by Bruce Bolton (on the Tiger 70, Mrs Jill Bee).

Velocette MAC (postwar)

Redesigned for 1953, the MAC Velocette is recalled as one of the most satisfactory motorcycles offered for sale in the decade after the end of the war. The rigid frame had been replaced by one with a full pivoted fork, on the pattern employed on the Velocette racers of the 1940s. At a time when many manufacturers were turning to the lugless, all-welded frame, Velocette retained their faith in plenty of lug work, with a particularly hefty example at the base of the seat tube, to take the bushes for the new rear-fork pivot. But in practical terms, the new Velocette frame was virtually faultless. Woodhead-Monroe spring units controlled movement of the rear wheel, with variation in ride stiffness available on moving the tops of the springs fore and aft in arcuate slots in the rear-frame extensions. At the front Velocette-designed and built telescopic forks took the place of older Dowty Oleomatics.

Twelve months earlier, before Charles Udall began work on the frame, the engine had been updated, losing something of its 1930s look with a fresh one-piece light-alloy cylinder head, rocker box, barrel and enlarged timing chest. Other distinguishing features of the new 349cc MAC were a fish-tail silencer and a two-level dual seat, the rear part an inch or so higher than the front.

Fast (for its time and cubic capacity), smooth and refined, the MAC was the most impressive 350 of the early 1950s, though not, of course, the best seller.

Specification, MAC: Single-cylinder, ohv, 349cc (68 × 96mm). 14.3bhp. Four-speed gearbox. Magneto/dynamo. 3¼g petrol, 5pt oil; dry sump. Telescopic/pf. tyres, 3.25 × 19in. 360lb. 76mph.

Velocette MSS

The salient facts, for this book, about the MSS are that it was a natural development of the 350 MAC, and had a road performance fully equal to that of the prestigious, and more expensive, cammy models. With a similar stroke measurement (96mm) to the MAC's, it achieved a capacity of 495cc on an 81mm diameter bore. The timing cover and rocker box were identical to those of the smaller model (though the MSS was the only one to suffer from cracking of the cylinder head, between exhaust valve seat and spark plug hole, because not enough "meat" had been left in the area). Non-Velo fellows were hard put to tell the two models apart.

There appears to be no reasonable basis for SS (super sports) in the 500's designation. The MSS certainly was not a sporting job in the way that a Rudge Ulster was, or an International Norton. Yet it was, as indicated, a match for Velocette's own sporting ohc 350.

In 1938 a KTS was timed at 78mph in top gear (5.66:1), with 70mph available in third (6.84:1). An MSS, tested within months of the camshaft model, also returned 78 in top, but at much lower rpm, because of its 4.4:1 gearing; and 71 in third gear.

MAC/MSS "timing side" layout.

A 1954 MSS once owned by motorcycle historian Jeff Clew.

Velocette MSS in 1937.

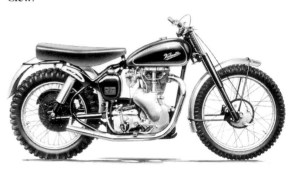

MSS scrambler in 1955: big, heavy and powerful – but seldom a winner.

The prices were £75 for the ohc 350, £69 10s for the MSS. Perhaps the unmistakable bevel-gear whine of the cammy was worth a fiver. C.E. Allen, for one, would argue that there was no contest . . . "Don't ask me why, but blindfold and with earplugs, anyone with a mechanical feel can pick out an ohc engine from a pushrod one. The feeling is that the engine can be revved and revved and revved without blowing up."
Specification, MSS (1938): Single-cylinder, ohv, 495cc (81 × 96mm). Four-speed gearbox. 3g fuel. Tyres, 3.25 × 19in. 78mph. £69 10s.

Velocette MSS (postwar)

The postwar history of the MSS can be seen as two chapters respectively headed 1945-48 and 1954-77.

In the earlier period the MSS was powered by virtually the original 1935-designed 495cc long-stroke (81 × 96mm) engine with high-camshaft operation of short pushrods and automatic advance and retard control for a rear-mounted magneto; the dynamo lived ahead of the engine and was driven by enclosed belt from the lefthand end of the crankshaft. In 1947 there was very little about the remainder of the bike to distinguish it from the last of the pre-war line. The frame, as before, was heavy, multi-lugged and very suitable for sidecar attachment. The saddle, the dismal Miller electrics, the smallish tank, the high-quality finish in black and gold: nothing had changed, or was to, until 1948 when the pre-war-pattern Webb fork was

changed for Dowty Oleomatics. However, within a year the MSS was withdrawn from circulation to give a clear field for manufacture of the revolutionary LE.

When the MSS returned, in 1954, the engine was in light-alloy, with a bonded-in iron cylinder liner, and had been reworked on "square" dimensions, at 86 × 86mm, to give a new capacity of 499cc. There were other new features too, like the hairpin valve springs, based on those used in the second-series MAC, reintroduced two years earlier.

The frame, with pivoted-fork rear suspension, and the front fork, tank and two-level seating were as prescribed for the 350.

A moderate performer, at 80mph in solo trim, the MSS was something of a favourite with the sidecar man who didn't want a revvy, vibratory twin.
Specification, MSS: Single-cylinder, ohv, 499cc (86 × 86mm). 25bhp. Four-speed gearbox. Magneto/dynamo. 3g petrol. 4pt oil; dry sump. Telescopic/pf. Tyres, 3.25 × 19in. 385lb. 82mph.

Velocette Model O

"Parallel twins like the Triumph," the outspoken – and prejudiced – Phil Irving wrote, "suffer from destructive vibration and broken crankshafts." It was this conviction that led the Veloce board, and Irving, in 1937 to plan their twin-cylinder successor to the Velocette singles along rather different lines from the Triumph. Yes, it was to be a parallel twin, but with two crankshafts, geared together and thus contra-rotating, which could be counterweighted to achieve near-perfect primary balance. As every commentator has since declared, the layout was like half an Ariel Square Four turned through 90 degrees.

Only one example of this machine was built. It remains a runner to this day and is, presumably, still capable of the 90-95mph which was achieved during test rides in 1938.

A single alloy cylinder head and barrels were held on an aluminium crankcase by eight long bolts, with a chain-driven camshaft set high between the barrels. Plain bearings supported the mainshafts, which were coupled by straight-cut gear wheels. To obtain reasonable "flywheel effect", a 7in auxiliary wheel was attached to one crankshaft. Modified 250 MOV gearbox internals running at engine speed were contained in a large shell which also accommodated the clutch and camshaft drive. Shaft drive to the rear wheel was arranged on the right.

Engine and transmission were fitted in a new frame with duplex front tubes and, at the rear, a stressed-skin monocoque. Full pivoted-fork rear springing had a patented adjustment involving movement of the tops of the spring units. The wheels were quickly detachable and carried 7in diameter brakes.

Tests of the prototype, known as the model O, indicated a power output of around 30bhp, with vibration-free running at any speed up to 80-90mph. There was none of the torque reaction that was a feature of another advanced shaft-driven twin of the day, the BMW. As war approached work on the model O was shelved.

Specification, Model O (1938): Twin-cylinder, ohv, 600cc. Four-speed gearbox. 3g fuel. Tyres, 3.25 × 19in. 90mph.

Velocette LE

The watercooled horizontally opposed side-valve twin appeared in 1949 in 150cc form. It had cast-iron barrels, and cylinder heads in light-alloy. The two-throw crankshaft ran on four main bearings. The backbone for the chassis was a 22-gauge sheet-steel pressing and carried the engine and 1¼ gallon fuel tank. A wide rear mudguard was welded to the backbone. The engine was started by a pull-up handle which was also linked to the centre stand; as the engine fired, so the LE was free to move off.

Legshields, footboards and a swept-back handlebar

The 192cc LE MkIII was impressive.

LE 150 – Velocette's first serious attempt at an "everyman" motorcycle.

added to the sedate air of this near-siLEnt side-valve. (Another interpretation is Little Engine.) A specially designed Amal helped to lower fuel consumption to 130mpg at 30mph.

In theory, the LE was everything that Mr Everyman had ever wanted, or asked for, in a motorcycle; but when it was offered to him, at only £125, he did not buy it.

At the end of 1950 the engine was enlarged to 192cc, which gave the LE more power on hills and when carrying a passenger, though little extra top speed.

Specification, LE: Horizontally opposed twin-cylinder, sv, 149cc (44 × 49mm); from November 1950 192cc (50 × 49mm). 8bhp. Coil ign/dc generator. 1¼g petrol, 1¾pt oil. Telescopic/pf. Tyres, 3.00 × 19in. 265lb. 48-52mph.

Velocette Valiant

When Alan Baker, an associate of the Institute of Mechanical Engineering, joined *The Motor Cycle* as technical editor, he stipulated that his "staff" machine was to be a Velocette Valiant. He had to settle finally for a Triumph twin; but his preference was an indication of the regard in which this little horizontally opposed twin was held by people with technical know-how.

Announced in 1956, the ohv Valiant shared much of the LE's design, with identical bore and stroke dimensions (50 × 49mm) giving 192cc, and an outwardly similar crankcase. The cast-iron cylinder barrels, air-cooled this time, carried light-alloy pushrod tubes, and the light-alloy heads had hemispherical combustion chambers in which domed-head pistons gave a compression ratio of 8:1.

Velocette Valiant, 1956, with maintenance-free rear shaft.

The Vogue, with glass-fibre bodywork, in 1955.

Valiant engine/transmission was based on the LE.

Eccentric adjustment was provided for tappet clearance.

Twin carburettors helped this 12bhp unit, housed in a tubular cradle frame, to propel the Valiant at up to 70mph, which was a performance in advance of that of most 250s of the day.

Handling was up to the usual high Velocette standards but the engine was noisy and a little fussy, and even the advanced technical specification, which came rather expensive at more than £200, was unable to keep sales going beyond 1963. A Veeline Valiant, with fairings, appeared in 1959 but sold less well than the standard version.

Specification, Valiant: Horizontally opposed twin-cylinder, ohv, 192cc (50 × 49mm). 12bhp/7,000rpm. Four-speed gearbox. Coil ign/alternator. 3g petrol, 1¾pt oil. Telescopic/pf. Tyres, 3.25 × 18in. 260lb. 68mph.

Velocette Vogue

The Vogue unfortunately never became the vogue. Fewer than 400 of these glass-fibre-bodied runabouts were sold during a production run of five years in the 1960s. It was a non-rusting, non-selling LE. The LE had made its name at a very different time; the Vogue as the scooter "boom" was dying and to a dwindling of interest in all things two-wheeled.

The large glass-fibre body, fronted by a tall Perspex screen, was made by Mitchenall Bros. It shrouded the internals from steering head to rear number plate, in which area it left approximately half the rear wheel exposed. Built-in valances for leg protection – it would not be fitting to call them mere leg shields – swept up from LE-style footboards to join a nacelle holding twin headlamps. Panniers could be had – and were later installed as standard equipment – in glass-fibre. The tank was made integrally with the middle section of the body.

The bodywork around the engine/gearbox was designed to come apart in sections, on release of Dzus fasteners, and was thick, strong and heavy. The frame was no lightweight, either – a very different affair from the LE's pressed-steel layout. On the Vogue a massive tube running back from the steering head made for a flexfree structure giving outstandingly good roadholding and steering. Not that owners were in a position to stress the Vogue to any extent. The all-up weight of panelling and chassis was enough to depress the spirits of the 192cc watercooled sv twin (the LE unit) to sub-50mph cruising and an all-out speed of no more than 60mph.

On early production bikes the electrics were 6-volt, but from 1966 12-volt Lucas equipment was installed.

Despite eulogies in the motorcycling press, the Vogue never caught on. David Dixon, of *Motor Cycle*, reporting continental grands prix almost weekly during a hectic road-race season, used one for a while. He enthused over the joy of being able to leave all-weather riding gear at home. But then, presumably, he ran short of time and had to get back to his speedy 500. The last Vogue was produced in late 1968.

Specification, Vogue: Horizontally opposed twin-cylinder, sv, 192cc (50 × 49mm). 8bhp. Coil ign/alternator. 2½g petrol. 1¾pt oil. Telescopic/pf. Tyres, 3.25 × 18in. 270lb. 55mph.

Velocette Viper

The 1950s MAC, Velocette's "cooking" 350, had no difficulty in matching, and usually surpassing, the sales of its 500 stablemate, the MSS. But a very different situation existed among the sporting Velos. At no time in its almost 15-year run did the 349cc Viper enjoy the popularity of Velocette's big sporting single, the Venom. The 350 deserved better of the public. It was arguably the better engine, for the good and sufficient reason that its 72 × 86mm top half was mounted on a

Velocette Viper sports 350 in 1955.

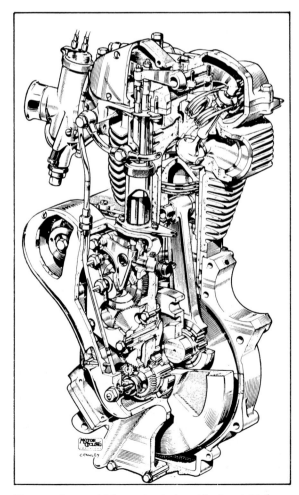

Viper engine was high-powered, almost "unburstable".

double of the Venom's bottom-end – crankcase, flywheels, crank, the lot – with all the benefits in smoother running, and an even greater degree of "unburstability", this conferred on the smaller unit.

Charles Udall, Velocette's designer, developed the Viper in 1955/56 with a bi-metal cylinder barrel, light-alloy head and hairpin valve springs. In later years it acquired, for a season or two, glass fibre panelling around the crankcase and gearbox which spoilt the bike's lines and, being black-finished, struck an odd, contrasting note with the all-chrome tank. Naked again, it got some extra tune, through revised carburation, a BTH racing magneto and a raised compression ratio. Finally it was saddled with a comprehensive fairing and christened Viper Clubman Veeline.

Specification, Viper: As MAC except for: higher-tune 349cc engine of 72 × 86mm, 26bhp, closer-ratio gears, 88-90mph.

Velocette Venom

A pre-Thruxton Velocette, the Venom in so-called clubman's trim had many though not all the aids to fast motorcycling featured in the later, top-of-the-range model. In 1958 the Venom could be bought with light-alloy wheel rims, BTH racing-type magneto (manually controlled, of course), Amal TT carburettor, rev-counter, special (noisy) exhaust system, rear-mounted footrests and close-ratio gears; top, being set at 4.4:1, made for effortless high speed at 16mph per 1,000rpm. A corollary of the high top was a correspondingly lofty ratio for first gear, which placed a premium on rider skill and some extra loading on the never-too-robust Velocette clutch.

John Griffith, a staffman on *Motor Cycling*, said that a Venom, from a standing start, should be travelling at 30mph before the clutch was fully home. It would top 70mph in second gear – in about 12 seconds – and carry on to around 105 in three-quarters of a minute. This may not make for impressive reading in the 1990s, but 30 years ago performance of this order was good enough to put the Venom among the top road-going 500 singles.

Specification, Venom: Single-cylinder, ohv, 499cc (86 × 86mm). 36bhp. Four-speed gearbox. Magneto/dynamo. 3g petrol, 4pt oil. Telescopic/pf. Tyres, 3.25 × 19in. 375lb. 105mph.

The 499cc Venom Clubman, a derivative of the MSS.

Velocette Thruxton

The fastest standard Velocette was the Thruxton, introduced in 1964. With its pushrod engine, so clearly derived from the pre-war MSS, the Thruxton produced more power than any of the firm's overhead-camshaft sports models. If the claimed 45bhp is true, it is safe to say that the Thruxton was the most powerful Velo of them all, racers included.

Velocette Thruxton, 1966: fastest of all roadster Velocettes?

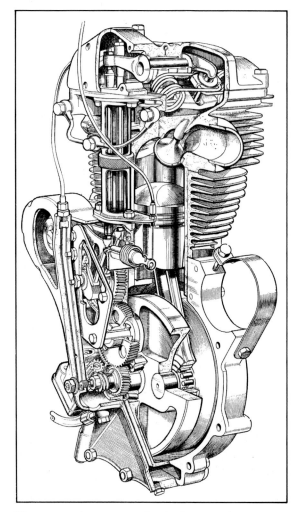

Thruxton engine; note overlapping hairpin valve springs.

Its immediate predecessor was the Clubman Venom, which could be purchased, or fitted, with some of the high-performance options that were incorporated as standard in the Thruxton. These included an Amal GP carburettor of 1¼in bore, so big and steeply angled that the fuel tank had to be cut away at one corner for clearance, a 10:1 cr piston, hairpin valve springs, close-ratio gears, hump-backed dual seat, narrow clip-on bars and light-alloy wheel rims. The front fork was a strengthened version taken from the moto-cross model and the front brake had twin leading shoes. The cylinder barrel was in cast-iron, the head in aluminium.

With its traditionally narrow, stiff crankcase, the Thruxton was free revving and comparatively vibration free. Though its performance was on a par with that of the equivalent Gold Star it was at all times more refined, if that is a suitable word for a near-racer, than the BSA.

Named of course after the Thruxton circuit in Hampshire, this model was finished in customary Velo black and gold, or in blue, and went on to win many production-machine races, even managing a TT victory in 1967, three years before it was dropped from the range.

Specification, Thruxton: Single-cylinder, ohv, 499cc (86 × 86mm). 40bhp/6,200rpm. Four-speed gearbox. Magneto/dynamo. 4¼g petrol, 4pt oil; dry sump. Telescopic/pf. Tyres, 3.00 × 19in(fr), 3.50 × 19in(r). 390lb. 105mph.

Indian Velo

This book is about British motorcycles. But when the engine of a bike known as the Indian Velo was as unquestionably British as the 500 Velocette, the machine surely merits a place here, no matter if much else was made in Italy.

The bike owed its existence to an American, Floyd Clymer, one-time race-promoter, publisher and, in his last years, motorcycle "manufacturer". His ambition was to resurrect the Indian motorcycle in full glory as a vee-twin. The Indian Velo was half-way house for him.

The Indian Velo 500: English-Italian-American hybrid.

More than 200 of the bikes had been assembled in Italy in 1970 at the time of Clymer's death, and most of these were shipped to the USA. There was no hope of continuing with the project, for the supply of engines was drying up as Veloce in Birmingham moved towards closure. Fifty were bought by a London dealer, Geoff Dodkin, long a Velocette specialist, and sold in the UK at the very reasonable price of £520.

Ironically this final Velo, despised by purists as a hybrid, was by any objective standard the best of all. The Velocette engine – sometimes a Venom unit, occasionally a special-order Thruxton – complete with Hall Green gearbox, primary drive and electrics was housed in an up-to-date duplex cradle frame that was at least 30lb lighter than the Velocette original and equipped with Marzocchi suspension front and rear.

Large-diameter brakes – the front made by race specialists Grimeca – in full-width hubs, light-alloy-rim wheels and, everywhere, the attention to detail that is a hallmark of Italian design and engineering further complemented the familiar high-camshaft power unit.

Lighter, a little faster, better braked and more comfortable than a "100 per cent" Velocette, Mr Clymer's 1970 hybrid was everything that the British-made product should have been in the 1960s.

Velocette Viceroy

The last of Velocette's postwar creations was the Viceroy scooter, on sale at £200 from 1960 to 1965. It had a zero impact on the market.

With its large (for a scooter) 250cc twin-cylinder two-stroke engine, big-tube frame, 12in wheels and generous bodywork, the Viceroy weighed more than 300lb. Ride and handling were exceptionally good even by motorcycle standards: among scooters, the Viceroy impressed like a TT winner. Unfortunately Velocette had misjudged the market, which consisted in the main of people who could not have cared less about TT standards but (a) were concerned that they should not strain any of the muscles left to them after years spent travelling by bus and train; (b) were reluctant to part with more than £100 – which happened to be the going rate for Italian scooters – for a powered two-wheeler; and (c) were convinced that "scooter" was merely another word for Vespa or Lambretta.

The Viceroy was a motorcyclist's idea of what a scooter should be. Not surprisingly, it failed to appeal to scooterists, who were a totally different breed.

VINCENT

The life and times of the Vincent motorcycle have a storybook quality. Here was a tiny firm, run by young men, which took on a wealthy industry and finally turned out what was, by consent even of its competitors, the best motorcycle of the day. The man who headed the company, P.C. Vincent, was an engineer and an inventor. He was also an idealist. And at first he had a useful amount of money. Over the years the idealism hardened into irascibility, an impatience of the compromises tolerated by other manufacturers.

Not for him the follow-my-leader path that led to single-lungers ("hopelessly outdated") or vertical twins ("worse than a single – those unbalanced forces – that vibration"), popular pivot-fork springing and telescopic front forks ("those weak arms – the whipping"). His masterpiece was to have none of these. No compromises. It was to be a "two-wheeled Bentley Continental, in which the comfort of the rider rated as high as any aspect of sheer performance". The words referred to the 1948 Black Shadow, but the philosophy was made clear much earlier.

The result was that the bikes were expensive: too few people bought them, and finally Vincents passed into other hands.

But that was in 1956, and it had been a 28-year-long story . . .

Philip Vincent made his first motor bike, with rear springing much in the style of that fitted to his last, on money provided by his father. The year was 1927 and

Velocette Viceroy, 1961. It was too large, and expensive.

Phil Vincent's second prototype, of 1928, had twin-port JAP engine and full rear springing.

he was an undergraduate at Cambridge. Twelve months later he was in business at Stevenage, and Vincent senior was keeping an eye on his investment.

The HRD part of the title that Vincent was to use for more than 20 years was acquired, cheaply, from Ernie Humphries of OK Supreme. Howard R. Davies' monogram had appeared on bikes he raced in Isle of Man TT races in the middle 1920s. Davies' business had failed but his reputation remained high. Vincent believed that the name might overcome motorcyclists' reluctance to buy an untried new model.

At first Vincent used JAP engines but in 1935, displeased with their varying quality, he abandoned them and designed his own 500. He had the able collaboration of Australian engineer Phil Irving. Together they built a high-camshaft 500 (with the double valve guides that were to be a hallmark of every Vincent thereafter) that was raced and later sold as Meteor (in standard tune), Comet (sports) and TT Replica (for racing). This engine was the basis for the Series A vee-twin, a double-up of the 500, with 47½ degrees between the cylinders. Handicapped by a standard 500 clutch and proprietory Burman gearbox, both unable to handle the twin's power for long, the Series A was sold to wealthy enthusiasts in the last years of the peacetime 1930s. Its top speed was almost 110mph. As a high-speed solo, with long-travel rear suspension, and clever design elsewhere, it was ahead of the other top performer of the day, the SS100 Brough Superior. But it lacked the style of the Brough. Vincent was irked when he heard that his bike was known as "the plumber's nightmare". It wasn't; and he was delighted to explain in crushing detail just why it wasn't; but the implication was clear, and he took it.

A 1927 TT HRD.

The vee-twin that he designed during the war and showed to the Press in April 1945 was very different. The vee had been opened out by a few degrees and the conventional down-tube frame abandoned. The bike was altogether smaller, yet more impressive. There was no lack of style this time. The engine, with a massive, internally strengthened crankcase, formed part of the whole, carrying the steering head and, at the rear, a sub-frame for the triangulated pivoted fork. As Vincent never tired of pointing out, no tubular frame could hope to rival the lateral, and torsional, stiffness of a 240lb engine/gear unit.

Among other items were a servo-action clutch, fit to take punishment from up to 60bhp, twin brakes per wheel (the wheels being interchangeable and quickly detachable on release of tommy-bar nuts), adjustable footrests, and twin prop stands. But above all, the bike had power, more power than an ohc racing Norton, giving tireless cruising at 100mph on continental motorways at little more than 3,500rpm.

After the Rapide came the Black Shadow, with output rising from 45 to 55bhp, a black finish for finning and crankcase, and an undisputed claim to being the fastest production motorcycle. In 1949 when the Series C twins, with patent Girdraulic forks in place of Brampton girders, were introduced they were in company with a new 500 single. The Comet amounted to the front half of a vee twin, with a separate Burman gearbox. It came into being in spite of Vincent's oft-stated prejudice against the average, ancient single because it was "so much better than the average, ancient single". Vincent had no need to be, and never was, a modest man.

Record-breaking at innumerable sprints, mostly with George Brown in the saddle, and over the shimmering miles of the Utah salt flats in the USA, ushered in production of an out-and-out racer, the Black Lightning, in 1950.

While achieving so much, Vincents remained underfinanced. When demand was high, they were short of manufacturing capacity. Injection of city funds meant temporary relief but a loss of company control for Vincent. In the early 1950s a concession for NSU mopeds and lightweights, sold under an NSU-Vincent label, brought in plenty of money. But, inevitably it now seems, the firm was moving towards closure. In 1956, less than a year after the arrival of the Series D, last and probably best of all Vincents, motorcycle production came to a halt.

Vincent-HRD Python 500

For some years following the formation of the Vincent-HRD company at Stevenage the considerable originality and flair of young Mr Vincent and his chief designer, Phil Irving, were devoted to the "cycle parts". A fully sprung 1931 500cc Vincent-HRD, although uncommon among hordes of rigid-frame roadsters, lost something of its distinction when the engine came in for scrutiny: it was, after all, very familiar in its usual setting, under a Rudge tank. Farmed out to other firms as the Python, the 85 × 88mm Rudge-Whitworth motor, with four radially disposed valves, was an energetic performer. When supplies of the Python were guaranteed, Philip Vincent was tolerably content to use it, though privately he bemoaned its harsh and noisy power.

The 1931 Python-powered Vincent retailed at £70, which was expensive at a time when an ohv Norton, with so-called TT-winning pedigree, cost no more than £60. Its frame, however, was better than any Norton's.

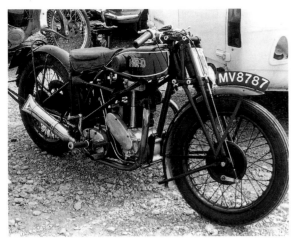

Vincent-HRD with Rudge Python 500 engine.

Vincent-HRD Model L and W

By 1933 Philip Vincent, still only five years a manufacturer, was disillusioned with motorcyclists. They professed admiration for his rorty 500s, with their revolutionary spring frames, but refused to buy them. It was enough to sour a more tolerant nature than Vincent's. Despairing of the good sense of the sporting fraternity, he turned to the commuter end of the market.

His 250s proved to be large, in the case of the aircooled model L, and both large and ugly when the L became the W, and acquired watercooling *and* enclosure.

A conservative public showed an approving interest in Vincent's creations, but continued to buy rigid-frame Nortons. It was frustrating for Vincent. He tended to blame the engines he had to fit for his lack of success. Much later he realized that innovation did not appeal to a complacent public.

In fact, the Python probably was the best of any proprietory engine available to Vincent and his friends at Stevenage. It had dry-sump lubrication, fully enclosed valve gear and developed about 25bhp – sufficient to give the Vincent a top speed of 75mph. The gearbox was a Burman four-speed, with positive-stop foot-change.

But, as indicated, it was the frame – the running gear – that gave the bike its appeal to a loyal, if restricted, following. Braced and triangulated in its front section, the rear part of the frame – a triangle also – pivoted on a large (11 × 2¼in diameter) single bearing, with taper rollers, set behind the gearbox. The two springs controlling movement of the rear frame were positioned at the apex of the triangle, with their forward ends attached to the saddle lug on the main frame. Total movement was around 4 inches and, with the massive bearing playing a major part in ensuring lateral stiffness, the Vincent could be hustled along at out-of-the-ordinary speeds. Press testers of the day were much given to standing in the saddle, hands on bars, while speeding over hummocky ground.

There were, of course, penalties in owning a machine produced by an individualist such as P.C. Vincent. Having obtained supplies of the latest Burman gearbox, with new foot control, and fitting it, reasonably enough, on the righthand side, he refused to move the rear-brake pedal to the other side. A gap – quite small – was left between the two, where the unhappy rider was supposed to insert his bewadered foot. The idiocy of this layout was plain to all except Vincent.

Vincent had looked at the 250s on offer from other manufacturers. He thought they were unduly small, and light; characteristic reasoning persuaded him that this was because the manufacturers believed 250 *riders* to be small and light; which brought him – equally characteristically – to the conclusion that his 250 ought to be uncommonly large. Thus the model L of 1932 had a 55in wheelbase, 30in saddle height and a spring frame that followed the pattern of those fitted to the 500s. There was also a measure of enclosure, mainly around the crankcase and extending up towards the saddle at the rear. Lighting was by a 30-watt dynamo, and ignition by coil. It cost only £39 10s, and would do 55mph, yet Vincent's biographer has recorded ". . . it failed to tempt any buyer at the 1932 motor cycle show".

P.C.V. swallowed his ire: the small-bike public, now shown to be no more intelligent or discerning than so-called enthusiasts, would be given a final opportunity to redeem itself. He brought out the model W, with Villiers watercooled 250 two-stroke engine enclosed

Vincent Model L 247cc two-stroke, 1933, with enclosure of crankcase and gearbox.

Vincent Model W watercooled 250 of 1934 had additional enclosure.

Specification, Vincent-HRD Python (1931):

Single-cylinder, ohv, 499cc (85 × 88mm). Four-speed gearbox. 2¾g fuel. Tyres, 3.25 × 19in. 70mph. £69.

by quickly detachable panels shaped to direct warm air from the radiator to the rider. This was a thoughtful design feature – known in the business as a rider's point – for a motorcycle intended for year-round use. But it failed to overcome a profound sales resistance aroused by the slab-sided look of the enclosure. Top speed of the model was around 65mph, and it could be ridden hard on the hottest day without undue heating-up.

Ignition was by flywheel magneto, with direct lighting, and the L's three-speed gearbox had been dropped in favour of a four-speed. The "all-in" price was £49 10s. Sales were negligible. P.C.V. "retired" it in 1935, devoting himself to more engrossing projects, such as the new Comet, with its "in-house" power unit. There were to be no further experiments for Vincent in the "tiddler" market until, nearly 20 years later, a connection was established with NSU.

Specification, Model L (1932): Single-cylinder, two-stroke. 250cc (63 × 80mm). Three-speed gearbox. 2¼g fuel. Tyres, 3.00 × 19in. 55mph. £39 10s.

Specification, Model W (1933): Single-cylinder, two-stroke. 250cc (63 × 80mm). Four-speed gearbox. 2¼g fuel. Tyres, 3.00 × 19in. 62mph. £49 10s.

Vincent-HRD Comet

Philip Vincent began to build his own engines following "harrowing" experiences with JAP-engined Vincents in the firm's first venture into TT racing, in 1934. After all-night sessions repairing troublesome components, the three-man team retired in the Senior race, following a succession of mechanical failures. P.C.V. and his staff wanted never to see another JAP. On returning to Stevenage they got down to designing a 500cc engine of their own. In fact, such a move had been contemplated for some time. It had been intended to proceed with a race engine while continuing to sell proprietary-engine road machines. Now the plan was to get new production-line engines on show at Olympia in October. They had little more than three months in which to do so.

They succeeded. The engines which they took to Olympia featured unique double valve guides and a high camshaft. The design was mainly the work of Vincent's Australian-born associate, Phil Irving. Vincent has pinpointed the advantage of the two valve guides per layout as offering "the valve support in double sheer against the rocking action of the rocker which with a single valve guide causes it to tilt and wear rapidly . . . thrust from the rockers merely makes the valve tend to move over to the opposite side of the guides, where it maintains continuous contact from top to bottom, thus resulting in a much slower rate of wear."

None of the several newly designed bikes taken into the Olympia arena had been started. Vincent did not think it necessary to mention this to the world. Instead he took a positive – mendacious – line and assured the

Press that the Comet had been tested at 90mph, the Meteor at 80. Years later he explained this away with an engineer's assurance. It was not a falsehood, he said, because there could be no doubt that the extra quality of his firm's handiwork, compared with Mr Prestwich's, *must* result in improved speed.

It was the gospel according to P.C.V.

He was, as it turned out, entirely accurate. The 1935 Comet was good for 92mph and would pull up from 30mph in about as many feet, thanks to four 7in-diameter brakes. No proprietory engines were fitted after the 1935 season.

Specification, Comet (1936): Single-cylinder, ohv, 498cc (84 × 90mm). Four-speed gearbox. 3¼g fuel. Tyres, 3.00 × 20in(fr), 3.25 × 19in(r). 92mph. £95.

Vincent-HRD Series A Rapide

The Series A Rapide was, in essence, two of the high-camshaft 500 singles mounted on a common crankcase. The scene in which the idea for the big one was born is dear to the heart of Vincent enthusiasts. It has a fascinating, filmic quality. The location is a drawing office of the Vincent-HRD company, in Stevenage, Herts. The year is 1936. Working at a desk is Phil Irving, a rugged Australian designer-engineer in his early 30s. Drawings of the 500cc engine have been disturbed, perhaps by a breeze from an open window, and have fallen in such a way that the two outlines of engines appear together, forming a vee. Irving notices this. He narrows his eyes, but because Australians are notoriously poker-faced, any pursing of his lips is barely detectable. He sets out the drawings, doodles them within the outline of a frame made up for record-breaker Eric Fernihough. Enter the young boss Philip Vincent (Harrow and Cambridge). It transpires that he has nursed a passion for vee-twin motorcycles since riding a McEvoy Anzani during his undergraduate days.

Vincent has explained the decision to make a thousand thus . . . "We were getting more demand for faster machines. We thought we could meet that demand with the Comet Special . . . but the trouble with a five-hundred is that with a reasonable silencer it's hard put to manage 100mph. Our only competitor would be Brough Superior. Our Comets were 10mph faster than any JAP-powered rival so I had no doubt that we could turn out a faster 1000 than Brough. We felt that any big bike we produced would have to be guaranteed to do at least 100mph, for I knew that the SS100 had to be on top form to achieve such a speed."

Within a few weeks, in the early autumn of 1936, the first Vincent 1000 engine was running, fitted in the frame which, as a Vincent biographer has noted, was no longer required by Fernihough. (He was dead.) Meteor "top-half" components were mounted on a new crankcase. The prototype achieved 108mph before troubles with the proprietary (Burman) clutch and gearbox brought testing to a halt. This was always to be the Achilles heel of the pre-war big Vincent. No matter how Vincent and his team toiled, no matter that highest-quality aircraft materials were specified – no Series A left Stevenage with the factory confident about the transmission. Slipping, or breakage, or both, would occur when an enthusiastic rider set out to verify some of the stories circulating about the tremendous performance of the "snarling beast". Between 70 and 80 vee-twins were manufactured from showtime 1936 to the summer of 1939.

Even the press testers of the 30s, possibly a little kinder to a maker's property than is the case today, and less ready to offend, were unable to avoid making some adverse comment on clutch and gearbox. In a 1939 report, for instance, *Motor Cycling*'s man was tactful enough to introduce the matter of clutch performance thus: "A glance at the graph will show the really amazing acceleration figures which were obtained . . ." but then went on, "the clutch being very carefully handled in the process. Anything approaching slipping the clutch to get quicker [sic] off the mark resulted in it continuing to slip for some time, and to avoid this the lever had to be released altogether before the throttle was opened appreciably." By 1939 standards this amounts to biting criticism.

Top speed on the 3.6:1 top gear was 110mph and average fuel consumption 45mpg. The 45bhp 1000 weighed about the same as a 1980s 250 Honda – 430lb.
Specification, Series A (1938): Twin-cylinder, ohv 998cc (84 × 90mm). Four-speed gearbox. 3½g fuel. Tyres, 3.00 × 20in(fr), 3.50 × 20in(r). 108mph. £142.

Vincent Rapide (post-war)

A month or two before the end of the war in Europe the editors of Britain's two motorcycle weeklies were on their way from London to Stevenage in Hertfordshire to inspect the new Series B Rapide. They were impressed by what they saw, and when write-ups and photographs were published so too was the motorcycle public.

Designed mostly by the brilliant Phil Vincent, with some original work by Phil Irving, the Rapide followed the pre-war Series A 1000, the so-called "plumber's nightmare", in being a vee-twin. However, the angle between the cylinders had been increased to 50° and in detail the engine was entirely new.

Now the 998cc engine, with bolted-on gearbox, was an integral part of the chassis, which meant that there was no longer a front down tube. Instead the massive unit, constructed mainly in light-alloy, was attached by long through-bolts to a box-section backbone member which extended rearward from the steering head and served as an oil reservoir. A triangulated rear frame pivoted against near-horizontal spring units; the front fork was a Brampton. Less obvious were the double guides for the valves (a feature retained from pre-war), the three-row roller big-end bearings, and the recently designed clutch with unique self-servo action giving more grip with increasing power input. Twin brakes

Series C Rapide, 1961 model, and Canterbury sidecar.

Rapide 998cc engine, and gearbox, 1951.

for both wheels (the wheels being quickly released by tommy bar action), finely adjustable setting for footrests and foot controls, and a special Feridax dualseat (when single sprung saddles were the rule) were other features that helped to make the 110mph Rapide a "superbike" before its time.

In Series C form (from 1951) the Rapide's Brampton fork was replaced by forged light-alloy Girdraulics, their movement controlled by long coil springs and a single damper. At the same time the friction dampers with handwheel control at the rear gave way to a hydraulic damper teamed with new spring units.
Specification, Rapide: Vee-twin, ohv, 998cc (84 × 90mm). 45bhp. Four-speed gearbox. Magneto/dynamo. 3½g petrol, 6pt oil; dry sump. Girder/Girdraulic. Tyres, 3.00 × 20in(fr), 3.50 × 19in(r). 455lb. 110mph.

Vincent Black Shadow

In May 1948 the new Vincent HRD Black Shadow was road-tested for *Motor Cycling* in the Isle of Man. In the report, written by Charles Markham, the Shadow was credited with a top speed of 122mph, confirming the Vincent vee-twin as the world's fastest production motorcycle. When *The Motor Cycle* got round to carrying out a test, the "top-speed" section in the published test panel was completed by the phrase, "Not obtained", which somehow was even more impressive than the rival publication's precise tabulation.

Vincent Black Shadow on test on a windy section of the TT course in 1948.

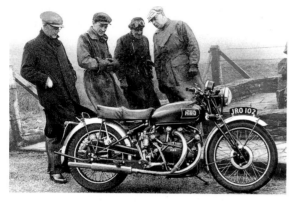

Drive side of the 1948 Black Shadow tested by *Motor Cycling*.

Black Shadow power unit. No wasted space . . .

Black Shadow's unique 150mph speedometer.

Very clearly a Rapide, but improved with some of the many modifications tested in the record-breaking model ridden by George Brown in 1947, the Black Shadow had highly polished rockers, ports and combustion chambers, and high-compression pistons (giving a compression ratio of 7.3:1). Big-bore (1¾in) Amals on bronze flanges looked impressive, and made their contribution to the 55bhp power output, but happily failed to depress average fuel consumption below 50mpg.

To cope with a top speed approaching 130mph, the brake drums were changed to a cast-iron, ribbed pattern.

Visually the Shadow was even more imposing than the Rapide, with a special baked-on black finish for the engine finning and crankcase, and what appeared to be, by comparison with the normal Smiths, an enormous speedometer, calibrated to 150mph. (It was of 5in diameter and was produced by Smiths for the Shadow alone.)

Vincent Comet (post-war)

Destined forever to be a poor relation to the big twins, the postwar single-cylinder Comet was named after the model originally introduced at Olympia in 1934. It appeared in 1948. Virtually half of the vee-twin, the inclined-engine 499cc Comet was assembled to Black Shadow tune, with a softer model, named Meteor, available also. Both were fitted with a separate four-speed gearbox made by Burman.

Despite a pleasing performance characterized by near-vibration-free running, and sporting successes notched up by the race-developed Grey Flash version in the hands of future world champion John Surtees, and George Brown, the "small" Vincent was a disappointing seller. Where the vee-twin was impressive in looks, as well as performance, cutting it in half resulted, in Comet guise, in an oddly unbalanced appearance which turned would-be

The Series C Comet 500 single in 1950.

buyers away, in search of more conventional singles. Underrated by the public, it carried on as a C series machine until the advent of the D in 1954/55, when it was dropped from production.

Specification, Comet: Single-cylinder, ohv, 499cc (84 × 90mm). 28bhp/5,800rpm. Four-speed gearbox. Magneto/dynamo. 3¾g petrol, 5pt oil; dry sump. Girdraulic/triangulated pf. Tyres, 3.00 × 20in(fr). 3.25 × 19in(r). 400lb. 88mph.

Vincent Series D

Ambitious, far-sighted, and having a healthy scepticism about what motorcyclists claimed they were looking for in their ideal two-wheeler, Philip Vincent was determined to make the Series D, successor to the Series C, as *different*, yet practical, as his firm's limited resources would allow.

He attended to the ignition, dropping the magneto in favour of coil ignition, and obtaining easier starting thereby; overcame fuel-dribbling by replacing the old-type Amals with Monobloc carburettors; and improved the rear suspension by fitting a long-travel Armstrong springing unit. The result was a better bike, but it was still, to all appearances, a Series C and as such hardly an adequate response to the pressure to turn out something radically new. That was, in any case, out of

1956 Series D Black Prince: last of the line.

the question, Vincent decided; there was too little money available. In any event the twin, so advanced when it was introduced a decade before, was still ahead of the pack.

However, any hope of an upturn in sales demanded a new look and new packaging. Thus was born the idea of enclosure. It would change the appearance of the bike, fulfilling the commercial object of the exercise. It could be turned to practical advantage, which would satisfy Vincent's determination to give the customer a better product for his money. Enclosure meant protection from the elements, less fatigue for the rider; it might even mean more speed; and lower fuel consumption. And underneath the plastic the bike would be, in the main, unchanged (which would save the firm's money).

The enclosed D models, named Black Prince (in Black Shadow form) and Black Knight (for the Rapide), were shown at Earls Court in 1954, where they received more praise than the designer had anticipated but, also, some merited criticism directed at the finish of the plastic panelling. This led to a delay in production while a new supplier was located.

By 1956, despite all the heartening interest evoked by the D series, the firm had ceased motorcycle production.

WATSONIAN

The compiler remembers a long-ago Winter when he travelled through snow and ice from London to south Wales on a Watsonian sidecar outfit. "Watsonian" applied not only to the sidecar but to the bike, which was fitted with a 996cc JAP side-valve vee-twin engine. It had been built in 1950 to answer the requirements of Ron Watson, managing director of Watsonian Sidecars, who saw it as prototype of a machine that might find a market among dedicated "sidecar men". Possibly he was right, but there was to be no finding out, for his plans to produce a number of these integrated outfits came to nothing when JAP let it be known that they were unwilling to devote further time to an engine of such limited appeal.

It was a 50° vee-twin with light-alloy cylinder heads. The frame had plunger rear springing, and the front fork was telescopic. The sidecar was built to take an adult and a child. Its brake (in a sprung wheel) was controlled by the rear-brake pedal on the bike.

On wintry roads, with grip at a premium, the Watsonian was able to proceed in good order when many four-wheelers were skidding, and only the bravest or most foolhardy of solo motorcyclists were abroad. With big flywheels and steam-roller torque, the engine would pull a high gear at minimum revs and appeared ready to take a half-ton of laden bike and sidecar up the Cresta Run.

But Winter is not a year-round blight; in better conditions the side-valve Watsonian was revealed as a modest, but thirsty performer when compared with 650cc vertical twins, which made light of sidecar hauling at 80mph, and 45 mpg.

WHITWOOD MONOCAR

Sixty years ago government, tradition, and authority in all manner of forms combined to influence the lives of ordinary citizens to a much greater extent than is the case today. In a similar fashion, leaders of the motor-cycle industry of the 1930s sought to impress their views of what was right and proper on the motor-cycling public. Their exhortations were aired via the columns of the press, usually during the week of the annual Olympia show, in much the way that Mr Balfour occasionally addressed the nation from the pages of *The Times*.

Whitwood Monocar: a two-wheeled car in 1934.

The manufacturers' "code" said that it was not a good thing to name names in the industry. With the exception of independent spirits such as Mr Edward Turner, who had no objection to making a splash in the wider world, little was known of the men behind the machines. When the editor of *The Motor Cycle* referred to the industry's top brass, it was usually as "Mr Manufacturer", a title that encompassed the entire world of managing directorship, from the panelled glories of BSA at Armoury Road to the dingy workshop of a one-man enterprise in Dalston Junction. The personality cult was not encouraged.

In 1934 the OEC concern – comprising, in the main, Mr Osborn and Mr Woods, though this was largely unknown outside their factory – having given the world the duplex steering system, was moved to benefit it further by a design for a kind of two-wheeler car.

Full descriptions of their vehicle, known as the Whitwood Monocar, appeared in the press, alongside details of new-season OECs. However, no connection between the two was to be inferred. Where the full address for Whitwood was given, that for OEC was omitted.

The Whitwood, it can be revealed, was largely Mr Woods' work. It was not the first of its kind to appear – A.V. Roe's Monocar had caused some interest in 1928 – and was far from being the last.

"A car on two wheels" was how the makers described it. One of the weeklies said that it was a praiseworthy attempt to meet the demand for a two-wheeler with complete weather protection. Simply described, it resembled a small boat running on two wheels, the hull being equipped with doors, screen and tandem seating. Secondary wheels, on outriggers, were present, to be lowered when necessary.

Initially, in 1934, its duplex steering ("made under licence," said *Motor Cycling*, mindful to name no names) was controlled, through a reduction gear, by a spring-spoke steering wheel. Four main tubes formed the frame, two coming down from the top cross-member of the steering, and continuing rearward, horizontally, to the rear-wheel spindle; below these tubes was a further pair, running back from the lower steering member. The engine, cylinder head to the front, was carried in a tunnel formed between the four tubes. The three-speed gearbox was fitted in tandem and the transmission was by chain throughout.

Seated at the steering wheel, the driver arranged his feet one on each side of the (road) wheel, while being protected from it by an inner shield. On the right side were gear-change lever and starting handle, the latter fitted inside the body.

The retractable undercarriage consisted of a pair of 10in-diameter wheels, controlled by a lever to the left of the driver. Petrol and oil were carried in the tail of the vehicle, which also held a locker.

As for the engine, it could be anything a customer cared to specify, from a 150cc two-stroke to a big twin. Prices in October 1934 ranged from £49 15s for the 150-powered version to £88 for a 1,000cc side-valve. "The prices are very moderate," said *Motor Cycling*.

A year later, and the design had been changed a little. The engine had left its midship position and was alongside the rear wheel, on the right, rather like the later Vespa; the gearbox was separate, mounted on the left and connected across the chassis by a shaft with flexible coupling. The new site for the engine gave a lower driving position. A folding hood was available. Twin lamps were mounted on the nose of the body.

It was an enterprising venture, and probably met the requirements of all those riders who had asked for something a little more sophisticated than the traditional two-wheeler. However, given the opportunity to buy a Monocar, they carried on buying traditional two-wheelers. Except, that is, for six adventurous people; that's how many Monocars were sold in the three-year life of the model.

WOOLER

Contrary to a widely held belief, a Wooler or two appeared on English roads in the 1950s. The Wooler ranks as one of the few outstanding designs of the postwar British industry, which was mainly content to rely on the ohv single for staple power and experimented no further than the single's close relation, the parallel twin.

It was the work of John Wooler, who in the previous 30 years had designed (and occasionally manufactured) fully sprung motorcycles powered by engines as diverse as a two-stroke single with double-ended piston driving twin connecting rods, a 350 ioe fore-and-aft flat-twin, and a single with ingeniously high cams.

Variations on the flat-four theme by Wooler, in the 1950s. The model with dual seat is, of course, the later machine.

But the Wooler planned for post-World War Two production was the most interesting of all. At first the design was for a flat-four having pistons attached by beams and links to a single connecting rod, power being transmitted through a torque converter to a shaft final drive. Technical writers despairing of anything new to say about Villiers-engined runabouts made almost a full-time job of monitoring the design and development progress of the Wooler, and incidentally provided much tantalizing news about its "imminent" production date, which fell back, year by year, to the middle 1950s.

Difficulties with the "beam" engine caused the designer and his son Ron to abandon that design and devote their energies to a marginally more conventional flat-four with plain, forked connecting rods and a four-speed gearbox. It was claimed that the entire bike could be dismantled using no more than a 10mm box spanner, and one other, from the standard toolkit.

In October 1954 the Woolers were still showing their bike, fitted with plunger rear suspension (albeit single plungers in place of the twin-unit layout of earlier models) and a spindly-looking telescopic front fork. Prices were detailed, to the nearest penny, and there was confident talk of such extras as a dualseat and a crash bar, to be available as extra fittings. But 1954/55 signalled the end, not the beginning, for the Wooler when plans to enrol a wealthy backer fell through.

ZENITH

Rescued from business doldrums in 1931 by an injection of cash from Writers Ltd., their main London dealers, Zenith thereafter had little choice other than to toe the retail line laid down by Writers. This meant less time being devoted to the preparation of record-breakers, and more to the "bread-and-butter" machines that were to bring customers into Writers' Kennington showrooms. A 172cc Villiers was brought in to power a modest addition to a range which traditionally had put more emphasis on up-market offerings, such as 680 vee-twins. No particular success accruing from this move, there was a return, by 1934, to a more interesting sales policy. This time, however, the range was more balanced than in the 20s, with a core of JAP-powered singles running from 250 to 500cc.

One such was the C5 model with 490cc ohv dry-sump engine inclined in a full cradle frame, with all-chain transmission, separate Burman four-speed gearbox, rear-mounted Magdyno and high-level twin exhaust pipes. The brakes, at 8in diameter, were larger than those fitted to many other machines of similar power, and the finish was much more attractive than the average, being a blend of purple, black and chromium.

With a top speed of 75-80mph, and priced from £58, it was a thoroughly decent motorcycle. As one

A Zenith with JAP 1,000cc sv engine.

The 1947 side-valve Zenith.

The 1939 500cc C5 model featured a single-cylinder JAP engine
designed by Dougal Marchant which had a cooling duct above
the exhaust port and cantilever valve springs.

observer described it in 1934 . . . "in its make up there
is nothing unorthodox, the design being, like that of
the rest of the Zenith models, perfectly normal and
straightforward."

It might, of course, have been straightforward to
the point of tedium, for sales never measured up to
Zenith's, or Writers', expectations.

Specification, C5 500 (1934): Single-cylinder,
ohv, 490cc (79 × 100m). Three-speed gearbox. 3g
fuel. Tyres, 3.25 × 19in. 74mph. £58.

It has been suggested that perhaps 250 Zeniths
were made and sold after the war. There is little
evidence on which to base a reliable estimate. In
magazines of the period the firm was credited, in
exactly the same way as, say, BSA, with undertaking
production runs for various models.

But whereas, after reading about the latest BSA,
motorcycle enthusiasts would very soon spot an
example in the showrooms or on the road, no
amount of reading on the subject of the latest Zenith
was ever, it seems, backed up by sight of one.

Yet somebody, somewhere must have a postwar
Zenith.

It was listed in 1945 as a 750 side-valve vee-twin
(the engine a JAP) with girder forks, later changed to
Dowty Oleomatics.